ABRAHAM AND ALL THE
FAMILIES OF THE EARTH

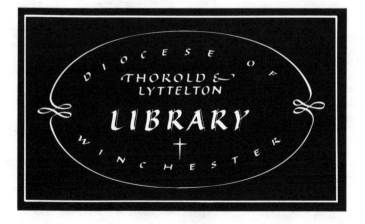

INTERNATIONAL THEOLOGICAL COMMENTARY

Fredrick Carlson Holmgren and George A. F. Knight
General Editors

Volumes now available

Genesis 1–11: From Eden to Babel
by Donald E. Gowan

Genesis 12–50: Abraham and All the Families of the Earth
by J. Gerald Janzen

Deuteronomy: Word and Presence
by Ian Cairns

Joshua: Inheriting the Land
by E. John Hamlin

Judges: At Risk in the Promised Land
by E. John Hamlin

1 and 2 Samuel: Let Us Be like the Nations
by Gnana Robinson

1 Kings: Nations under God
by Gene Rice

Ezra and Nehemiah: Israel Alive Again
by Fredrick Carlson Holmgren

Proverbs and Ecclesiastes: Who Knows What Is Good?
by Kathleen A. Farmer

Song of Songs and Jonah: Revelation of God
by George A. F. Knight and Friedemann W. Golka

Isaiah 1–39: The Lord Is Savior: Faith in National Crisis
by S. H. Widyapranawa

Isaiah 40–55: Servant Theology
by George A. F. Knight

Isaiah 56–66: The New Israel
by George A. F. Knight

Jeremiah 1–25: To Pluck Up, To Tear Down
by Walter Brueggemann

Jeremiah 26–52: To Build, To Plant
by Walter Brueggemann

Ezekiel: A New Heart
by Bruce Vawter and Leslie J. Hoppe

Daniel: Signs and Wonders
by Robert A. Anderson

Hosea: Grace Abounding
by H. D. Beeby

Joel and Malachi: A Promise of Hope, A Call to Obedience
by Graham S. Ogden and Richard R. Deutsch

Amos and Lamentations: God's People in Crisis
by Robert Martin-Achard and S. Paul Re'emi

Micah: Justice and Loyalty
by Juan I. Alfaro

Nahum, Obadiah, and Esther: Israel among the Nations
by Richard J. Coggins and S. Paul Re'emi

Habakkuk and Zephaniah: Wrath and Mercy
by Mária Eszenyei Széles

Haggai and Zechariah: Rebuilding with Hope
by Carroll Stuhlmueller, C.P.

ABRAHAM AND ALL THE FAMILIES OF THE EARTH

A Commentary on the Book of

Genesis 12–50

J. GERALD JANZEN

WM. B. EERDMANS PUBLISHING CO., GRAND RAPIDS

THE HANDSEL PRESS LTD, EDINBURGH

First published 1993 by Wm. B. Eerdmans Publishing Company,
255 Jefferson Ave. S.E., Grand Rapids, Michigan 49503
and
The Handsel Press Limited
58 Frederick Street, Edinburgh EH2 1LS

Printed in the United States of America

Library of Congress Cataloging-in-Publication Data
Janzen, J. Gerald, 1932-
Abraham and all the families of the earth; a commentary on
the book of Genesis 12–50 / J. Gerald Janzen.
    p.   cm. — (International theological commentary)
Includes bibliographical references.
ISBN 0-8028-0148-X
1. Bible. O.T. Genesis XII-L — Commentaries. I. Title. II. Series.
BS1235.3.J36 1993
222'.1107 — dc20   93-13846
CIP
Handsel ISBN 1 871828 ?? ?

For
Holly and Daniel

And of Zion it shall be said,
"This one and that one were born in her."
— Psalm 87:5

CONTENTS

ABBREVIATIONS

JPS	Jewish Publication Society translation
KJV	King James (Authorized) Version
mg	margin
NRSV	New Revised Standard Version
RSV	Revised Standard Version

EDITORS' PREFACE

The Old Testament alive in the Church: this is the goal of the *International Theological Commentary.* Arising out of changing, unsettled times, this Scripture speaks with an authentic voice to our own troubled world. It witnesses to God's ongoing purpose and to God's caring presence in the universe without ignoring those experiences of life that cause one to question God's existence and love. This commentary series is written by front-rank scholars who treasure the life of faith.

Addressed to ministers and Christian educators, the *International Theological Commentary* moves beyond the usual critical-historical approach to the Bible and offers a *theological* interpretation of the Hebrew text. Thus, engaging larger textual units of the biblical writings, the authors of these volumes assist the reader in the appreciation of the theology underlying the text as well as its place in the thought of the Hebrew Scriptures. But more, since the Bible is the book of the believing community, its text has acquired ever more meaning through an ongoing interpretation. This growth of interpretation may be found both within the Bible itself and in the continuing scholarship of the Church.

Contributors to the *International Theological Commentary* are Christians — persons who affirm the witness of the New Testament concerning Jesus Christ. For Christians, the Bible is *one* Scripture containing the Old and New Testaments. For this reason, a commentary on the Old Testament may not ignore the second part of the canon, namely, the New Testament.

Since its beginning, the Church has recognized a special relationship between the two Testaments. But the precise character of this bond has been difficult to define. Thousands of books and articles have discussed the issue. The diversity of views represented in these publications makes us aware that the Church is not of one mind in expressing the "how" of this relationship. The authors of this commentary share a developing consensus that any serious explanation of the Old Testament's relationship to the New will uphold the integrity of the Old Testament. Even though Christianity is rooted in the soil of the Hebrew Scriptures, the biblical interpreter must take care lest he or she "christianize" these Scriptures.

Authors writing in this commentary will, no doubt, hold varied views concerning *how* the Old Testament relates to the New. No attempt has been made to dictate one viewpoint in this matter. With the whole Church, we are convinced that the relationship between the two Testaments is real and substantial. But we recognize also the diversity of opinions among Christian scholars when they attempt to articulate fully the nature of this relationship.

In addition to the Christian Church, there exists another people for whom the Old Testament is important, namely, the Jewish community. Both Jews and Christians claim the Hebrew Bible as Scripture. Jews believe that the basic teachings of this Scripture point toward, and are developed by, the Talmud, which assumed its present form about 500 C.E. On the other hand, Christians hold that the Old Testament finds its fulfillment in the New Testament. The Hebrew Bible, therefore, belongs to both the Church and the Synagogue.

Recent studies have demonstrated how profoundly early Christianity reflects a Jewish character. This fact is not surprising because the Christian movement arose out of the context of first-century Judaism. Further, Jesus himself was Jewish, as were the first Christians. It is to be expected, therefore, that Jewish and Christian interpretations of the Hebrew Bible will reveal similarities *and* disparities. Such is the case. The authors of the *International Theological Commentary* will refer to the various Jewish traditions that they consider important for an appreciation of the Old Testament text. Such references will enrich our understanding of certain biblical passages and, as an extra gift, offer us insight into the relationship of Judaism to early Christianity.

An important second aspect of the present series is its *international* character. In the past, Western church leaders were considered to be *the* leaders of the Church — at least by those living in the West! The theology and biblical exegesis done by these scholars dominated the thinking of the Church. Most commentaries were produced in the Western world and reflected the lifestyle, needs, and thoughts of its civilization. But the Christian Church is a worldwide community. People who belong to this universal Church reflect differing thoughts, needs, and lifestyles.

Today the fastest growing churches in the world are to be found, not in the West, but in Africa, Indonesia, South America, Korea, Taiwan, and elsewhere. By the end of this century, Christians in these areas will outnumber those who live in the West. In our age, especially, a commentary on the Bible must transcend the parochialism of Western civilization and be sensitive to issues that are the special problems of persons who live outside of the "Christian" West, issues such as race relations, personal survival and fulfillment, liberation, revolution, famine, tyranny, disease, war, the poor, and religion and state. Inspired of God, the authors of the Old Testament knew what life is like on the edge of existence. They addressed themselves to everyday people who often faced more than everyday problems. Refusing to limit God to the "spiritual," they portrayed God as one who heard and knew the cries of people in pain (see Exod. 3:7-8). The contributors to the *International Theological Commentary* are persons who prize the writings of these biblical authors as a word of life to our world today. They read the Hebrew Scriptures in the twin contexts of ancient Israel and our modern day.

The scholars selected as contributors underscore the international aspect of the series. Representing very different geographical, ideological, and ecclesiastical backgrounds, they come from more than seventeen countries. Besides scholars from such traditional countries as England, Scotland, France, Italy, Switzerland, Canada, New Zealand, Australia, South Africa, and the United States, contributors from the following places are included: Israel, Indonesia, India, Thailand, Singapore, Taiwan, and countries of Eastern Europe. Such diversity makes for richness of thought. Christian scholars living in Buddhist, Muslim, or Socialist lands may be able to offer the World Church insights into the biblical message — insights to which the scholarship of the West could be blind.

The proclamation of the biblical message is the focal concern of the *International Theological Commentary*. Generally speaking, the authors of these commentaries value the historical-critical studies of past scholars, but they are convinced that these studies by themselves are not enough. The Bible is more than an object of critical study; it is the revelation of God. In the written Word, God has disclosed himself and his will to humankind. Our authors see themselves as servants of the Word which, when rightly received, brings *shalom* to both the individual and the community.

— GEORGE A. F. KNIGHT
— FREDRICK CARLSON HOLMGREN

AUTHOR'S PREFACE

This commentary grows out of two decades of classroom work on the book of Genesis with many different groups of students at Christian Theological Seminary in Indianapolis, Indiana, U.S.A. I am indebted to all who have participated in these classes, and dedicate this commentary also to each one of them. Several people have made a more recent contribution to both the form and the content, by reading and critically annotating an earlier draft: Shirley Gilson and Jay Southwick, former students in my Genesis class and now teachers in the church in Indianapolis, whose concern for and involvement in congregational ministry and witness make them treasured dialogue partners in biblical interpretation; Patrick D. Miller, Jr., of Princeton Theological Seminary, whose sane judgments I value even when I do not have the sense to abide by them; and Fredrick Holmgren and George Knight, editors of this commentary series, whose initial encouragement, subsequent patience, generous latitude, and, at the end, incisive attention to detail have modeled the sort of divine providence I have thought to discern in Gen. 12–50.

INTRODUCTION

This is a theological commentary. It is not primarily a commentary on the many sources and traditions out of which the text of Gen. 12–50 may be shown to have been formed (though on occasion I will refer to them). Nor is it a study of the historical events and social situations which may be reconstructed as lying behind those sources and traditions (though on occasion I will refer to them). Such commentaries and studies, of which there are many, are important and valuable in their own right, and they can contribute much by way of background knowledge to the task of theological interpretation. But this commentary has been written in the conviction that the final form of the text is greater than the mere sum of its sources, and that the theological vision which it presents is greater and more profound — more ripe or mature — than can be gained simply from studies of the historical events and social situations out of which the text arose.

I subscribe to the view emerging among a number of scholars that the Bible in its present form displays a complex integrity of its own, which calls for analysis and interpretation according to principles and methods which guide the reading of literary texts generally. However, a reading which remains at the literary level is, in my view, incomplete. Indeed, the theological concern which permeates the Bible calls for theological reflection and religious response. The "narrow gate" to such reflection and response, in my judgment, is by way of a literary reading. The theological meaning of the text cannot be neatly detached from its literary form, any more than a person's spirit can be neatly detached from one's body. Just as one's body informs, expresses, and conveys one's spirit, so too, *how* the text means is part of *what* it means.

Accordingly, I have tried to pay attention to the literary form of the narrative, as expressive of its theological content.

In this introduction I shall confine myself to a few comments on the literary and theological relation between Gen. 12–50 and the parts of the Bible that precede it (Gen. 1–11) and follow it (Exodus-Malachi; in the Hebrew Bible, Exodus-Chronicles).

THE RELATION BETWEEN GENESIS 1–11 AND 12–50

In the introduction to his commentary in this series, *From Eden to Babel,* Donald E. Gowan characterizes Gen. 1–11 as "the preface to salvation history" (Gowan, 4; also 2). This salvation history begins with Abram in 12:1-3 and extends through the rest of the OT and (for Christians) on into the NT. Gowan considers that, although the Priestly and the Yahwistic traditions that form a large part of chs. 1–11 continue into chs. 12–50 and beyond, the first eleven chapters are "compartmentalized" and set off from what follows. "The authors of the OT do not draw upon them, except for the teaching that Yahweh, God of Israel, was Creator of the heavens and the earth" (Gowan, 3). Gowan implies that this was because Israel, and therefore most of the OT, was concerned primarily with "God's dealings with his people Israel" (4). It was not until the period between about 200 B.C. and A.D. 100 (when the Jews no longer enjoyed national independence, but lived among the nations) that Jewish writings — and then also early Christian writings such as the NT — began to draw heavily on Gen. 1–11 and to interpret it through elaborate retellings of its themes.

In this commentary I adopt a different view of the literary and theological relation between Gen. 1–11 and 12–50. To be sure, the ancestral narratives contain few explicit references to the earlier chapters, of the sort that Gowan identifies elsewhere in the Bible. But explicit reference does not begin to exhaust the relations between texts within the Bible. Indeed, in regard to such relations, explicit references are only the tip of the iceberg. Michael Fishbane (*Biblical Interpretation in Ancient Israel*) has shown in great detail how earlier parts of the Hebrew Bible are interpreted in later parts, sometimes indeed through explicit quotation and commentary, but often through allusion and echo. One may compare also Robert Alter's chapter on "Allusion and Literary Expression" in his book *The World of Biblical Literature*. Similarly, Richard B. Hays (*Echoes of Scripture in the Letters of Paul*) has shown how the OT underlies and informs the thought in Paul's letters in ways far beyond his explicit quotations and references. To detect this, to hear such "echoes" of the OT in Paul, we need to come to know the OT as intimately as Paul did. Just so, in my view: Gen. 12–50 everywhere presupposes the reader's familiarity with the preceding chapters, in such a way that scene after scene in the ancestral narrative receives its depth and precise nuance of meaning from the way it takes up and repeats or transforms themes and images anchored in Gen. 1–11.

I shall offer only a few examples here. When in Gen. 12–50 we repeatedly come across the genealogical or narrative heading, "these are the generations/descendants (*toledot*) of X" (e.g., 25:12, 19) or "this is the history (*toledot*) of X" (e.g., 37:2), we cannot help remembering 2:4a, "these are the generations (*toledot*) of the heavens and the earth when they were created," and the headings in 5:1; 6:9; and 10:1. The relationship between 2:4a and all the following headings suggests that for the Priestly editor there is ultimately one all-encompassing story, which has its origin in the mystery of divine creativity. This heading also suggests the central theme of this all-encompassing story. It is the story of the *toledot*, the "generations," of heaven and earth. The noun *toledot* comes from the verb *yalad*, "to bear, give birth." In Gen. 1 the heavens and the earth are portrayed as fruitful places where the earth brings forth vegetation that can reproduce itself (v. 11), the waters and the heavens bring forth fish and birds that are blessed with the capacity to reproduce themselves (vv. 20, 22), the earth again brings forth animals (v. 24), and finally God makes earthlings in the divine image and blesses them with fruitfulness and the commission to have dominion (vv. 26-28). Throughout, the picture is one of a divinely given power to receive life and to pass it on through the blessing of fruitfulness or "generativity."

The all-encompassing story of heaven and earth, following its initial creation, is fittingly summed up in the word *toledot*. The animating principle and fundamental moving energy in this story is the generative power of which conception and birth are the prime embodiment. This generative power can take many forms and operate at many levels, as when one speaks of conceiving how to solve a problem, or coming up with a fruitful idea, or when a social or economic structure so serves the purposes of life that it can be called a blessing.

The word *toledot*, of course, is variously translated, depending on whether it introduces a genealogical list or an extended narrative focusing on a specific individual and his family. The relation between genealogy and narrative can be thought of in terms of how we may view a videotape. The genealogy is a "fast-forward" movement through many generations, in such a way that the emphasis is on the primary events of birth, parenting, and death. In contrast, the narrative can become so detailed as to look like a "slow motion" study of a single highly important action within the life of a single person or generation of people. When such a narrative is introduced by the the *toledot* heading, it is implied that — not only at the beginning of life, but throughout an individual's life and the interaction between individuals and groups — the divinely intended governing principle is the power of blessing. Insofar as the narratives show other principles and motives at work which threaten life and render it barren, the story of heaven and earth becomes ambiguous and its outcome appears uncertain. This ambiguity is clarified and the progress of the story is steadied by the genealogies which, sprinkled throughout the narratives, reassert the continuing efficacy of the original divine creative intent and action.

By the device, then, of the *toledot* formula that runs throughout Genesis, the Priestly editor firmly connects specific persons and their descendants in chs. 12–50 to the Creation narrative. These persons have their specific and mutually diverse vocational purpose and status in the world in relation to the generic human status announced in 1:27 and the generic commission given in 1:28-30. Such a connection is underscored by the loud echoes of 1:28 in ch. 17 (referring to both Isaac and Ishmael; see commentary); 28:3; 35:11; and 48:4 (and see Exod. 1:7) — all of these passages involving promises of abundant children to one or another infertile couple.

The connections between Gen. 12–50 and Gen. 1–11 are more allusive in the Yahwistic strand of tradition, yet they cannot be missed. The portrayal of the Jordan valley as "well watered everywhere like the garden of Yahweh . . . , before Yahweh destroyed Sodom and Gomorrah" (13:10) presupposes the reader's familiarity with Gen. 2 on the one hand (the blessing of fruitfulness) and Gen. 3 on the other (the curse of relative barrenness on the ground). Similarly, when Sarah says of herself, "after I am old . . . shall I have pleasure (*'ednah*)" (18:12), the imagined "pleasure" of childbearing would be her participation in the fruitfulness of Eden as the garden of God (cf. Isa. 51:2-3), while her actual barrenness is implicitly her participation in the destiny spoken of in Gen. 3. Thus Sarah in 11:30, and Rebekah, Rachel, and Tamar, are all presented in implicit connection and problematical contrast with Eve, whom Adam names in 3:20 as "the mother of all living."

Both Gen. 1 and Gen. 2 present the world, and humankind within it, as a place of blessing and fruitfulness. Whereas Gen. 1 (the first Creation account in Gen. 1:1–2:4a) uses the word "bless" three times to refer to this fruitfulness, Gen. 2 does not use this word at all, but instead provides the garden as a picture of the total blessedness of creation. That this is a picture of primal blessing is implicit in the fact that its opposite is the repeated occurrence of the word "curse" in ch. 3, and that the latter word refers to a reversal of the garden's fruitfulness. When the so-called "salvation history" begins in 12:1-3, its agenda is announced in the fivefold repetition of the word "bless/blessing." This fivefold repetition answers to the fivefold reference to "curse" in chs. 1–11 (3:14, 17; 4:11; 5:29; 9:25), signalling that the agenda of the salvation history is to counteract the workings of evil in the world and to restore the world to its divinely intended blessedness. In this respect, then, chs. 1–11 are not the preface to the main story called salvation history; rather, the salvation history is a remedial process within the larger story of God's creation.

Again, consider how God's word to Abraham, "I will make your name great" (12:2), echoes "Let us make a name for ourselves" (11:4). The new community through which "salvation history" begins is set in some sort of contrast with communities that would secure their status through an economic empire based

5

on skill with weapons (see 10:8-12) and rendered safe behind awe-inspiring city fortifications (11:4). One cannot fully appreciate the character of Abraham's vocation to "go from your country . . ." (12:1) unless one hears this call as a contrast to the fearful defensive steps taken in 11:4 "lest we be scattered abroad upon the face of the whole earth." Whenever Abraham's descendants begin to emulate 11:1-9, they will betray their vocation.

In short, I take Gen. 1–11 as much more than a preface to the rest of the OT, which is then understood as primarily the story of the relation between God and Israel. The earlier chapters are the foundation and the continuing frame of reference for that particular story. If they are not often explicitly referred to in Gen. 12–50, that is because they are everywhere presupposed and echoed.

THE RELATION BETWEEN GENESIS 12–50 AND EXODUS-MALACHI

R. W. L. Moberly has written a book that has broken fresh ground on a number of important issues: *The Old Testament of the Old Testament: Patriarchal Narratives and Mosaic Yahwism.* As the title suggests, Moberly argues that Gen. 12–50 relates to what follows in the OT on the analogy of the relation between the OT and the NT. (Or, to turn it around, we may understand the relation between the OT and the NT on the analogy of the relation between Gen. 12–50 and Exodus-Malachi.) Just as the NT focuses on Jesus Christ as the fulfillment of divine promises presented throughout the OT, so God's acts on behalf of Israel beginning with the Exodus fulfill the promises made to the ancestors in Gen. 12–50. Again, just as Jesus Christ may be said to be typologically prefigured in the OT as a whole, so God's later relation to Israel, and the events in Israel's history, are in some sense typologically prefigured in the ancestral narratives.

I consider Moberly's thesis to be sound and profoundly suggestive in its main lines, and set forth with admirable theological concern and sensitivity. (In this commentary I have attempted to show how aspects of later salvation history are foreshadowed in aspects of the ancestral narrative, e.g., when Gen. 12:10–13:1

foreshadows the Exodus.) But in one aspect of Moberly's argument I am less confident that he is correct. Since the issue at this point bears directly on the status and significance of Gen. 12–50 in the Bible as a whole, I shall quote extensively from this one aspect of his argument:

> The thesis I wish to propose is that the relationship of patriarchal religion in Genesis 12–50 to Mosaic Yahwism in Exodus onward is analogous to the relationship of the Old Testament as a whole to the New Testament. Or to put the same point differently, the position of the adherent of Mosaic Yahwism with regard to the patriarchal traditions in Genesis 12–50 is analogous to the position of the Christian with regard to the Old Testament. *Each case gives the sense of looking back on a previous period of salvation history from the perspective of a new period that has in some ways superseded the old.* (126, italics added)

> In the terms *Old Testament* and *New Testament* the epithets *old* and *new* are not primarily chronological judgments. . . . Rather, the terms are first and foremost a theological judgment to the effect that the content of the Old Testament belongs to a period and mode of God's dealings with the world that has been in some ways superseded by the coming of Jesus Christ in the New Testament. (156)

> It is as necessary for the Christian that the faith centered on Jesus in some ways supersedes the religion of the OT as it was for the adherents of Mosaic Yahwism that their faith in some ways superseded patriarchal religion. . . . The new religions, respectively centered on Christ and Torah, have normative status for their adherents and relativize the significance of the former dispensation. (161)

There is much to ponder in these statements; and I am half-inclined to agree with them. However, two sorts of biblical emphasis combine to give me pause.

(1) In the letters of Paul many texts can be brought forward

to support Moberly's view that the Mosaic (or Torah-centered) "mode of God's dealings with the world . . . has been in some ways superseded by the coming of Jesus Christ in the New Testament" (156). By the logic of supersession, this should mean that Christians are twice removed from the religion of Israel's ancestors, and that that religion should be even more relativized for Christians than it was for adherents of the Mosaic Torah. Yet, strikingly for our purposes, in Paul's view the ancestral religion gains in prominence vis-à-vis Mosaic religion in the light of Christ. In what many consider his two most important letters, Galatians and Romans, Paul "relativizes" the Mosaic Torah, not only with reference to the grace of God enacted in Jesus Christ, but also by appeal to the ancestral traditions of Gen. 12–50! In Gal. 3:15-18, for example, the Mosaic covenant in no way supersedes or "annuls" the Abrahamic covenant or makes its promise "void" (see Rom. 4:13-14). So far as Paul is concerned, the theological core of the ancestral religion remains foundational, and the theological core of Mosaic religion, however great in importance, does not annul or supersede it. The difference between Paul and his fellow Jews who do not follow Jesus is precisely that, in Paul's view, they have allowed the Mosaic dispensation to supplant the Abrahamic. The result is that the Abrahamic frame of reference is not able to help them recognize Jesus as the fulfillment of God's primary agenda in the world.

It is the same in Romans. As C. E. B. Cranfield shows in his commentary on Romans (International Critical Commentary [1975-1979]; abridged [Grand Rapids: Wm. B. Eerdmans and Edinburgh: T. &. T. Clark, 1985]), the argument in Rom. 9–11 moves from the statement in 9:15, "I will have mercy on whom I have mercy," to the conclusion in 11:32, "God has imprisoned all in disobedience so that he may be merciful to all" (NRSV). But of course, while the OT quotation in Rom. 9:15 is from Exod. 33:19, Paul brings it in immediately after his brief survey (Rom. 9:6-13) of God's dealings with Isaac and Ishmael, and Jacob and Esau, as though already in the ancestral period God's relation with humankind depended ultimately on divine mercy rather than human will and merit (v. 16). The fact that Mosaic religion with its Torah serves to "imprison all in disobedience so that [God] may be merciful to all" (Rom. 11:32, NRSV) shows that Mosaic religion fulfills a particular and necessary function within the larger compass of ancestral religion but does not supersede it. In 11:28, having written, stringently, that "as regards the gospel they are enemies of God for your sake," Paul goes on to write, "as regards election they are beloved," not for the sake of the Mosaic covenant and the Torah, but "for the sake of their ancestors" (NRSV).

(2) However, Paul's view of the relation between ancestral and Mosaic religion, especially in Rom. 9–11, is already foreshadowed in the book of Exodus. In Exod. 32–34, when Israel breaks the newly made covenant by making the calf, it is *for the sake of God's promises to the ancestors* that Moses asks Yahweh to forgive Israel (Exod. 32:13). In response, Yahweh sets forth the divine nature in 33:19 as "I will be gracious to whom I will be gracious, and will show mercy on whom I will show mercy." This characterization of God as gracious and merciful, and "abounding in steadfast love and faithfulness," is then reiterated in Exod. 34:6-7 and from there echoes throughout the OT (e.g., Jon. 4:2; see Mic. 7:18-20). But the divine attributes of steadfast love and faithfulness do not emerge for the first time in Exod. 34:6, for they appear already in Gen. 24:27 (see commentary). Their appearance in Exod. 34 applies to the specific problem of idolatry and sin, but these two attributes represent a divine character that is appealed to already in the ancestral period. The problem with sin and idolatry is that it threatens to abort the divine redemptive agenda which begins with the ancestors, the agenda of restoring creation to its intended blessing. God's method of dealing with sin at Sinai, like God's dealings with the ancestors, is grounded in steadfast love and faithfulness.

For the relation between these two eras from the perspective of the people we may consult the book of Nehemiah, in which the Sinai covenant and the "book of the law of God" (e.g., Neh. 8:18) appear to stand at the very center of the people's life. Thus, on a day of fasting and confession of sin, they read from the book of the law for a fourth of the day, and for another fourth they make confession and worship. When this confession reaches its climax in the prayer of Ezra (Neh. 9:6-38), he begins, "Thou art Yahweh, thou alone." We expect a recital of the Exodus from

Egypt and the covenant at Sinai, followed by reference to the idolatry of the calf and subsequent sins of the people. This is indeed what appears in Neh. 9:9-37; but that is not how Ezra begins or ends. He begins by celebrating Yahweh as maker of heaven and earth and as calling Abraham from Ur of the Chaldees. Then he calls God's attention to the fact that "thou didst find [Abraham's] heart faithful (*ne'eman*) before thee, and didst make with him the covenant to give to his descendants the land of the Canaanite . . . ; and thou hast fulfilled thy promise, for thou art righteous" (Neh. 9:7-8). It is as though the community rests its current standing before God, not on its own compliance with the laws of Sinai, but on the fact that God has found Abraham faithful and made a promissory covenant with him. This agrees with the way in which the repeated references and appeals to God's grace and mercy in Neh. 9:17, 19, 27, 28, and 31 (cf. v. 32) echo Exod. 33:19; 34:6-7 and thereby indirectly continue the reference to God's faithfulness to the ancestors. Then Ezra ends the prayer as he began. As Fredrick Holmgren has shown, the choice of language in the last sentence picks up the theme of Abraham's faithfulness: "Because of all this, we make a firm covenant" — literally, "we enact an *'amana* — a 'faithfulness.'" As Holmgren writes, "Although the influence of the Sinai tradition is easily observable in Neh. 9:6–10:1[9:38] (see, e.g., vv. 13-14, 16, 26), it is the covenant made with Abraham that determines the basic movement of the text" (Holmgren, "Faithful Abraham and the *ʾᵃmānâ* Covenant," 252). If it is the period of Ezra and Nehemiah that gives such great prominence to Sinai and its laws for subsequent generations, nevertheless Ezra's prayer at this point both echoes the book of Exodus and anticipates Paul in placing Moses and Sinai within the continuing theological framework of the relation between God and Abraham.

At the level, then, of specific forms of religion in one period or another, one may wish to speak of supersession. (Cf., e.g., Jer. 3:15-18, where in the return from exile the ark of the covenant "shall not come to mind, or be remembered, or missed; it shall not be made again.") However, the term "supersession" is misapplied when used to identify what is at the core of God's dealings with the community of redemption. (Thus, if the ark is not to be made again, that is because its function is taken up and continued by the city of Jerusalem [Jer. 3:17].)

The great merit of Moberly's thesis lies in its basic formula, which I consider to be sound: Ancestral religion is to Mosaic religion what the OT is to the NT. By the above remarks, I hope to have nuanced Moberly's thesis in two respects: First, the relations between ancestral and Mosaic religion, like the relations between OT and NT, are not unilinear but complex, and not helpfully illuminated by the introduction of the notion of supersession. If it is the case that "the New is in the Old concealed, the Old is in the New revealed," the reverse is also the case: "the Old is in the New concealed, the New is in the Old revealed." That is to say, the revelation of God presented in the OT is hidden in Christ (the way yeast is hidden in dough, or the way the fundamental teaching of the OT concerning the reign of God is again and again hidden like a messianic secret in the parables of Jesus). It is as Christians read and reread the OT that Jesus becomes increasingly clear in his person and work. So, in my view, the OT and the NT — like the ancestral and Mosaic dispensations — stand in a relation of mutual illumination.

Moreover, the ancestral narratives of Gen. 12–50, by their intermediate position between the accounts of creation and universal history in Gen. 1–11 and the accounts of Mosaic religion that follow them, hold a unique position in Scripture. Genesis 12–50 is indeed the beginning of salvation history. Yet given its relation to Gen. 1–11 (as I have argued earlier), this means that the whole of salvation history serves universal history and the redemption of the whole creation. The issue here can be pinpointed in a sentence contained in the first quotation from Moberly: "Each case [the Mosaic Yahwist, and the Christian] gives the sense of looking back on *a previous period of salvation history* from the perspective of *a new period* that has in some ways superseded the old" (126, italics added). The language of supersession, with its inadequate way of dealing with relations between "old" and "new," goes hand in hand perhaps with a preoccupation with "salvation history." For a long time biblical interpreters have contrasted what they have seen as the nature- or creation-centered religions of Israel's neighbors with what they have seen as the history-centered religion of Israel. There is a genuine issue here which such a contrast tried to clarify. But that way of conceiving the issue has been unfortunate, tending among other things to relegate Gen. 1–11 to the status of a mere "preface" to the salvation history which is taken to be the main story of the Bible. When Gen. 1–11 is so relegated, it becomes increasingly difficult to prevent the following salvation history, with its focus in Israel and then in the Jesus of the Church, from becoming just another divisive and thereby problematic force in the world — a source of curse rather than blessing.

The remedy for this danger is to keep salvation history in perspective. That perspective is the all-encompassing story of God's creation inaugurated by the heading, "these are the *toledot* — the many and diverse narratives and representative genealogical summaries — of heaven and earth." It is the distinctive function of the ancestral narratives in Gen. 12–50, I propose, that they sustain the literary and theological connection between Gen. 1–11 and Exodus-Revelation. Held in such a connection, salvation history with its elect community loses nothing of its historical particularity, but that elective particularity is placed in service of the wider story of God and all creation. Moreover, by the way in which it narrows the universal scope of Gen. 1–11, and the national scope of much of Exodus-Malachi, to focus on individuals and their families amid other families and nations, Gen. 12–50 offers every individual and family a gate of entry into the story for themselves. As we read of the individuals and families in these stories — Abraham and Sarah, Hagar and Ishmael, Isaac and Ishmael, Abraham's faithful servant, Isaac and Rebekah, Rebekah's faithful wet nurse, Jacob and Esau, Jacob and Leah and Rachel, Judah and Tamar, and finally all Jacob's reconciled children in ch. 50 — we may learn to walk as they learned to walk in the ways of "Yahweh, the God of heaven and of the earth" (Gen. 24:3, 7). That such a path leads from Abraham to Christ is Paul's argument in Gal. 3:1-28. That this path then turns and leads from Christ back to Abraham is Paul's conclusion in Gal. 3:29, for "if you are Christ's, then you are Abraham's offspring, heirs according to promise."

COMMENTARY

12:1-3

It is said that the journey of a thousand miles begins with a single step. The biblical story of redemption, as it begins in Abraham, is a journey in blessing from a single person to all the families of the earth. This journey is set in motion by a call from God. For all its brevity, this call is of immeasurable importance, for it both anchors the journey and guides our interpretation of each step along the way — Abraham's, his descendants', and our own steps as we join the journey.

As so often in poetry and in narrative prose, the shape or structure of the passage is a guide to its content and meaning. Therefore, the first step in commenting on this passage will be to consider its structure.

The key to Yahweh's call to the founding ancestor lies in the pattern of its primary verbs: a twofold repetition of one *imperative* followed by three *result* clauses:

> I. Go from your country and from your kindred and from your father's house to the land that I will show you,
>> a. that I may make of you a *great* nation,
>> b. and that I may *bless* you,
>> a'. and that I may make your name *great*;
> II. and be a blessing,
>> b. that I may bless those who *bless* you
>> a. — but the one who *belittles* you I will curse —
>> b'. and that by you all the families of the earth may *bless* themselves. (author's translation)

In I sentences a and a' are marked by the common term "great." Enclosing sentence b, with its "that I may bless you," a and a' together show how God will bless Abram: Abram will become a great nation with a great name. The "name" echoes the concern for a name in Gen. 11:4, just as "great" (Heb. *gdl*) echoes the tower (*mgdl*, literally "great structure") in 11:4, 5. The people in ch. 11 seek to make a name for themselves by building a great defensive tower and walled city. There is a vivid contrast between God's opposition to human attempts to make a name for themselves and God's intention to give Abram a great name. This contrast matches the contrast between fearful human attempts to safeguard their unity in one place by building a walled city, "lest we be scattered abroad upon the face of the whole earth" (*erets*), and Abram's willingness to follow God's call to leave his own place and people and go to a land (*erets*) he does not yet see. The separation from familiar place and faces, which the people in 11:4 see as filled with danger, is a separation that to Abram is filled with promise.

In I Abram receives blessing; in II he is to be a blessing to others. The theme of blessing in the enclosing sentence I.b becomes the theme of the enclosing sentences II.b.b'. The theme "great" in the enclosing sentences I.a.a' becomes the contrasting theme "slight, belittled" in the enclosing sentence II.a (the Hebrew verb *qll* means "to consider or treat as trifling, as of no account, to belittle"). Section I focuses directly on only two parties, God and Abram. But third parties are hinted at, for a name is meaningful only where there are others who are familiar with it, know what it stands for, and can and do use it. These third parties come into focus in section II, both in their actions toward Abram and God, and as objects of divine action. They are shown as relating to Abram by blessing him or cursing him (II.b.a). They are also shown as relating to both Abram and God by using Abram's name when asking God to bless them (II.b'). (The verb "bless themselves" means here to ask a blessing upon themselves by the use of Abram's name.) Finally, the third parties are shown as recipients of God's blessing or curse, depending on how they relate to Abram.

It appears at first, then, that these third parties are defined only in their relation to Abram. They are referred to only as "those who bless you" and "the one who belittles you" (II.b.a), as if they have no identity in their own right but only in relation to Abram. Yet in the final sentence they are identified in their own right — "all the families of the earth." They are families. They belong to communities, each having its own origin, history, location, and identity. Each community is presented as seeking divine blessing upon itself. There is a movement of the focus in vv. 1-3: from just God and Abram (with other peoples only barely

16

hinted at), to others described only as those who bless and curse Abram, and then to these others in their own lives and concerns as well as in their own relation to God as they seek God's blessing upon themselves. This widening movement suggests a deep relation between the call and destiny of Abram and his descendants, and the call and destiny of all human communities. (It is to be remembered that the God who here calls Abram is the God who has called all creation into existence [Gen. 1], and who has called all humankind to stewardship of that creation [Gen. 1:26-28; 2:15, 19].) On the one hand, the relation between God and all the families of the earth depends on the attitudes and the actions of these others toward Abram and his descendants. On the other hand, Abram and his descendants are called to serve the well-being of all human communities, by becoming the kind of community they all would like to become (cf. Deut. 4:5-8). To bless oneself "by" Abram is to use Abram's name when asking a blessing from God, as in saying "O God, make us like Abram and his descendants." (Similarly the people in Ruth 4:11-12 bless Ruth "by" Rachel and Leah and bless Boaz "by" Perez.)

The blessing asked is first of all God's gift of fertility. This gift is rooted in, and is a specific form of, the fruitful goodness of all creation (Gen. 1 and 2). To ask this blessing in Abram's name is to seek it when, as in his case, the fertile goodness of the human creation has given way to barrenness. Thus Abram's name is associated with the restoration of the goodness of creation when it has broken down. Further, to seek this restoration in Abram's name is to be willing to receive it from God in the way Abram received it — not in fearful grasping, but in faithful trust and obedience.

In Gen. 1 and 2 the fruitfulness of the various forms of life is emphasized by the threefold repetition of the word "blessed" (1:22, 28; 2:3). (The sabbath, which celebrates the completion and wholeness of creation, is itself blessed. This suggests that in some mysterious way that day is itself "fruitful.") In Gen. 2 that blessedness is not named but it is shown in the fruitfulness of Eden, a name that may mean "abundance, plenty." In Gen. 3–11 the contrary word *'rr*, "curse," occurs five times (3:14, 17; 4:11; 5:29; 9:25) to emphasize the growing crisis that threatens life in the created world. Abram's role in the story of redemption is shown in the way the five references to curse are matched by the fivefold reference to blessing in 12:1-3. Even here the curse still finds a place, for the drama of redemption after the call of Abram still unfolds outside of Eden and within the ambiguities and conflicts of history. Yet we should notice the shift from plural to singular (those who bless you; the one who belittles you) and the way II.a is set off by itself, apart from II.b.b'. These shifts suggest that blessing is God's primary universal intention, while curse is a secondary specific provision for dealing with an evil which even then is presented as less prominent (as though God were taking a generous view of humankind).

The universal use of Abram's name in blessing takes on additional redemptive significance, beyond the concern for fertility, when read in relation to the Babel story. In 11:1-9 the original unity of the human family was expressed in its common speech. This common speech, however, was used (11:3, 4) to build a walled city which shattered the one human community by dividing insiders from outsiders. The confounding of the unified speech of the city builders into mutually strange languages (11:7; cf. Ps. 114:1) came both as a sign of the divisiveness embodied in the city walls and as God's judgment on that divisiveness. Now Abram's name is to serve as a seed word in the reunification of the human family (cf. Gal. 3:28-29). All human families, however much their speech may differ, will have in common this one word "Abram" when they use it to ask God's blessing upon themselves. Thus they will begin to receive through this common word what through common speech they earlier sought to sustain but in fact lost. They will find a unity, a solidarity, that cannot be shattered by being scattered across the face of the earth. The benefit that is to come through Abram, then, has to do with two basic aspects of human life — biological descent and social interrelatedness (or nature and politics).

In all, God's speech to Abram contains eight primary verbs: two relate Abram's action (*"go," "be"*), five relate God's action (*"make," "bless," "make great," "bless," "curse"*), and one relates the action of others (*"bless themselves"*). God's and Abram's actions together add up to seven. Like the repeated *imperative + result* pattern already referred to, this numerical pattern also suggests that the completion of God's purposes calls for divine-human "synergism" or "working together" (cf. Paul's term "co-workers [*synergoi*] with God" in 1 Cor. 3:9; 2 Cor. 6:1). It is the joint or synergistic action of God and Abram that is the basis for the eventual well-being of "all the families of the earth" (II.b′), as they seek their life from God in connection with their relation to Abram. (Among all these "families," Jews, Christians, and Muslims already have Abram in common — whatever else may divide them.)

The ancestral narrative begins, as the narrative of cosmic origins in Gen. 1 begins, with a word of divine command (in 1:3 "let there be" has the force of a third person indirect imperative). The mystery of vocation, like the mystery of creation, turns on the way God calls to "what is not," and in so calling to it conveys to it the power to respond (if it will) and, in responding, to "come to be" (cf. Rom. 4:17). The mystery of faith turns on whether the one called will step forth from the familiar sterility and despair of nonbeing, where he or she has been "at home," and venture the risk of the promise of existence offered in God's call. Faith is the womb into which the word comes, the womb that receives and carries the word, shaping one's bodily actions in such a way as to give the word of promise a place to grow toward its birth into actuality (Heb. 11:1).

But toward what actuality is Abram invited to live? In what sense is he to become a great nation and to have a great name? Is it in the same sense that the builders of Babel sought to achieve these goals? Or is it by making a name for great defensive might, a name that strikes fear into the hearts of their enemies and provides the basis for imperial ambitions? (Gen. 11:6 can be translated, "nothing that they propose to do can now be defended against.") It is not clear whether Abram himself, at this point in his life, would know how to answer such questions. We may be sure that the builders of Babel earnestly and sincerely sought the blessings of creation. But they sought them with a harmful wisdom, misunderstanding what is meant by both "blessing" and "a name." If Abram is to be the means of healing what has gone wrong in the human community and in its care of creation (compare 1:28; 2:15 with 3:17-19; 6:5-7, 11-13), part of what will be called for is a reeducation in what is meant by blessedness and greatness. The rest of the ancestral narratives give ample evidence — in Abram and his family, as well as in those who come into contact with them — of the slowness and painfulness with which that reeducation must proceed.

12:4-9

"Abram went, as Yahweh had told him." How did God speak to Abram? What became identified for Abram as God's voice? How was it distinguished from all other voices? Reflection on such questions is guided in part by the way Gen. 12:5 retraces essential elements of 11:31 (the RSV is altered here to show the parallels in Hebrew):

11:31 a. Terah took Abram . . . and Lot . . . and Sarai . . .
      b. and they went forth . . . to go to the land of Canaan
      c. and they came to Haran and settled there.
12:5 a'. Abram took Sarai . . . and Lot . . .
      b'. and they went forth to go to the land of Canaan
      c'. and they came to the land of Canaan.

The son completes an agenda begun but left unfinished by the father. This is an old story, sometimes analyzed today in terms of "scripts" or "agendas." Parents develop a script for their lives which they then pursue, and this script is passed on or "enscripted" in their children like a family "genetic code" through all manner of influence, from explicit instruction and advice to indirect communication, silent example, and even (or perhaps most strongly) subconscious messages.

Abram is called by God to separate himself from his past — to go from his country and kindred and father's house. Yet in doing so, he does what his father did before him in leaving Ur. There is this difference: Abram leaves at the explicit direction of God, while the narrator gives no such indication of Terah's motives. But this contrast is not absolute. The narrator prefaces Terah's departure from Ur with two vital facts: his youngest son has died,

and his oldest son has no children. What is the relation between
these two calamities and Terah's move? Did he seek a change in
fortunes by a change of place? Whatever Terah's motives, was
God at work in and through them? Is the difference between
Terah and Abram one between life shaped by secular considerations and life shaped by divine guidance? Or is it that what was
implicit and unreflectively spontaneous for Terah came into explicit consciousness for Abram and thereby into the realm of
responsive freedom?

The connections between 12:5 and 11:31 suggest that it is
one-sided to read 12:1-4 simply as a break with the past initiated
only by God. God's call to "go from" picks up Terah's earlier
decision to "go from," and so imitates and connects with Abram's
past. It is equally one-sided to suppose that Abram's name (which
means "the [divine] father is exalted") identifies his God simply
as his human father writ large — as though the aims and values
of God are simply the aims and values of the community projected
onto the sky. Abram's going forth to a new life is not to be
explained only in terms of God's action, nor only in terms of
human social aims and values and scripts, but in terms of their
mysterious interaction.

The similarity between Terah's agenda and Yahweh's call of
Abram suggests that God works in and with the forces and
circumstances of human life. That Abram's completion of his
father's agenda is not simply the working out of parental and
other social scripts, but is also a response to God as source of his
own freedom as a personal agent, is suggested by the difference
between the narrator's silence about God in 11:31 and the prominence of God's voice in 12:1-3. Abram's free action, by com-
pleting Terah's agenda in response to God, fuses grace and nature,
freedom from the past and continuity with it. In short, Abram's
action embodies *hesed* — freely given loyalty. (I shall comment
more fully on *hesed* later. Cf. Pss. 118, 136, RSV.)

If Gen. 12:4-5 invite reflection on the relation between Abram
and his familial and geographical past, vv. 6-9 shift the focus to
Abram in relation to another people and another geography, the
Canaanites and the land of Canaan. He arrives at the "place" — a
cult place — at Shechem with its oracle tree (Moreh is from the

21

hiphil form of Heb. *yarah*, "to point out, show, direct, teach").
The relation between the Canaanites, their gods, and their land is
symbolized in two ways: by the humanly built cult place, and by
the oracle tree rooted in the earth. The gods of Canaan, the land
of Canaan, and the people of Canaan exist in an organic web of
meaningful existence that is both natural and cultural, both growing and constructed. This meaningful web is expressed through
the symbols of sacred growth and sacred structure: the tree and
the cult place. Later the narrator will begin to evaluate this web of
existence, but here it is only identified in its essential features.

Into this web comes Abram — and Yahweh. In the vicinity of
the teaching tree Yahweh appears to Abram and instructs him
concerning his relation to this land. Once again the question
arises: What is the relation between Yahweh's appearance here
and the character of the tree? Does the general sacral character
of the "place" and the oracle tree predispose Abram for divine
visitation? If it does, he distinguishes his God from the deities of
the place and its tree by building an altar to Yahweh who has
appeared to him. Yahweh's word to Abram and his response in
setting up the altar together tear the seamless web connecting
gods and people and land in Canaan. Yahweh promises this land
to Abram's descendants, and the new altar at Shechem — to all
appearances like the other altars there — becomes for Abram a
sign of eventual possession of that land. For the present, the
Canaanites occupy the land in fact and in sacred symbol, while
Abram occupies it in symbol only.

Thus God's future first becomes present in the earth in the
form of symbols that are given their meaning by God's promise
and human response. One way of measuring the truth of symbols
is by measuring their correspondence to the way things actually
are. By that measure, the Canaanite cult symbols at Shechem seem
more true than Abram's altar. Their symbols correspond to the
present settled fact of Canaanite occupation, while Abram's altar
corresponds only to the promise he believes himself to have heard
by the oracular tree. The narrative in v. 7b, however, invites a
different measure of the truth of symbols, a measure that takes
account of time as the passage from a settled past into a changing
future known only in promise and symbol. The truest symbols

identify not only what is settled and actual in the present, but also what is in the present only as vision and possibility. What is present in that way is the seed of the future, like a promise in the womb of faith. The Canaanite symbols speak of the settled present and a future arising in unchanging continuity with the past. Abram's altar speaks of a future rooted in the past, but not merely an exact extension of that past.

Settling in a plain in Shinar, earlier migrants had built a city there, and so had sought to secure their dwelling there against the possibility of being scattered (11:1-4). Abram secures his future at Shechem, not by building a rival city but by building an altar. Having symbolically rooted his future there, he is free to move on to the mountain east of Bethel, where he pitches his tent between Bethel and Ai. (The symbolic character of this act becomes clear from the references to Bethel and Ai in the book of Joshua.) Whether or not the mountain itself contains Canaanite cult places, Bethel is such a center, as its name "house of god" indicates. This time, in contrast to Shechem, Abram builds an altar on his own initiative and then invokes Yahweh. This inversion invites the inference that religion and its symbols arise in two ways: in response to divine initiatives, and as human initiatives seeking divine presence and activity in human life. In other words, religion is a genuine dialogue between heaven and earth, with either side capable of initiating a given exchange. Insofar as the second episode with its human initiative follows upon the first with its divine initiative, the dialogue as a whole is rooted in the intention and self-communication of God.

From Shechem, by way of Bethel, Abram now moves on to the Negeb by stages (so the Hebrew text). These stopping places are not identified, nor is mention made of any interaction there between Yahweh and Abram. Such is the process of the emergence of a new identity inhabiting its Promised Land only in expectation: one moves and stops, moves and stops, in stages often unmarked by special significance except as they occur against the backdrop of significant exchanges with God at a Shechem and a Bethel. Through these repeated actions, which leave their trace like sediment on the ocean floor of the soul, faith begins to form character and the strange new world of promise slowly becomes familiar.

12:10–13:1

Abram, whose marriage is barren, now discovers that the land of promise can itself become barren. Like any transient pastoral group responding to local famine (and like his father before him), Abram seeks better fortunes in a change of place. In such circumstances, such conventional wisdom or common sense may generally be assumed to embody the wisdom and implicit guidance of God. However, God has promised this land, barren or not, to Abram. Given that promise, does Abram act in faith or in doubt? The narrator tells us he goes down to Egypt to sojourn, not to settle. Apparently he does not give up on the Promised Land. He is able to leave it in trust that he will return. The theological question is, When does faith act according to common sense and when according to uncommon sense? Common sense in part is peculiar to specific communities, as the wise distillation of their own peculiar trial-and-error experience and reflection. When is faith called to act upon a sense that as yet is uncommon but in time will become common wisdom for a community?

While Canaanite agriculture cannot feed his family, Abram soon realizes that Egyptian society also threatens their safety. Sarai may be barren, but she is beautiful; and as everyone knows, powerful rulers like to collect wives, both to ensure dynastic succession by not relying on only one mate to produce an heir and to provide themselves with an abundant diversity of marital pleasure. The Mesopotamian king Gilgamesh, in his "unbridled arrogance," "leaves not the maid to her mother,/The warrior's daughter, the noble's spouse" (Gilgamesh Epic I.ii.13, 16-17, 24, 28-29). We see the same sort of royal practice in David's affair with Bathsheba, and it is reflected in Solomon's acquisition of many wives (1 Kgs. 11), so that in the Deuteronomic provision for modified kingship it is explicitly prohibited (Deut. 17:17). All this suggests that Abram's suspicion of Pharaoh has its commonsense reasons. How narrowly self-regarding is Abram's fear, and how are we to assess his proposal to Sarai? Does he basely treat her as a means to his own safety? Given her beauty and his relative powerlessness as an alien in Egypt, Abram cannot ensure her safety, so that she may well wind up in someone else's household. The realistic question is whether Abram is to die and leave Sarai and the rest of his household to be absorbed into Egypt, or whether he can contrive to survive and at least preserve the possibility of some kind of positive outcome, for himself and his household and perhaps even for Sarai.

Abram might offer some such commonsense reasoning to justify his proposal. What he cannot know is whether this particular pharaoh will act typically of rulers (in which case Abram's commonsense proposal is prudent) or will show uncommon respect for a marriage bond if he is told of it. The question is, When should faith interpret the motives of other social groups on the basis of one's own fear and suspicion, and when does such suspicion merely perpetuate and intensify a human drama driven toward evil by fear, defensiveness, and manipulation? When is faith called to break this vicious cycle by a social interpretation arising out of trust, and to accept the risks of such an interpretation?

Abram's address to Sarai is punctuated twice by the Hebrew particle *na*, which is untranslated in the RSV but appears in the KJV as "Behold now" (Gen. 12:11) and "I pray thee" (v. 13). This particle indicates that the address it punctuates "is a logical consequence, either of an immediately preceding statement or of the general situation in which it is uttered" (Thomas O. Lambdin, *Introduction to Biblical Hebrew* [New York: Scribner's, 1971], 170). In other words, the speaker regards his or her command or request, not as arbitrary, but as logically called for given the situation or given what has just been said. With this particle the speaker appeals to the hearer to recognize the rightness-in-context of what is being asked or ordered.

There is no question, of course, but that Sarai is the pivot on which the whole episode turns ("because of you," and "on your account," v. 13; "for her sake," v. 16). As such, the weight of the episode falls on her. The question is whether Abram orders Sarai or asks her to act as his sister, and whether she hears and agrees with the logical appeal in his twofold *na*. Does she read the situation as he does, and does she see that her husband's ploy offers a margin of hope also for herself? Does she cooperate because she must, or because she will? In this passage only Abram and Pharaoh are speakers, while Sarai, like God, acts but is silent (in vv. 1-3 and 7 God speaks; in v. 17 God does not speak but only acts). As the story of Abram and Sarai unfolds, gradually she will emerge as both actor and speaker in her own right before God and in society. (Indeed, in ch. 16, where she first breaks into speech, she uses the same form of speech to Abram as he uses toward her in 12:11-13: "Behold now" [16:2]; "I pray thee, go in unto my maid" [16:2, KJV].) Here the actions and speech of others frame Sarai's silence and veiled behavior, the interior character of which the reader is left or invited to wonder about. What is clear is that, taken into Pharaoh's harem, she not only saves Abram's life but enables his sevenfold enrichment (12:16, listing seven sorts of possessions).

If the actions of Abram and Pharaoh center on Sarai, so does the action of God, who afflicts Egypt with great plagues "because of Sarai, Abram's wife" (v. 17). Otherwise referred to only as "woman" or "wife," Sarai is named in her own person at two points: when Abram addresses her with his twofold *na,* and when the narrator in v. 17 gives the motivation for God's affliction of Egypt. If Abram asks her to agree to his ploy for his sake, God acts for Sarai's sake. To be sure, insofar as she is identified not only as "Sarai," but as "Abram's wife," the divine motivation does not focus exclusively on her. But here a first slight narrative clue is given concerning an issue that will emerge prominently later on. In a patriarchal culture permissive of many wives and/or concubines, Abram might suppose that the promise to him of descendants can be fulfilled through some other woman. Sarai herself is not integral to the promise. If God is moved to act for Sarai's sake as well as Abram's, a first signal is given here that Sarai is integral to the divine agenda with Abram.

The passage begins "Abram went down to Egypt" (v. 10), and ends "Abram went up from Egypt" (13:1), foreshadowing the Exodus story in its main lines and even in some of its details (descent to Egypt on account of famine; threat to male and sparing of female Hebrews; plagues on Egypt; the verb *shillah* to describe Pharaoh's "release" of the Hebrews; leaving Egypt with many possessions). Such narrative similarities connecting widely separated events and generations — the earlier foreshadowing the later, and the later recalling the earlier — represent a deep conviction about the course of time. The sequence of events in human experience is not just "one damned thing after another," as Henry Ford is said to have defined history. For all its disjointedness, experience spins a meaningful thread of time, the different phases of which have meaning in light of one another. That thread is woven together with other strands that may change in specific texture and color, as the problems and circumstances of one age differ from those of another; but the Weaver remains constant. Though the crisis facing a whole Hebrew subculture (Exod. 1–2) may differ in many respects from the crisis facing a family (Gen. 12), the experience of each displays affinities with that of the other. The self-identification of the God who appears to Moses at the burning bush ("I am . . . the God of Abraham, the God of Isaac, and the God of Jacob"; Exod. 3:6) is an invitation to the Hebrews in Exod. 1–4 to find in such a story as Gen. 12:10–13:1 the grounds for hope that they too will come out of Egypt. These two stories thus anchor a narrative line along which other stories within the Bible will fall, in relation to other types of crises (e.g., Jer. 23:7-8; Mark 12:18-27). Such individual episodes grow into a connected, living, and growing whole, a kind of narrating "oak of Moreh" or oracular tree, through which God may speak to us as we seek to act in our own time and to make sense out of a history marked by both change and continuity.

13:2-18

This chapter contains one complex episode with a major and a minor thread. The major thread runs through Gen. 13:2-4, 14-18, the minor through vv. 5-13. The episode begins in 13:2 by picking up the theme of possessions from 12:5, 16. This theme is not immediately developed. Instead, the narrative then picks up themes from 12:6-9 concerning Abram's tent and altar and his invocation of Yahweh at Bethel. The threefold repetition in 13:3-4 of the word *sham*, "there" (RSV "where . . . where . . . there"), and the repeated "at the beginning . . . at the first," call attention to the place and to the significance of his stop there. On first coming from Haran, Abram had arrived in Canaan as a stranger to that place, and his altars at Shechem and Bethel had served as inaugural markers. Coming now from Egypt, Abram's arrival at Bethel has the character of a return and a recognition, and his invocation of Yahweh has the character of a reenactment. The strange has begun to become familiar. If the life of Abramic faith consists in part in the appropriation of the future through symbols which arise in response to God's promise, then here we see how those symbols become a kind of home to which one can return after events that seem to have taken one away from that promise. The Canadian poet Earle Birney, lamenting his country's comparative newness and lack of deep history such as Europe enjoys, has written of Canada as a country haunted by its lack of ghosts. For Abram, Bethel is becoming a home haunted by memories of promises which sustain hope.

Immediately the narrative breaks off to resume the theme of v. 2, the "also" of v. 5 juxtaposing Lot's livestock and tents alongside those of Abram. Drought-prone Canaan is unable to sustain two such sizable herds "dwelling together" (twice repeated in v. 6), and strife erupts as economic constraints threaten social peace. The note concerning the Canaanites in 12:6 is sounded again (13:7b), a reminder of their present control of the land and an implicit critique of the prospects for the future of this community of promise in this place if it cannot solve the emerging problem of insufficient space (cf. Exod. 1:7-11).

On entering Egypt Abram had dealt with a possible threat by a proposal to Sarai, the logic of which (in the twofold *na*) was clear to him but is questionable to many readers. Now he addresses Lot in similar fashion (Gen. 13:8, "Let there be *na* no strife"; v. 9, "separate thyself *na*"; see KJV). Abram's appeal (v. 8) rests in the assumption that kinfolk ought not to fight with one another. What is the logic of his proposal in v. 9? One can imagine other solutions based on Abram's senior status in this patriarchal extended family, solutions embodying the premise that power and rank are served first, with others getting what is left over. In offering the choice of grazing land to Lot, Abram reverses that premise and embodies an understanding of power as a capacity both to enable and to accept the decisions of others. The generosity of this action stands in contrast with his fearful prudence in

12:10-16. This may be a function of the contrast between Lot as male and Sarai as woman, or of the contrast between Lot as kin and Egypt as foreign. Or Abram's generosity may be an act that cannot be reduced to a function of the situation or of his own character. It may be an act of freedom and grace that helps to transform the situation, creating openness for a peaceful solution where, a moment ago, economic constraints had everyone locked in conflict.

Lot chooses what he sees — a land watered and lush, reminiscent of the Egypt from which they have just come and, at a deeper level, reminiscent of the "garden of Yahweh." What he does not see is that its city-dwellers are wicked and will bring down divine judgment on that area. The comparison of the land with the garden of Yahweh, the theme of evaluating and choosing what is seen, and the mention of wickedness and judgment draw this subplot into interpretive connection with Gen. 2–3 and the latter's focus on the problems of appearance and reality and of false and true wisdom. This is not to suggest that Lot's decision is obviously wrong or foolish, for what he ends up choosing is not prohibited. But his decision is naive. The reliable logic built into the original good creation — what is good to look at is good to eat (2:9a) — has been complicated and contaminated by a "wisdom" which can make what is bad appear good (3:6). In his naive innocence Lot makes an obvious choice that will turn out to place himself and his house at risk. Abram, for motives that are veiled from view, contents himself with Canaan.

Upon Lot's departure, Yahweh calls on Abram to "lift up your eyes *na*" (13:14). Abram has seen the land already, more than once. But he is to look again, to see this drought-prone land under the word of divine promise, and so to recognize in it a desirability contrary to appearances and contrary to what is suggested by its unfavorable comparison to the land Lot has seen and chosen. That God can value things contrary to appearances is reinforced by the contrast between the "foreverness" of the gift to Abram and the hinted fate of Sodom and Gomorrah.

Following on 12:1, 7, this is the third time God promises Abram the land. The repeated verb *r'h*, "see" (RSV "look," 13:14; "see," v. 15), takes up and reasserts the motif in 12:1 (where RSV "show" translates *r'h* hiphil, "cause to see"). In this way, 13:14-18 brings to a brief resting point the journey of faith initiated in the first call and promise. Abram is now urged to move about in the land and enjoy it freely. This he does, moving to Hebron and settling there by the oaks of Mamre, where he builds an altar to Yahweh. The cluster of motifs in v. 18 (tent, oak, altar, and the word "there") signals the conclusion of the episode that began in vv. 2-4.

The pattern of local encounters with God is significant: In 12:6-7 God appears to Abram by the oak of Moreh at Shechem to repeat the promise, and Abram responds by building an altar. In 12:8 Abram pitches his tent near Bethel, builds an altar, and calls upon God. In 13:3-4 Abram returns to Bethel and again calls on God at the altar there. In 13:14-18 the pattern reverts to that concerning Shechem, as the altar in the vicinity of the oak is built in response to God's promise. These three places lie along mountains that run through the part of Canaan west of the Jordan, points of special contact with God and with that part of the earth God has promised to Abram. As such, these places symbolize the inseparability of the spiritual and material dimensions of human existence and concern. The pattern of movement between these places, and away from them and back to them, is the rhythm by which a people becomes ready materially and spiritually — in body and in soul — for the arrival of a future in deep continuity to a past which it does not simply repeat.

14:1-24

The account of the creation of heaven and earth in Gen. 1:1–2:3 was followed by a heading (2:4a) that introduced the whole sweep of the following "history" of creation. In chs. 2–11 this history was presented in very broad and inclusive terms, beginning with a representative human couple in the garden, moving through human "families" (10:32), and coming to a climax in the spread of nations across the face of the earth (ch. 10; 11:1-9). Since 12:1 the narrative has narrowed sharply to focus on Abram and his household. Other "families" or peoples have been mentioned only in passing (12:3, 6; 13:7, 10, 13) or as they relate directly

30

to Abram (12:11-20). If one forgets 12:3 (and it is easy to do so), the Genesis story seems really to be about Abram and his promised descendants — as if the whole story is "for" them. Now the narrative shifts dramatically in focus and in scope, away from Abram, and once again embraces the affairs of city-states and empires. Those affairs are marked by the pursuit of defensive and aggressive policies that involve groups of alliances to wage war where it is necessary to success. By the way in which it narrates at some length a specific series of military engagements between two city-state coalitions, ch. 14 reminds us of the human agenda which has become widespread and characteristic since 10:8-12 and 11:1-9.

So long as we read Genesis only through the experience of Abram and Sarai and their descendants, it is easy to assume that in the Bible the human story has its center in them, and that other peoples are only a context or a frame of reference for these ancestors of faith and their descendants. What 14:1-12 does is to remind us that the human story has as many centers — and as many particular stories — as there are peoples. For example, in ch. 13 Sodom and Gomorrah are introduced only in relation to Lot, as the cities of the region in which he chooses to live; but in ch. 14 they are introduced in their own right, as members of a five-state Canaanite coalition attempting to rebel against the imperial overlordship of Chedorlaomer enforced by a four-state Mesopotamian coalition led by the king of Shinar (cf. 10:10; 11:2). In such a perspective, Abram and Lot are only one group among many; their fortunes are easily caught up, swept along, and swallowed up in the fortunes of the larger human agenda (14:12). God may have called the community of promise into existence in redemptive response to the rise of city-states with their aggressive and oppressive forms of power. Yet here the community of promise seems at the mercy of those states and their power. Divine promise seems to be no match for human power in the shaping of human affairs.

When Abram "the Hebrew" is told what has happened (v. 13), he gathers his men to rescue Lot by force (vv. 14-15). This seems a natural thing for anyone to do (like the common sense that led him to pass off Sarai as his sister in Egypt). Is it the right thing

31

for Abram as recipient of the divine promise and in time the new name of human blessing? How does the narrative invite us to view his action? A number of clues may guide us. First, the narrative describes him as "Abram the Hebrew" (v. 13). In the Bible the term "Hebrew" is used to distinguish this people from other people sociologically. It does not draw attention to their inner identity or character as the people of Yahweh. So in 14:13 the narrative presents Abram to us, not as a bearer of divine promise, but simply as leader of one social group among many. Second, as such a leader he is presented as standing in a defensive alliance with a number of local Amorites, an alliance much like the alliances of the small states in vv. 1-12.

Third, in rescuing Lot Abram acts like any small allied power. In contrast to ch. 13 where he settled the rise of strife peacefully, here he is willing to resort to force of arms to assert his claims against his enemies. Is the community of promise to be like any other community, jostling for position by force of arms? What then does Yahweh's promise of name and blessing mean? Does it mean that, among human communities competing under the so-called law of survival of the fittest, the community of Yahweh is promised success and survival over against all others?

Abram's return (14:17) is described as "the defeat of Chedorlaomer and the kings who were with him." Much here depends on point of view. From the point of view of the king of Sodom, Abram's action probably would hardly have been noticed — at the fringes of Chedorlaomer's withdrawing troops, a few insignificant prisoners were stolen away by a local gang. From Abram's point of view, the rescue of Lot and family and goods is a victory over a whole empire, and is remembered as such. From the point of view of the reader, who has been led to look at Abram as God's redemptive alternative to the tangled human agenda of strife and counter-strife, Abram's victory may be viewed as a step in the direction of becoming "like all the nations" (e.g., 1 Sam. 8:5). Will Abram take another step in that direction when, on his return, he is met by the king of Sodom? Will he expand his defensive alliances to embrace this king too? Given the character of Sodom (Gen. 13:13) and the future that lies ahead of it (v. 10), such a possibility would be fateful. With the king of Sodom on the horizon and the reader alert to see how Abram will meet him, the development of this scene is suddenly interrupted by an encounter with Melchizedek which changes things.

Melchizedek is a king — of a city-state identified only as Salem (Jerusalem? the possible hint is not made more clear). He is also priest of God Most High, that is, of El Elyon, who is chief god of the Canaanite council of gods and as such is worshipped as "maker of heaven and earth." In the name of this god Melchizedek feasts Abram's success. In 12:1-3 Abram was told by Yahweh that his name would become a means by which all families bless themselves. In 12:6-8; 13:4, 18 he had carefully distinguished his worship of Yahweh from local gods and their cult places. Now, feasted and blessed in the name of another god, Abram responds with a tithe, as if to accept such a blessing and to make an offering through the priest of this god. What has happened to Yahweh?

Now the king of Sodom arrives. Will the Abram who a moment ago had positive dealings with the king of Salem and his god go one step further in positive dealings also with this king? The king asks that Abram return the people who had been taken by force from his city, but offers to let him keep the recovered goods, perhaps to establish some sort of standing relation. Abram's response is abrupt. He is content to let his Amorite allies benefit from this king, but by his own refusal he distances himself both from the king of Sodom and from those allies. Thus Abram halts his drift in the direction of becoming simply another society among all the other societies, indistinguishable except in name. What leads him to do this? Is it something that happened in the course of his interaction with Melchizedek (14:22)?

Apparently, in receiving Melchizedek's blessing and offering a tithe through him, Abram had in his own mind associated the whole affair with his own god Yahweh. It is as though he thought to himself, "the god whom you worship as El Elyon, maker of heaven and earth, I worship as Yahweh, God Most High, maker of heaven and earth." Further, it is as though the offered tithe conveyed Abram's vow to give up all claim to the people and the goods he had rescued. The contrast in Abram's dealings with these two kings thus makes more complex the question of how the community of promise interacts with other communities of faith and of ultimate meaning. In one instance, Abram seems willing to act in a pluralistic spirit, acknowledging and interacting with another community's forms of faith while preserving his own identity as a Yahwist. In the other instance, he is concerned to distance himself. What leads him to these two different interactions? We are not told. It is as though we are left to interpret the narrative in light of the larger story — just as in our own encounters with other groups we are left to discern what we should do in light of the larger human story as set in the perspective of the divine promise.

This much is clear: In vv. 13-16 Abram resembled any other small power using force of arms to recover people and goods. By the end of the chapter the Abram who benefitted from his interaction with Egypt (12:16, 20; 13:1-2) knows how not to seek his welfare at the hands of such as the king of Sodom. He has relinquished both people and goods, and becomes again the Abram we saw in ch. 13, content not to impose his acquisitive will, but to live by the promise of his God.

15:1-21

The chapter is introduced as a vision (15:1). What is distinctive about a vision is that what is seen within it is different from what is seen by ordinary eyes. It is possible, for example, to have a vision during the day in which what is seen in the vision occurs at night. Thus, the night within Abram's vision (v. 5) may be followed by awakening from the vision (perhaps at v. 6) and further interaction with God during late afternoon descending into dusk which shades off into another kind of darkness (vv. 12, 17). It is also possible that the vision lasts for the whole chapter. In that case the shift from night in v. 5 to late afternoon in v. 12 is typical of what can happen within visions and dreams, where events can unfold in odd ways and scenes can change without warning. I take the whole chapter, then, as one complex episode. For convenience I will comment on vv. 1-6 first by themselves.

15:1-6 The importance of ch. 15 is signalled in several ways. (1) The phrase "after these things" often marks a noteworthy stage or turn in the story (e.g., 22:1, 20; 39:7; 40:1; 48:1; Josh. 24:29). (2) A number of terms that are central to the biblical story occur for the first time here, and thereby receive a foundational definition: "vision," "believed," "righteousness," and the expression "the word of Yahweh came to _____." The latter expression frequently introduces a prophet's reception of the divine word. Here it marks Gen. 15 as prophetic and Abram as a prophet. Long before the rise of prophets in Israel as distinct from priests, sages, judges, warriors, kings, and so on, Abram and his community are described as prophets (see Ps. 105:15). Long before prophecy has to do with critique and judgment, it has to do with God's promise, God's faithfulness to that promise, human response to that promise, and the meaning of "righteousness" in such a context.

God's word comes to Abram "after these things" — presumably after all that has happened since Gen. 12:1-3, but especially after ch. 14. Among "these things" two motifs stand out: Abram continues to acquire goods; but in spite of God's repeated promise (12:7; 13:16) there is no sign of children. Does Abram's response to the king of Sodom in 14:22-24 reflect a disinterest in more goods because of his preoccupation with childlessness? Such a preoccupation is presupposed in the divine address: "Fear not, Abram."

As a divine word, "fear not" has been traced to a cultic setting, where it comes as a priestly "oracle of assurance" in response to a worshipper's petition. In what life situation was the assurance "fear not" at home before it was taken into the cult? I take it that such words belong to the universal language of parenthood, and are at home therefore in the religion of Abram with its emphasis on God as divine parent. The human parent — most often but not only the mother — soothes the hungry, wet, cold, or anxious infant with cradlings and croonings that convey reassurance long before words can convey anything. The croonings become short general expressions like "there, there, everything will be alright" and "don't be afraid," so that specific provisions for specific needs are nested in the deep generic provision of parental assurance. Such assurances convey the sense that the parent is there for the child, and they encourage the child to trust.

In the developmental psychology of Erik Erikson, the development of the capacity for "trust" is identified as the first psycho-social task of the child. Unless this capacity is developed, all other psycho-social capacities will be imperfectly learned. Even where it is well developed at that stage, the challenge to develop other capacities at later stages calls for trust all over again. Life continuously leads us beyond what we know and can deal with familiarly. At each stage, with its accompanying anxieties, the word of God comes: "fear not." Thus the whole of one's life, and of a community's life, is a process of learning to trust in the deep assurances of the God who gives life and who calls and promises in the face of what threatens life.

It is within the bosom of this generic assurance that God repeats the promise. This time it is merely "your reward shall be very great" (15:1). Does this refer only to more goods? Has Abram mis-heard the earlier promise in thinking it included children? Has God reconsidered and withdrawn the promise of children? Or is this the voice of a parent who senses the child's inner disquiet, and purposely speaks in general terms to draw out that disquiet? Is Abram's response (v. 2) an act of doubt or of trust? Deeply anxious children cannot afford to express doubt to their parents. A challenge to parents is a sign that the child feels secure enough to remind them of their earlier promises and to hold them to them. The repetition in vv. 2 and 3, by the way it echoes the repetition of the promise in chs. 12, 13, and here, may reflect a repeated questioning of God that has been going on since 12:1-3. Such questioning, sometimes subconscious and sometimes conscious, rises now to the intensity of a vision in which God deals with it.

In contrast to 15:1, God now responds unambiguously. In 13:16 the promissory image "dust of the earth (*erets*)" corresponded to the promise of land (*erets*, vv. 15, 17). To what does the image of the stars of heaven correspond (15:5)? In a culture where the stars were often worshipped as divine powers that determine times and seasons and fates, Abram may have begun to fear that his and Sarai's barrenness was "in the stars" and that in the face of such cosmic divine powers Yahweh their familial God was ineffectual. Such a focus for his fears is then drawn into the language of assurance. In place of aloneness and helplessness under the stars comes a sense of numerical likeness with them. Abram and Sarai's future is indeed "*in* the stars," but not *from* them. Rather, it is from the creator of heaven and earth (14:22).

Abram, the narrator tells us, believes God (15:6). The Hebrew word "believe" is a form of the verb *aman,* which most basically means "to nourish (as a foster father or nursing mother), to support (as a pillar)." It refers to what is enduring, reliable, and trustworthy. In its present form (the hiphil stem), the verb means "to take another as reliable, and to rely upon that one." As a subjective act, such belief expresses its conviction of the objective reliability of what is believed in. In view of the repeated promise, and the continuing delay in its fulfillment, Abram's belief rests on no evidence other than the word that comes to him once again. In that sense, Abram's belief is itself the only evidence to any third party of the reality of Abram's God. Abram's God is that divine reality who, in the absence of visible evidence, is able to continue to claim Abram's trust and loyalty.

The dynamics of assurance and trust often bond members of a family together in ways that seem unjustified to outsiders. In the midst of great hardship and danger, parents may soothe their children in the recognition that even if they can give them nothing else they can give them generic assurance. In such acts they embody the conviction that, in the face of all that may go wrong, there is a divine goodness in which one may trust without measure. Conversely, in such situations children may cast themselves upon such assurance, in hope that the goodness conveyed through it is deeper than the situation that threatens them. Such assurance and such trust are the seed and the womb of a future for which visible factors in the situation show no promise.

The second line of v. 6 is open to several interpretations. Four questions are at issue: (1) Do the "he" and the "him" refer to God and Abram, or to Abram and God? (2) To what does "it" refer? (3) What is the precise meaning here of the verb *hashab* (RSV "reckon")? (4) What is the precise meaning here of *tsedaqah* (RSV "righteousness")?

The word *tsedaqah* refers in general to "right relations." It can describe one who is in right relations to another, or it can describe a whole web of right relations in society, in the natural world, or in the world of nature and humans together. The distortion of those right relations calls for action leading to their reestablishment. If that action is legal, the result is "righteousness" or "justice." If that action is military, the result is "victory" or "deliverance." If that action converts poverty into plenty, the result is "prosperity"; and if it converts barrenness into fertility, the result is "posterity." (For the last, see, e.g., Job 8:6; Isa. 48:18-19; 51:1-2.) The verb *hashab* means "to think; to devise, plan, intend, or mean; to esteem, value, or regard; to charge, impute, or reckon." Given these ranges of meaning of the two words, Gen. 15:6b may be understood in at least three ways.

(1) "He believed in God, and he [Abram] reckoned it [the promise] to him [God] as righteousness." In this interpretation (as in much Hebrew poetry), the second line parallels the first and spells it out more fully: Abram's belief in God means that he took God's word at face value and trusted it, thereby showing that he believed God to be "righteous," that is, to be acting in a right relation to Abram. One persistent theme in the Bible is the question of human righteousness. But just as persistent, whether as divine assertion or as human question, is the theme of God's righteousness. Abram may be shown here as believing in God's righteousness against the contradictory evidence of the lack of fulfillment of the promise. The "right relation" that *tsedaqah* here speaks of, then, is the still-to-be-demonstrated faithfulness of God to God's own promise to Abram.

(2) "He believed in Yahweh, and he [God] reckoned it [the believing] to him [Abram] as righteousness." According to this interpretation, God considered Abram's belief the appropriate response to God's promise. (To draw this interpretation into a discussion of "faith and works" is perhaps to impose on this story a set of issues which arise elsewhere and may be left to be dealt with there.) The "right relation" that *tsedaqah* here speaks of, then, is Abram's trust in God's promise to him.

(3) "He believed in Yahweh, and he [God] meant it [the promise] to him [Abram] as posterity." According to this interpretation, the verb *hashab* here functions as it does in 50:20:

"God *meant* it for good, to bring it about that many people should be kept alive." God's intention as reaffirmed in this visionary encounter is to set right the fruitful order of creation (Gen. 1:28a) at the point where it has gone wrong in the barrenness of this human couple. The "right relation" that *tsedaqah* here speaks of, then, is the fruitfulness of this couple as part of the restored order of God's creation.

Which of these possibilities is the right interpretation? The question cannot be decided simply from the grammar of the verse itself. This is a case where the right reading of an element in the story depends on how we read the whole story of which that element is a part. Uncertainty over the meaning of this verse, then, should drive us more widely and deeply into the whole biblical story. Even then, various parts of that story may each in their own way support one or another of the above interpretations. Is it possible that the text means to throw us in turn to one possibility and then to another, as though to lift up more than one dimension of this pivotal event? Such a possibility may be disturbing to some readers — and to some preachers who would rather proclaim only certainties. But where trust rests on deep assurance, perhaps we can learn to live at times with interpretive uncertainty, as itself part of the promissory call of God to the community of faith. Such uncertainty borne in questioning trust may become the womb out of which further insight into the meaning of the text emerges at a later time.

15:7-21 With the promise of children reaffirmed and believed, the narrative moves on without pause to reaffirmation of the promise of land. Since he continues to be a wanderer, Abram responds again in the spirit of 15:2-3. A moment ago he had believed. Now he seeks to know. What happens next teaches what it means for Abram's community to "know." It has been said that knowledge is power, enabling its possessor to control the future through action. For the community of Abram, knowledge is not unilateral possession of inert fact; it is a relation between personal agents, bonded by each agent's commitment trusting in the other's fidelity. It is this mutual commitment and trust that makes the relation fruitful.

Instead of simply being told something, Abram is asked first to do something (cf. John 8:31-32). It is a symbolic act, in which he cuts in half each of three animals but leaves two birds intact. Then, "as the sun was going down," a "deep sleep" (*tardemah*) falls on Abram, of the sort we see in Job 4:13; Dan. 8:18; 10:9. It seems to involve a sleep of the ordinary senses and a descent into the depths of the self where human freedom and intentionality have their hidden roots in the likewise hidden presence of God. At that depth, God's presence is felt and seen only as a dread and intense speaking darkness.

God's "know of a surety" (Gen. 15:13) introduces a strange word. It would have Abram "know" of a long delay involving exile from the land of promise, and oppression, and only then the making good of the promise. Yet Abram will be able to die in peace. Hebrew *shalom* connotes wholeness, which in the case of promise includes completion. Though God's promise will achieve *shalom* only much later, Abram will die in *shalom*. Already in this founding act of covenant, we see the characteristic biblical connection between the "not yet" and the "already" of God's redemptive purposes. It is possible to know a *shalom* that is of a piece with and on the way to a larger *shalom*.

This divine word is followed by another reference to the setting sun and the following darkness, as though the narrative seeks to suggest Abram's ever deeper descent into the depths of this encounter with the holy. Now the symbolic act reaches its dramatic pitch and meaning. When covenanting parties pass through the halves of sacrificial animals, they bind themselves to one another in such a way that covenant disloyalty will tear each of them in two as the animals lie cut in two. Fire and flame (like birds) often symbolize the vital soul. Here, the smoking fire pot and the flaming torch may represent Abram and God as the two parties.

The difference between the two symbols fittingly suggests the disparity between Abram and God. What is astounding is that, in the face of such disparity, God and Abram should be shown engaging in such an act of mutuality and parity. The symbolism, in which two parties of such disparate stature still engage in an act of such mutuality, suggests both the humility of Yahweh, however flaming, and the dignity of Abram, however smoking.

Henceforth the wholeness of each (suggested by the undivided birds?) is defined by fidelity to the covenant relation. The event as narrated becomes the matrix for a community that understands itself as drawn in hope and self-commitment into a personal knowing with the God whose purposes work themselves out over long reaches of time and through strange reversals of fortunes. As read again and again, by descendants of Abraham, the narrative can become an event into which the later community may enter for renewal, as often as it finds its own hope flagging and its own commitment weakening.

16:1-16

To this point (except for Gen. 14:1-12) the main narrative line since 12:1-3 has remained focused on Abram. Indeed, the phrasing of 12:1-3 gives the impression that it is in God's dealing with this individual that "the families of the earth" are to see the hand of his God. When Sarai comes into the picture in 12:11–13:1 it is easy to look upon her as merely an adjunct to Abram, though already there are hints that the narrator and Yahweh view her in more than adjunct terms (see above). Now Sarai begins to come into focus in her own right. The presentation of her role in succeeding episodes will invite the conclusion that it is God's dealing with Sarai that is the crucial element in God's dealing with Abram for the welfare of all the families of the earth. Such a conclusion in turn will invite the suspicion that it is the note at 11:30 that anchors the whole ancestral story. However, the present chapter does more than begin to draw Sarai into narrative focus. While it begins with her, it ends with Hagar, in a way that is of profound theological importance.

In ch. 12 Sarai did not speak. Even her actions were veiled from view, as Abram and Pharaoh dominated the episode in both action and speech. Now it is Sarai who speaks and initiates the action: "Behold, *na* . . . , go *na* in to my maid. . . ." Her imperative speech is punctuated by the same particle of persuasion that Abram had used in ch. 12. Then Abram had called on her to act on his behalf. Now Sarai calls on him to act on her behalf, that she might have children. Moreover, she herself acts in giving

41

her handmaid to Abram. He obeys (he "hearkens to her voice"), and Hagar conceives. From Gen. 2:18 one might gain the impression that woman is created to be a helper or adjunct to man — though even there the term "fit" (RSV), translating Heb. *neged,* "opposite to, corresponding to," suggests a peer helper, in contrast to animals on the one hand or divinity on the other. Comparison of 12:11-13 with 16:2-4a suggests that we may interpret Gen. 2:18 as a reciprocal relation: Male and female are called to help one another.

If we may view Abram and Sarai as peer helpers, how are we to view Hagar? She is introduced as an Egyptian maid — presumably acquired in Egypt (12:16; 13:1). One can hardly suppose that Hagar was an Egyptian free-woman reduced to servanthood. Rather, she was likely to have been a servant already in Egypt and was simply transferred from one household service to another, doubly removed thereby from her own native origin and identity. In the whole chapter Abram and Sarai never refer to her by her name, but only by her function as a handmaid. In contrast, the narrator and the angel of God always include her own name in reference or address to her. This difference in her status already suggests something of Hagar's narrative and theological importance. On the one hand she is a social functionary, serving the needs and agendas of others; on the other hand she is a person in her own right, with her own hopes and frustrations.

By conceiving, Hagar has the opportunity to contribute to Sarai's recovery of well-being by giving her child to Sarai according to the custom of the times. In return, by the same custom Hagar is to enjoy the domestic status and security that goes with providing a child for a barren mistress. Instead, she takes her pregnancy as an opportunity to gain a personal and social victory over her mistress. Hagar "looks with contempt" on Sarai. The Hebrew verb, a form of *qll,* is the same verb as occurs in 12:3, "him who curses you," which I have translated "belittles" (see above). Two things are signalled by the recurrence of this verb: (1) The belittling is a wrong that is done to Sarai (16:5), not to Abram. This means that the provisions of 12:1-3 refer not only to Abram, nor only to Sarai as his adjunct, but also to Sarai in her own right. (2) Hagar, who is subject to Abram and Sarai as their maidservant, might have been blessed through them in blessing them with the presentation of her child to them. Instead, by belittling Sarai she brings herself under the judgment of 12:3 and renders herself liable to curse. In her condition — and given the frequent association in the Bible between blessing and fertility, and curse and sterility — that judgment might imply the possibility of miscarriage.

Sarai's inability to bear children has been felt as a cause for shame. That shame has been intensified through the attitude of her maidservant. In such a circumstance, where her husband might well favor the fertile servant over the barren wife, how shall Sarai's honor be upheld? She appeals to Yahweh. In a patriarchal culture she might have interpreted developments to mean that the God of her husband is on the side of her husband and the servant, and against her. Had this God not prevented her from bearing (16:2)? In appealing to Yahweh, Sarai challenges the partriarchal God to be her God in her own right.

Is Abram's response (v. 6) an abdication of his responsibility for justice, or a recognition of Sarai's claim and of her own power of action? Is Sarai's action on her own behalf (v. 6) an appropriate exercise of the justice due her and the judgment under which Hagar has placed herself? "Dealt harshly" translates a form of the verb *'nh* which occurred already in 15:13. In that chapter, the verb described the oppression of the Hebrews as slaves in "a land not theirs" (which readers will know is Egypt). In this way the narrative implies an evaluation of Sarai's action toward Hagar. Anyone who can sympathize with the Hebrews' later flight from Egypt into the wilderness of Sinai is invited to sympathize with Hagar in her flight from this domestic oppression. Yet the fact remains that she wronged Sarai, so that our moral sympathies remain divided between these two women in a way that is not easily reconciled.

Water in the wilderness (16:7) is frequently an earthly sign of divine good news: of fertility in the face of barrenness, and of encouragement in the midst of danger. Given the prominence of well/spring episodes in Israel's ancestral stories (e.g., Gen. 24, 26, 29, 37; Exod. 2; 15:22-27), it is remarkable that the first such episode focuses not on a Hebrew but on an Egyptian fleeing from harsh treatment by a Hebrew. The spring lies near Shur, a border outpost just short of refuge in Egypt. Here an angel of the God of Abram and Sarai finds her. Is heaven (like the spring) on her side, or is this heaven's posse come to arrest Hagar's flight and return her to slavery? The initial address is ambiguous: The angel addresses Hagar by her own name, but also as "maid of Sarai." Yet the angel does not command; it inquires, as if to leave the way open for Hagar to respond. The two questions, as to her origin and her destination, touch her own self-understanding and identity. Who is she? She could lie, but she does not. Hagar tells the two-sided truth: She is a servant, and she is fleeing her servitude. In her "I am fleeing" lies a plea to heaven for justice (similar to Sarai's in Gen. 16:5), for flight implies harsh treatment (cf. Deut. 23:15-16).

In this exchange between Hagar and the angel the reader may trace the dialogue between dimensions of conscience. If the voice of conscience arises out of the voices of one's various social relations, how does the voice of heaven come? When is the voice of heaven heard in and through the clamor of the claims of one's social relations, and when is it heard over against them? This is Hagar's dilemma. "From my mistress Sarai" is the voice of one who has been socialized to the relation of servanthood. "I am fleeing" is the voice of one who acts in response to the call of a different voice. Whose is that voice? Is it only her own inner self? Or is it her inner self as called and claimed by the voice of God?

The first address of the angel, by its "Hagar" and its "maid of Sarai" (Gen. 16:8), seems to reaffirm both dimensions of who Hagar is: She is both herself and a servant of another. If then both dimensions claim her, what is Hagar to do? The angel's second address to Hagar comes in a threefold utterance (vv. 9, 10, 11) that again touches both dimensions, as if to signal the complexity and the momentousness of the action asked of her. The first utterance matches Sarai's action of v. 6 in its harshness: "Return to your mistress, and submit to her." The second verb, "submit," translates another form of the verb *'nh*, which in v. 6 means "deal harshly." Here it means "place yourself again under her power, however harsh it may be." One may recall that Hagar has wronged Sarai. If Sarai has wronged her in return, then all

Hagar's flight has done is to leave two women alienated from one another, adding further to the fund of resentment and animosity that mars relations between different ethnic groups and different social roles.

If the ancestral narratives of Genesis are the opening chapters in the story of the redemption of humankind, then this chapter is noteworthy for how it deals with the sort of conflict in which Sarai and Hagar are caught. The turn in the conflict is to come with Hagar's return to Sarai. She had fled from an affliction imposed on her. Now she is to place herself under that affliction, for the sake of what may follow. We may detect here a first profile of the suffering servant spoken of later in the tradition.

The second utterance of the angel (v. 10) dramatically balances the harshness of the first. Also, by the way it echoes words earlier spoken to Abram, it counteracts the disparity between Hagar and her domestic superiors. Indeed, it invites the hope that her offspring will enjoy a destiny in some way parallel to that of the offspring of Abram. (This will be underscored in ch. 17.)

The third utterance (16:11-12) spells out the second. The son Hagar now carries she will bring to birth — as though by her return to Sarai she will come out from under the judgment of 12:3 incurred by her action in 16:4. She will give the son his name, and the name *Ishmael* will celebrate the fact that Yahweh (Abram's God!) has given heed (*shama'*, "heard") her affliction. The word "affliction" translates *'ny*, a noun from the same root as the verb *'nh* in vv. 6 and 9. The same God who calls Hagar to return to serve under Sarai's heavy hand is the God who has heard and will hear her in that affliction. Her child, born in her servitude, will be free: He will be a wild ass of the wilderness, not a domestic; he will not be under anyone's power (hand), but will enjoy parity with those who act against him; and he will dwell alongside his own kin. Thus, his freedom is conceived and born in the womb of Hagar's free obedience to the call of God. Thus, the story of Hagar and her descendants in 16:9-12 parallels in miniature the story of Abram and his descendants in 15:13-16.

Hagar's response to the angelic call is as remarkable as the call itself. She names God (16:13): "Thou art a God of seeing." As in Exod. 2:23-25, Yahweh is a God who hears (Gen. 16:11) and sees (v. 13) and acts accordingly. Not only does God see Hagar, but (cf. Exod. 24:9-11, after 2:23-25) Hagar sees God and lives. The importance of the occasion is sealed in the fact that the well comes to bear the name she gives to the God who sees her: *Beer-lahai-roi,* "Well of the Living One who sees." The question raised by Gen. 16:7 has been answered: In the earthly well and the heavenly angel alike, Hagar meets a source of life that issues in a future that outstrips what she had hoped.

By the way the whole passage ends, with Abram naming the child (vv. 15-16), one may suppose that Hagar's brief entry into the narrative limelight is eclipsed as the focus returns to Abram. A number of elements in these verses suggest otherwise. First, Hagar's name occurs three times and Abram's four times in these two verses, to bring the chapter to a rounded positive conclusion (seven personal names). Second, Hagar is mentioned only by her name, and not as servant to Sarai or woman to Abram. Third, of the four active verbs in these verses, three are in the repeated expression "Hagar bore," thereby holding the focus on her maternal relation to the child. Fourth, though Abram names the child Ishmael, "God hears," and no doubt supposes the son to be born in answer to his prayers, the reader knows (along with Hagar and the narrator) that Abram is only serving an agenda established already between heaven and Hagar. The name does not draw Ishmael into Abram's future, though he may suppose it does, but testifies silently to Ishmael's own future outside Abram's household. Through this ironic conclusion Hagar's story retains its own full integrity, its own inner identity and freedom, even while she lives as a servant within a people not her own.

To sum up this most remarkable chapter, we may note how, with the human roles reversed, it anticipates the story in the book of Exodus. The first, sobering lesson is that the very community of promise and hope, of redemption and liberation, the community of Abram and Sarai, is itself capable of becoming a community of oppression. Indeed, it can become so in seeking to cooperate with God in moving toward the fulfillment of the promise and the hope held out to it. When that happens, such a community is reminded by this story that it has no monopoly on God's redemptive concern, let alone God's promises. Nor does its reception of God's promises become a basis for justifying its actions toward others when those actions run counter to God's redemptive aims for "all the families of the earth." We may move this discussion to the NT and Paul's reference to Hagar in Gal. 4. In his concern to affirm the liberating power of the Gospel, Paul draws on the Hagar of Gen. 21 as a negative foil. How might he have used Gen. 16? By way of doing justice to Hagar, how may our use of her story balance Paul's?

The second lesson of this chapter rests in the fact that Israel's story includes within it this episode which Israel tells against itself. In this way, here and elsewhere, Israel's story contains within itself elements that should guard against that story becoming an ideological weapon against other peoples. To the degree that Israel's story can become an idol — a narrative way of converting Israel's God into a mere projection of its own wishes and powers over against other people — episodes such as this one serve to shatter the idol, and to set the biblical story free to testify to a God who is not possessed by nor captive to any partisan community. Or perhaps the story testifies to a God who goes into captivity with those who are called to "return . . . and submit," in order that God may empower such suffering servants to live in hope and eventually to bring forth their Ishmaels. In this way of looking at it, the story of Abram and Sarai and the story of Hagar and Ishmael make common cause at the deepest level.

17:1-27

Genesis 16 marked a double shift in focus, from Abram to Sarai and from Sarai to Hagar. The words in vv. 10-12 promised her a future through Ishmael and his descendants distinct from, but in some ways similar to, the future promised to Abram. Yet in naming Ishmael (v. 15), Abram seemed to claim the boy for his own future. The chapter thus ended on a note of tension that introduces ch. 17. This chapter belongs to the Priestly tradition, which gave us the Creation story in 1:1–2:4a and the story of the covenant through Noah in 9:8-17. If the first two stories are universal, including all humankind and indicating the general human vocation on earth before God, this story focuses on the community of Abram as distinguished from all other peoples by circumcision (17:14). The question arises: What is the relation between the universal human vocation to be God's image on earth (1:26-28) and the particular vocation that comes through Abraham? The tension at the end of ch. 16 becomes the context for the treatment of this larger question in ch. 17.

As seen in, e.g., 1:1–2:4a; 9:8-17; Exod. 6:2-8, the Priestly tradition shapes its stories in carefully patterned ways, including repetition of key words and organization of sections in threes (or multiples) and sevens. For example, in 1:1–2:4a the verb "create" occurs seven times. When the verb occurs three times in 1:27, this draws attention to the importance of humankind in creation. The verb "blessed" occurs three times to mark the generative powers of nonvegetative life (v. 22) and of human life (v. 28), and of the sabbath (2:3). The expression "it was good" occurs seven times, the seventh time marked by the term "very" (or "exceedingly" — *me'od*). Chapter 17 is also shaped by such patterns, which will offer clues to the relation between particular and universal human vocation. For now we note that, after God's opening address to Abram and his response in vv. 1-3a, the divine address is marked off into sections by the threefold "and God said to him/Abraham": vv. 3b-8, 9-14, 15-16 (cf. 9:8-11, 12-16, 17).

17:1-3a The meaning of the divine name El Shaddai (RSV "God Almighty") is uncertain. Some link it ultimately to the Semitic word for "breast." Such an overtone, and passages such as Gen. 49:25-26 (see below), may point to God as giver of fertility. That capacity was demonstrated in Abram's case through Hagar. Now, in words that echo the pattern of the call in 12:1-3 (imperatives followed by result clauses), God calls on Abram to "Walk . . . and be . . . that I may make . . . and that I may multiply . . ." God's purpose comes about through divine call and human response. The response looked for has a cultic ring: "before me" and "blameless" (*tamim*, "complete, sound"; in P more than forty times of a sacrificial animal "without blemish"; e.g., Exod. 12:5). Abram's response is in the form of ritual: he falls on his face (Gen. 17:3a). Then comes the first of the three divine addresses, repeating in Priestly tones the promises with which Abram and the reader have by now become familiar.

17:3b-8 Coming after the birth of Ishmael, and echoing 16:10, this passage seems to swallow up the promise to Hagar by drawing it along with Ishmael into Abram's story. Twice (but not three times) he is called "father of a multitude of nations" (vv. 4-5), and this is the meaning of his new name. Whatever historical linguists may rightly decide about the origins and meaning of the name "Abraham," a proper understanding of the name in the context of this story depends on our willingness to allow the name to be redefined by the narrative in which it is introduced (cf. 11:9; 17:17-19; 25:25-26, 30; Exod. 2:10, 22; 3:14-15; and often). Before moving to the second address, in Gen. 17:9-14, we may note the pattern formed by the keyword "covenant": It occurs three times in vv. 3b-8, six times in vv. 9-14, and three times in vv. 19-21; and it is called an everlasting covenant in each section (vv. 7, 13, 19). God is said four times to "make" or "establish" the covenant (vv. 2, 7, 19, 21); and the covenant partner is said twice to "keep" it (vv. 9, 10) and once to "break" it (v. 14). Thus the possible breaking of the covenant is signalled by the way the verb "break" destroys the wholeness of a sevenfold pattern made up of fourfold positive divine initiative and threefold positive human response.

17:9-14 If God's part in the covenant is to "multiply" Abraham "exceedingly" and to "make him exceedingly fruitful" (vv. 2, 6), Abraham's part is to practice circumcision. This ritual marks off his community from other communities. Is it an arbitrary marker, or is there something about circumcision that symbolizes what the community of Abraham stands for amid the peoples of the world? Historians of religion tell us that circumcision was in fact practiced by many peoples, so that physically it would not mark his descendants distinctively. Scholars also offer a variety of explanations as to the meaning of this mark. If Christian baptism (which resembles many other practices of ritual washing) gains its distinctive meaning from the Gospel story in which it arises, and if the rainbow gains its biblical meaning from the Flood story, perhaps we should look for the distinctive meaning of biblical circumcision in the story in which it arises. This story has to do with barrenness which issues in fertility and the promise of communal greatness among the families of the earth. It is in relation to this story that circumcision becomes a covenantal sign.

This sign marks the male generative organ, which in a patriarchal culture is the organic instrument and symbol of social power and status. In such a culture, identity, authority, and wealth (i.e., inheritance in every sense) are transmitted through it. As the first evidence of natural potency, the firstborn enjoys both natural and social preeminence. Thus, primogeniture is the cornerstone of patriarchal society, and is the focus of such a society's conception of the wisdom and the power by which the world arises and is sustained. That the firstborn may come through any female — first or second wife, wife or female domestic — underscores the principle of transmission through the male. So we might suppose that circumcision has something to do with social organization and transmission of power and authority as centered in the male. We might suppose that, applied to Abraham, circumcision celebrates the restoration of his community to such conventional organization and future prospects, after the sterility of Sarai had threatened to bring it to an end. It would be for such a restoration through Hagar to recognized forms of life that circumcision would be a sign, and that "all the families of the earth" would bless themselves in Abraham's name (12:3). That ch. 17 gives circumcision a quite different meaning, however, is suggested by vv. 15-16.

17:15-16 The first sign of a shift in focus is that Sarai too gets a new name. Then, not once but twice, God says, "I will bless her." Through the son she gives to Abraham, Sarah shall become "a mother of nations." This designation, parallel to Abraham's in vv. 4 and 5, shows Sarai to be integral to the divine purpose with Abraham. From the way v. 16b echoes v. 6b, it is clear that this son and not Ishmael will be the heir. With one stroke God subverts two of the bases of patriarchal identity and power: (1) primogeniture is displaced, and (2) inheritance is tied to the mother as well as the father. The point of circumcision begins to emerge. If the male generative organ is the instrument and symbol of conventional wisdom and power, then circumcision may be the mark of a radical reconception of the wisdom and power at the base of God's new society and indeed of creation itself. That reconception may be reflected also in the Hebrew word *tamim* (RSV "blameless") in v. 1. If a sacrificial animal is to be "without blemish," in a redemptive irony it is by mutilation of the male organ of social identity and power that Abraham will be "without blemish" or blameless! This symbolic reversal of conventional understandings accords with the double subversion in vv. 15-16 as analyzed above.

When God springs the surprise of vv. 15-16 on Abraham, the patriarch responds outwardly as before, falling on his face. But he laughs. Why? Laughter arises over the difference between the expected and the unexpected, between the conventional and the incongruous. Laughter is a play of the spirit in the space opened up within that difference; it is a dance of levity amid life's gravity; it is a springing fountain amid waters that fall or run downhill. Even bitter or ironic laughter achieves a moment of "elbow room" in a confining situation. Why does Abraham laugh? He is struck with two implausible discrepancies, one social, the other natural. Socially, he resists the notion that primogeniture (and his own role in it) is to be disregarded (v. 18). This is the objection he presents to God. The deeper discrepancy, which he thinks he keeps to himself, is between God's promise concerning Sarah and her own natural state of barrenness. Abraham too, thirteen years after Ishmael's birth, is probably too old (v. 17). Can even God reverse such a long proven natural inability? By his laughter, Abraham briefly entertains the prospect of God's acting against the conventions of nature and of society, and at the same time hesitates to believe it.

The laugh is on Abraham. His laughter, like his rhetorical questions, opens up within him a brief space of humorous possibility. Though he means the laughter and the questions as doubt or denial, God seizes on them and transforms them into affirmation. As for Isaac, his name gives him his identity and his vocation. He is the embodiment of that laughter and that questioning which, starting in the human breast as humorous doubt, in God's hands is transformed into hope. As such Isaac is the bearer of a transformed understanding of the wisdom and the power at the base of nature and society. The Isaac of later chapters strikes many as an unimpressive character, measured in conventional narrative or dramatic terms. Perhaps the explanation for this is to be sought here in ch. 17. Like the servant of Isa. 53:2, Isaac does not impress the eye that is as yet untutored to God's wisdom and power.

What then of Ishmael? With further irony, God addresses Abraham in words that echo the divine answer to Hagar: "I have heard you." Given what is said in Gen. 17:15-16 and in vv. 19, 21, it is clear that God is free to make good on what was said to Hagar. But the wording of v. 20 gives Ishmael's story an even more remarkable status. The universal vocation that was given to humankind in 1:28 began, "God blessed them, and God said to them, 'Be fruitful and multiply.'" The promise to Abraham and to Sarah had echoed various elements of 1:28: "I will multiply you exceedingly" (17:2); "I will make you exceedingly fruitful" (v. 6); and "I will bless her . . . I will bless her" (v. 16). Only in Ishmael, however, do these three elements converge, accompanied by the third use of "exceedingly": "I will bless him and make him fruitful and multiply him exceedingly" (v. 20). In narrative terms, the thematic energy drawn from Gen. 1:28, and trickling through 17:2, 6, 16, flows into this verse as one climax of this chapter. The covenant is with Isaac; but Ishmael, too, fully enjoys the human mandate of creation. Moreover, it is only in Ishmael that this chapter precisely echoes 12:2: "I will make him a great nation." It is as though every rhetorical means is used to balance the particular covenant in Isaac with the general creation blessing in Ishmael.

What then is the point of belonging to the community of Abraham, and what is the risk of not belonging to it (17:14), if God's intent for humankind can be realized in so unqualified a way through Ishmael? There is no point if the meaning of such belonging depends on the special advantage over others it bestows on those who belong. But belonging to such a community may have great meaning if the vocation of that community is properly understood. The context of that vocation has two dimensions, one natural and one social. Socially, the context is the sort of divisive advantage-seeking typified by the builders of Babel (11:1-9). Naturally, the context is the sort of disadvantage typified in the barrenness of Sarai (11:30). In a world where the actual conditions and conventions of nature and society often frustrate God's purposes for the whole creation, the call to belong to the community of Abraham and Sarah is a call to undergo God's transforming wisdom and power. Conventional power is challenged to reconceive itself; and conventional barrenness is promised fruitfulness. As the firstborn, and through the social convention of a surrogate wife, Ishmael fulfills God's purposes through predictable processes of nature and society. As the secondborn, and through God's laughing reversals, Isaac fulfills God's redemptive purposes in their unpredictable faithfulness.

18:1-15

According to 12:4 and 16:16, Abram lived for eleven years in hope of the promise given him in 12:1-3. According to 17:1, he lived for thirteen years assuming the promise had begun to be fulfilled in Ishmael through Hagar, only to discover that the child of the promise was yet to come, and was to come through Sarah. The divine visitation in the form of the three men now at last draws the long drama toward its conclusion.

The scene in 18:1-8 portrays the courtesies of hospitality in a traditional society. The specific courtesies may vary from people to people, but the widespread practice of the unwritten law of hospitality in traditional cultures testifies to a basic human awareness. This awareness is of a common humanity that runs deeper than customary distinctions of kin and stranger, friend and enemy. This common humanity calls for a response in which one treats the stranger and the enemy as one would treat kin. When outsiders few in number and far from their home are in need of sustenance, one may not ignore their need or take advantage of them, but must give them food and shelter and send them peaceably on their way. Such hospitality may be taken to reflect a sense — however obscure — that all people enjoy divine hospitality through the life heaven gives them and the food and shelter by which they are sustained in the world. Such divine hospitality may be taken as the motive and ground of God's creating purpose and the form of God's sustaining providence.

Human hospitality thus is that response which images God in one's relation to others. It is not surprising, then, that Abraham's hospitality to three men should turn out to be his hospitality to God. As God is imaged in human relations, God becomes present in them. (By these comments on human hospitality as imaging God, I mean to suggest one way of understanding the narrative's shift in focus from three human figures to God. The suggestion turns in part on the assumption, among Israel and its neighbors, that the divine is present where the divine is imaged. In this scene, God becomes present in the unnamed strangers who seek hospitality and in Abraham who extends it.) The scene takes place by the oaks of Mamre, those sacred trees which speak of the fruit and shade that earth hospitably offers humankind. This scene thereby establishes the double theme of hospitality and fruitfulness for the scene that follows.

After the meal, the point of the visitation begins to emerge. If it concerned Abraham, the visitors would pursue it directly with him, as in previous divine visitations. Instead, they ask, "Where is Sarah your wife?" as if to address her indirectly (for she is within earshot). Why this indirection? Two factors may be at work. First, the customs of courtesy toward the host in a patriarchal society would inhibit speaking directly to his wife. Their indirect approach works through such social customs so as to work around them. Second, when one addresses another in the third person, a special kind of communicative situation is established. This strategy is frequent in communication between parents and children, and between estranged parties who might be open to mediation if not approached too directly. Where the one to be addressed is shy, or alienated, third person address respects that one's interior consciousness by not intruding directly upon it. Standing "outside the tent," so to speak, and speaking (as if) to someone else, the speaker allows the hearer to entertain what is said hospitably, but without the pressure and claim — or intrusion — of direct address. To this point we have heard from Sarah only twice, both times in her concern to redress her own unenviable case (16:2,

5). Otherwise we have been left to guess (if we have cared enough to guess) what has been going on within her. The indirect address comes as a tentative first overture to Sarah's veiled attitude.

Since 18:1 Yahweh's name has receded, and Abraham entertains "three men." Now, after Abraham's "she is in the tent" (v. 9), Yahweh speaks (v. 10), promising not Abraham but Sarah a son "in the spring," literally "in the time of life." Spring is called "the time of life," because then vegetation turns green and begins to grow fruit after the winter sleep; and animals then give birth. In Canaanite religion, for example, it is the season when the worshippers of Baal, seeing nature in its renewed greenness, know that he is alive and the god Death has no permanent hold on him. Though humankind gives birth in all seasons, spring symbolizes the generative potential humans share with all creatures. But for Sarah, past the change of life (v. 11), spring intensifies the settled certainties of despair. The annunciation in v. 10 is so incongruous as to move her to the momentary relief of bitter laughter and a rhetorical question whose answer, she thinks, should be self-evident.

"After I have become worn out with use [so the Hebrew], and my husband is old, shall I have pleasure?" (The last word [Heb. *'ednah*] echoes the proper noun Eden, which names a fruitful garden [cf. Isa. 51:1-3]. By this echo, Sarah's barrenness is set in ironic contrast to the general intent for creation represented by that garden.) She knows her own worn-out body. The bitter gap between it and what is promised to it becomes a space filled with her laughter and her doubting question. Though spoken to Abraham, God's response betrays by its content that it is really directed to Sarah. Her laughing question turns on both her age and the age of Abraham; but in quoting her, God ignores her reference to Abraham and repeats only the matter of her own age (Gen. 18:13). The unfolding scene thus draws her ever more fully into its focus.

Now the real problem emerges: "Is anything too hard for Yahweh?" (v. 14) At the burning Bush, Moses' reluctance to get involved in what he regards as a hopeless cause in Egypt is based on his self-knowledge, expressed in the form of a skeptical rhetorical question, "Who am I?" (Exod. 3:11). When God promises

55

to be with Moses (v. 12), the "Who are you" of v. 13 is answered, "I will be who I will be." The real issue for Sarah, as for Moses, is the identity, the character, and the capacities of God. Is Yahweh to be measured by and contained within what one knows of oneself and the world, or does response to Yahweh lead one out beyond those limits?

From Gen. 18:9 to v. 12, Sarah has taken the speaker to be addressing only Abraham, and so has felt free to laugh and voice her thoughts to herself. By the way they echo what she has been thinking, God's words in v. 13 awaken her to the realization that the speaker is in fact interacting with her. Becoming afraid, she denies that she has laughed. Why the fear and the denial? One feels free to laugh in disbelief at a wide discrepancy between what one certainly knows and what is improbably proposed. But something in what God has said in vv. 13-14 alters Sarah's perspective. Now she feels herself claimed by a presence and a possibility beyond her capacity to measure and assess, a presence who can be "known" only in the response of trust, if she dare trust. Doubtful of this possibility, but no longer sure of her old negative certainties, she is suspended in the middle. Now her laughter becomes a sign of her uncertainty, and she tries to hide it by putting on a face of belief. At this, God finally addresses her directly: "No, but you did laugh." The laughter must not be denied. Arising in despair, it may not yet signal trust, but for now only uncertainty. Yet as with Abraham, it signals a "quickening" of her spirit (like the movement of the spirit over the face of the waters in 1:2). God's generative word can call forth new life from Sarah only as it enters into her despair through the opening of her laughter. This opening must not close too soon, for it is this laughter that conceives Isaac. Abraham and Sarah's matching laughter and matching rhetorical questions offer a felicitous portrayal of man and woman as peer helpers of one another (2:18) in their comparable encounters with God.

The scenes in 18:1-8 and 9-15 are connected by the theme of hospitality. In the first scene Sarah serves as auxiliary (v. 6) while Abraham offers hospitality to God in entertaining three visiting strangers. In the second scene Abraham is auxiliary to the interaction between God and Sarah, as the supposed recipient of words actually addressed to her. If in the first scene he is the host, in the second scene she is invited to be the host, in entertaining the possibility of a child in spite of her longtime inability to conceive. Insofar as the two scenes come to a climax in the exchange between God and Sarah and the question of her openness to the divine annunciation, they suggest that a woman's willingness to host the presence of another human being in her body, and to nurture it there until it goes on its own way, is the primal model of faith as hospitality toward God. In the act and the stance of faith, the hospitable creature images the hospitable Creator. As hospitality, faith is the willingness (however uncertain) to allow the word of divine hope to enter one's soul; and it is the willingness (however tentative) to bear that word through time, trusting in God to bring forth a future which is beyond one's own unaided powers.

18:16-33

Since ch. 14 the narrative has focused in various ways on the promise of children to Abraham. Now the narrative resumes a theme introduced in 13:10-13 and woven into ch. 14 (vv. 2, 8-12, 17, 21-24), the theme of Sodom and Gomorrah. These cities occupy a place in the ancestral narratives of chs. 12–50 analogous to the place occupied by the story of Babel in chs. 1–11. If Babel typifies the city-state form of human condition in contrast to which Abraham and Sarah are called to found a new community, Sodom and Gomorrah appear in their story as a continuing contrast to what that new community is to be.

In 13:10-13 the ambiguity is that the region is fruitful as the garden of Yahweh (cf. Isa. 51:3), yet its cities stand under judgment for their great wickedness. In Gen. 14 their leaders are shown carrying on state "business as usual" (i.e., power politics) with other states and attempting to draw Abram into such business; but Abram declines to play that game. Now, immediately after the scene marked by Abraham and Sarah's hospitality to the three strangers (and thereby hospitality to God), God's business with these cities comes to a head. By the way it draws Abraham into the process, God's dealing with these cities shapes our understanding of divine providence (literally, *pro-vide*, "foresee," or "see to in advance").

Living with a sense of divine providence involves the recognition that human knowledge and insight cannot penetrate to the full depth and width of all the forces and agencies that shape the story of the world, its communities, and its individuals. The question is whether we are simply at the mercy of those many unknown forces and agencies, or whether there is a divine knowledge and agency operative in and through them, which we may both trust and serve. In the present passage the narrative first takes us behind the veil of Abraham's ignorance, to where God engages in providential soliloquy (18:17-19). Then we are shown God's disclosure to Abraham concerning Sodom and Gomorrah (vv. 20-21). Finally we are shown Abraham's intercessory response and thereby his participation in God's providence.

The question in v. 17 may be compared with, e.g., Amos 3:7; John 15:14-16. The motive for the unveiling lies in the purpose of Abraham's call (Gen. 18:18; see 12:1-3). What does it mean to become a great and mighty nation? To imitate the great states and empires of history and legend, like those of Nimrod (10:8-12), or of Amraphel and Chedorlaomer (14:1-2), or of local coalitions unafraid to mount a heroic if unsuccessful rebellion against their overlords (14:4)? Lot has been attracted to the region of Sodom. Abraham has declined its attractions and its overtures. What of his descendants? They are "chosen" (18:19, RSV) for a greatness, for an understanding of "righteousness and justice," which means that they must not be kept in the dark about God's judgments on the sort of human self-understandings that prevail in the world's Sodoms and Gomorrahs. In terms of John 15:14-16, Abraham and his descendants are to become "friends" of God.

"I have chosen him" (Gen. 18:19). The Hebrew text reads, "I have known him . . . that he may . . . so that Yahweh may. . . ." God's election comes through God's knowing — more precisely, through God's fore-knowing (cf. Rom. 8:29). Does this mean God knows in advance all details of all actions and events, so that Sodom, and Abraham, and all God's world, are merely acting out a totally fixed script which includes the illusion of freedom, agency,

and responsibility? Such a view of divine foreknowledge is dis-
couraged by such passages as Gen. 18:20-21; 22:12.

Perhaps we should think of God's elective knowing as a divine
envisioning of human life, calling humankind to aspire to a certain
qualitative character but declining to foreknow all details, leaving
at the center of that envisioning a void to be filled by the free
actions of human agents. This void is opened up by God's gift
of genuine spirit and freedom, which may be exercised in faithfulness and justice or in self-serving injustice. Thus, God knows
or envisions Abraham and Sarah and their descendants as a certain
kind of community. It is this divine knowing that establishes the
horizon of their sense of "being known" by God, and that calls
forth their response to God. (In Rom. 8:29, RSV, "predestined"
translates Gk. *prohorizein*, literally, to "pre-horizon" or mark off
the bounds of a territory. God predestines and calls, by knowing
or envisioning humans according to a generic image of what it
is to be human. The tension between God's providence and
human activity arises out of the fact that God's generic image of
what it is to be human is at odds with the human self-image that
so often sets human goals and shapes human behavior.)

Now God discloses the intention to respond to the outcry
(Gen. 18:20-21; cf. Exod. 2:23-25) of those suffering at the hands
of these two cities. The question is not over the fact of injustice,
but over its extent. It is "great" and "very grave"; but is it
"altogether" (cf. Gen. 6:5 with its "every . . . only . . . continu-
ally")? It appears that divine providence, in envisioning
humankind as moral agents, establishes a horizon of freedom
within which evils and oppressions may arise. But that horizon
serves also as a limit to such evil. Have the cities "altogether"
reached that limit? God does not unilaterally decide whether they
have, but allows these cities to show whether they have through
how they respond to the divine visitation ("I will go down") in
the form of two strangers seeking hospitality. Even in their grave
sin, the cities exist within a horizon of divine knowing which, by
declining to know and thereby determine their response in advance, leaves them room to respond humanely if they will.

As often noted, the original text of 18:22 seems to have read,
"So the men turned from there, and went toward Sodom; but

Yahweh still stood before Abraham." The present text is marked in Hebrew Bibles as a scribal alteration made out of a deferential desire not to see God in an inferior position (cf. v. 8, where Abraham waits on the three guests). Yet this is the point of the whole passage. The God who will not decide the fate of the wicked cities apart from their treatment of two strangers, also will not decide apart from the agency of this called person. The God who appears before city-states as one seeking hospitality appears before Abraham as an attendant awaiting instructions. The God who elects to know Abraham as an intercessor waits to see how as an intercessor he will concern himself with "righteousness and justice" (v. 19).

Has Abraham heard in Yahweh's words to him (vv. 20-21) the critical balance, between divine displeasure at the cities' wicked oppression and the small opening for repentance to be explored by the coming visitation? Does he feel in God's attendance upon him an implicit invitation to enter this opening? Or is he aware only of his own concerns for justice? His concerns, of course, are not first for the wicked, but for the righteous swept away in a general judgment. As badly as they are now oppressed by the wicked, to share in the judgment on the wicked would be a greater injustice. For their sake Abraham is willing to countenance the cities' continuing existence.

Abraham's intercession through several stages of negotiation is dramatically interesting for its portrayal of such a haggling between "dust and ashes" (v. 27) and the "Judge of all the earth." One should note how Abraham's concern for a remnant, in shrinking from fifty eventually to ten, mirrors in reverse God's concern over the expanding mass of wickedness (vv. 20-21: "great . . . very grave . . . altogether"). Does this mirror image suggest to the reader that, whether or not he knows it, Abraham participates in God's concern?

One is reminded of Job, whose agonized questions over God's justice are his unwitting participation in God's (agonized?) questions over human piety and rectitude. Both there and here, God's justice seems not to turn on exact retribution. The pathos implicit in Abraham's plea in vv. 23-25 reaches a delirious pitch on Job's lips (Job 24:1-12). Strikingly, only in Job (30:19; 42:6) and here

(Gen. 18:27) is humankind imaged as "dust and ashes." Is it not the height of presumption for dust and ashes to think it can question God about justice in the world? Or is it precisely when dust and ashes concerns itself in this way over justice that it images God? Where the massed forces and agencies in great cities, states, and empires come to work such injustice that in the providence of God they are swept away, but where that momentum threatens also to sweep away the innocent, shall not God's image cry out in protest? Is it not in such protest that the image shines forth and (whether it knows it or not) knows God even as it is known and called by God?

19:1-29

It is clear from a comparison of 19:1-3 with 18:1-8 that the test of Sodom turns on the question of hospitality. The way Sodom fails the test becomes clear through a study of the similarity and difference between these two episodes. For example, each opening section leads to a question, "Where . . . ?" (18:9; 19:5). Then the differences begin. In 18:9 it is the visitors who ask after Sarah within the tent, content to talk about her and indirectly to her through the closed door, seeking to win her response to the word they bring. In 19:4-5 it is the locals who ask after the visitors within the house, insisting on a direct "contact" with the visitors and not waiting for their consent. In 18:24-32 Abraham's concern for a "shrinking righteous remnant" mirrors in reverse and thereby participates in Yahweh's concern for the cities' "expanding sinfulness" (18:20-21). In 19:4 the action of the men of the city involves "young and old, all the people to the last man." Such a triple emphasis on the all-inclusiveness of the assembly suggests the "altogether" that is still in doubt in 18:21.

The contrasts between the two episodes continue to mount up. When Yahweh "goes down" to "know" (18:21) the city's moral condition as reflected in how it receives the two visitors, the city responds by pursuing a quite different sort of knowing (19:5). Whereas Yahweh's knowing is bilateral — waiting to see how the city will respond, and then knowing it in its response — the city's approach is unilateral. Its men "knowing" the visitors does not depend on the visitor's response, let alone their consent. The knowledge in question is the exercise of a certain kind of power — the power to impose one's will coercively in a domination that subordinates and humiliates.

It is important to place the intended homosexual rape in the wider context of the motives and logic of city-state existence as assessed in the biblical narrative. The specific form of "knowing" that the men of Sodom seek is symptomatic of the general character of the city's wickedness. According to 11:1-9, the motive for a walled city is to render a community invulnerable to those it fears, while providing a base from which to impose its rule over those beyond its walls. (Gen. 11:6 reads literally, "now nothing they plot to do can be defended against.") There is an old saying that knowledge is power. The reverse is also true: power is knowledge. That is to say, the sort of power a person or people exercises shapes its knowledge of itself and the world. A people that can impose its will coercively on another people achieves a self-knowledge and identity which it worships in the form of gods who are understood as creating the cosmos through battle and defeat of the dragon of chaos. The incessant warfare between city-states (e.g., ch. 14) typically comes to a climax in the battering down of walls and gates with siege engines, and forced entry into the very bowels of the city under attack. The inner spirit of such power, such political "virtue," is embodied in the rape and pillage of the defeated inhabitants. In such a context, rape is the diabolical sacrament of a whole way of being in the world, individual and social, a whole way of understanding what it is to be human. It is diabolical in that it desecrates its victims in a world which according to the Bible arises and is sustained within the hospitality of God. Specifically, rape desecrates the sanctity of human sexual relations. The sanctity of those relations consists in the mutuality of consent — the mutuality of entrusting one's body vulnerably to the other and offering tender hospitality to the body of the other. Of course, sexual relations need not take the form of rape to fall short of such an ideal. Nor need politics issue in war and its devastation to consist in systematic violence. There is a deep connection between sexual and political relations, in spite of some tendencies to consign the first simply to private and second simply to public spheres. The connection is seen again when the dangers of monarchy in Israel are signalled by the David-Bathsheba-Uriah affair. In the present instance the men of the city of Sodom, by their act of "knowing," aim to assert their political power and identity by their degrading treatment of these strangers.

Lot is schooled in a different ethos, an ethos in which family and clan relations are the model for all other human relations. Accordingly, he is horrified at the prospect of such a violation of his hospitality. But his appeal to the men's sense of common humanity ("my brothers," v. 7) is brushed aside by their retort concerning "this fellow" (literally, "this solitary individual") who has "come to sojourn" and who now has the impertinence to "play the judge" (v. 9). The irony is that it is precisely this lone sojourner whose presence in the city's midst is the moral measure of that city's ethos.

But what of Lot's daughters? Are they not, in turn, the moral measure of Lot's appalling proposal (v. 8)? Can any father not recoil in horror at his callousness? Whether to excuse or to accuse a society capable of telling such a story, some recent commentators have observed that in those days women were not valued as highly as men, so that Lot would be taken to propose a commonly understood lesser of two evils. If that is the case, any truly theological function of this text can lie only in the (unintended) revulsion it might evoke in readers of a different ethos. The present reflection proceeds from a different reading of the point of v. 8 in its context. Before proceeding further, it may be helpful to refer to the similar episode in Judg. 19.

In Judg. 19 three details may be noted. First, the primary issue is not sexuality but relations between citizens, sojourners, and transient strangers (vv. 11-21). Second, though the host (like Lot) offered his virgin daughter and his guest's concubine to the local men to avert "so vile a thing" (vv. 23-24), it is only the guest who in fact shoves his concubine out the door. Was, then, the host's offer meant literally? Or was it meant rhetorically to shock the local men to their moral senses? If in fact the host meant his offer literally, there is a third detail which signals the narrator's view of such an offer. That detail is the mutely telling depiction of the dead concubine's hands: "There was his concubine lying

63

at the door of the house, with her hands on the threshold" (v. 27). Why this detail, if not to draw the reader sympathetically into the violated woman's desperate point of view? She sought sanctuary in the hospitality of the house, and did not find it. Like his action in v. 25, the Levite's speech (v. 28) is callous beyond measure. The narrator's attention to the concubine's hands invites us to view both the Levite's action and his speech in that way. Such considerations lead me to hear in this story a note of profound pathos and moral outrage almost toneless with intensity.

Similarly, it may be — but we cannot be sure — that Lot in Gen. 19:8 seeks to shock the men of the city to their senses, by apparently offering for gang rape two young women whom they as "my brothers" should recognize and treat as the daughters of a neighbor. In that case, if vv. 4-5 establish the quantitative measure of the city's wickedness, v. 8 suggests its qualitative measure. Lot's apparent offer would aim to show up the city dwellers' intentions against the visitors as even worse than the "altogether" morally unthinkable act of the gang rape of a neighbor's daughter. Thus, by offering his daughters to those who should view them as their sisters, Lot may hope to awaken his neighbors to the common humanity they share with those whom they view only as strangers, therefore enemies, and therefore fit objects of their power.

Whatever Lot's reasoning and motives, the men of Sodom persist in their aggressive intentions. Thereupon the two visitors — leaving us in no doubt at least as to God's view of the whole matter — hustle Lot, daughters, and wife out of the town. The escape of this small remnant echoes the escape of Noah and family from the Flood (compare, e.g., the motif of the door in v. 10 with 7:16); and it anticipates Israel's deliverance from the final plague of death on Egypt (compare, e.g., the motif of the un-leavened bread in 19:3 with Exod. 12:39). The narrowness of the escape is underscored in two ways: by the fate of the sons-in-law, who suppose Lot to be jesting (literally, "laughing"; cf. Gen. 17:17; 18:12; 21:6); and by Lot's wife who, ignoring the warning, looks back on the city and shares its fate (19:26b; in ancient treaty texts, salination of the earth is a symbol of judg-ment). While Sarah — all her life barren — will soon have *'ednah* (see above on 18:12), this region — once like "the garden of Yahweh" (13:10) — now becomes barren. More than the Flood story or Babel, the fate of these cities becomes proverbial (Deut. 29:23; 32:32; Isa. 1:9-10; 3:9; 13:19; Jer. 23:14; 49:18; 50:40; Lam. 4:6; Ezek. 16:46-56; Amos 4:11; Zeph. 2:9; Matt. 10:15; 11:23-24; Luke 10:12; 17:29; 2 Pet. 2:6; Jude 7; Rev. 11:8).

However, the stringency of the judgment is qualified. In Gen. 18:22-33 Abraham has prayed that Sodom might be spared for the sake of even ten righteous. Thus a wicked city would be spared for the sake of a righteous remnant. In fleeing Sodom, Lot asks to be allowed to hide in Zoar because the hills are too far. In so doing, by the logic of the righteous remnant in Abraham's intercession (19:29), Lot's presence in Zoar is instrumental in Zoar's escaping the destruction that falls on the other four cities (cf. 14:2, 8). If the four cities become proverbial of final judgment, then the lesson of the providential sparing of Zoar for Lot's sake perhaps resurfaces in the parable of the wheat and the tares (Matt. 13:24-30).

19:30-38

The first human couple, for their own sin, were driven from the first "garden of Yahweh" to a barren land. Lot and family are led from their "garden" (Gen. 13:10) to escape the judgment on its cities and its land (19:25). While Zoar is spared for their sake, Lot's family soon leaves that human stronghold for natural refuge. Walled cities arise from the natural and good instinct of fear seeking safety. But they are monuments also to the pride and power in which this fear vests itself. As such, like lightning rods, they attract divine judgment. In a cave in the bosom of the earth, Lot seeks a safety that is free from the evils that destroyed the cities of the plain (cf. Isa. 2:12-22).

Now the initiative shifts to Lot's daughters. His concern has been for the safety of the family; theirs is for its continuation. The "way of all the earth" (Gen. 19:31, Hebrew) is for a man to "come in to" a woman — in to her chamber and in to her body — that the blessing of life may pass to another generation. But for these women there is no man save their father, who is

65

excluded from such a role by an incest taboo. In this extreme situation, what is to be done? Which is the stronger imperative? The powerful taboo against incest? Or the primal mandate to be fruitful and multiply and fill the earth? Norbert Lohfink has argued that the mandate in Gen. 1 addresses the need to rebuild diminished communities so that they may be large and strong enough to be viable (*Great Themes from the Old Testament* [Chicago: Franciscan Herald and Edinburgh: T. & T. Clark, 1982], 167-182). In the present instance the women's motivation is clear: "that we may preserve offspring." They do so by a striking set of initiatives. First they ply Lot with wine, so that his participation may be unknowing. Then (reversing the common idiom) they "go in" and lie with him.

The development of the scene is as delicately nuanced as its ethics are extreme. The firstborn speaks three times of "our father" — as if to accustom herself to her proposal by feeling it again and again on her lips. Yet in the crucial clause she lightly veils the proposal with her pronominal "let us lie with him." Then the narrator takes over. First both of the daughters, finding support and reassurance in each other's help, "made their father drink wine." Then (of necessity) the action narrows to the one who "went in, and lay with her father" — he in his drugged state unknowing, she having only the veil of night. In the morning even that veil is set aside, as she says candidly, "I lay last night with my father." Then she helps her sister to do likewise. From this double stratagem come two sons, founders of Moab and Ammon "to this day."

How are we to read this story? One may suspect an earlier tale told as a put-down of Israel's oft-time enemies, Moab and Ammon, by impugning their ancestry (cf. the deadly charge in John 8:44, retorting the charge in v. 41). Is that the function of the story as it now stands in Genesis? I think not, for a number of reasons. (1) Other relatives of Abraham who are the founders of parallel peoples, such as Ishmael and Esau, are given their own proper place in the world (Gen. 16:11-12; 17:20; and 27:39-40, on which see below). (2) This is underscored in Deut. 2:2-8a (where Moses refers to Esau as "our brothers") and 2:8b-22 (similarly, of Moab and Ammon). (3) The actions of Lot's daughters are to be interpreted in the context of similar concerns on the part of Hagar, Sarah, and later in Genesis, Rachel, and Tamar. (Tamar, David's ancestor, is particularly instructive here, as the narrator has Judah belatedly vindicate her extreme action.) (4) The actions of Lot's daughters stand in sharp contrast to those of the men of Sodom, both in aim and in approach. (5) The drugging of their father to draw new life from his body echoes, however ironically, the deep sleep into which God placed the first man toward a similar end.

On the one hand, the extreme nature of the circumstances of this story should prevent anyone from taking it as a pretext for casual violation of the incest taboo. On the other hand, the story reminds us that social conventions, however wise and deeply ingrained, are not absolute. Read with due sensitivity for the pathos of its circumstances, this story may help Israel to appreciate that is problematical relations with Moab and Ammon and its attitudes (and stories) about them, however deep-rooted, may be open to revaluation under a God within the bosom of whose providence the "way of all the earth" sometimes moves forward very strangely.

20:1-18

It would at first appear (20:1) that we are resuming the story of Abraham and Sarah from 18:15. But as ch. 16 turned out to be Hagar's story, ch. 20 turns out to be Abimelech's. This is suggested by several features. (1) After the stage is set in vv. 1-2, vv. 3 and 18 frame the episode itself in terms of the "death" and the restoration of Abimelech and his house. (2) Whatever the reader's allegiances in the ancestral narratives overall, here one must sympathize with Abimelech, who has unwittingly been drawn into jeopardy. (3) In this chapter God speaks directly only to Abimelech. (4) Abimelech's plea in v. 4, "wilt thou slay a righteous [so the Hebrew] people?" echoes Abraham's concern in 18:23-25. Thus we are reminded that, while from one point of view the Abimelech affair is an episode in the story of Abraham and Sarah, from another the Sarah affair is an episode in the story of Abimelech. We may recollect that, according to 12:1-3, the whole saga of the community of promise is a component (to be sure, a redemptive component) in the story of humankind which encompasses "all the families of the earth." In that light, the story of Abimelech (like that of Hagar) serves to keep the reader's concerns and valuations from narrowing too finely — and ideologically — on the community of promise.

The story of Abraham and Sarah moves from 18:15 to 21:1. In between stand the stories of Sodom and Gerar, each city the recipient of a divine visitation, and each city the burden of Abraham's intercession. The similarities accentuate the differences between the two cities, in character and in destiny. Again, Abraham's repetition of the "wife-sister" ploy associates Abimelech with the pharaoh of 12:10-20, and with the general theme of the people of promise sojourning under foreign rule. As we shall see, not all such rulers come under the same judgment, for not all such rulers behave in the same way.

As they approach Gerar, Abraham uses the ploy with Sarah's cooperation (20:5). Given what happened in Egypt, how are we to think of their rationale? Do they suppose Abimelech will not take Sarah into his house? Do they trust that Yahweh will somehow deliver her again? In any case, Abimelech in this respect acts true to royal form. (One may think of David as also acting true to royal form in taking Bathsheba, though, unlike Abimelech, he knows of her marriage to Uriah.) This time the divine visitation comes in a dream, "you are a dead man." The "death" (cf. 30:1 and commentary) consists in the closing of all the wombs in Abimelech's house, and apparently extends to Abimelech himself, God deadening any desire he might have had for Sarah (20:6).

Abimelech's protest rests on his claim to have been unaware of violating any existing marital relation. How can actions done with a clear conscience be wrong? Yet the objective structure of human relations runs deeper and is more widely woven than the reach of ordinary daytime consciousness. That objective structure has been violated, and it cries out wordlessly with its own protest. This cry comes to voice in a dream of the night, at one and the same time the disclosure of the objective facts and of the voice of God.

In Abimelech's view there is a direct causal move from the

integrity of his heart to his actions (v. 5). The way God modifies this view is telling. Acknowledging the integrity of Abimelech's heart, God inserts between this integrity and Abimelech's following actions the observation, "it was I who kept you from sinning against me." If Abimelech has placed his house in jeopardy through unawareness of the deep objective structure of human relations, he also has been kept from worse jeopardy by a yet deeper objective divine presence and activity of which he has likewise been unaware. If God intervened in view of the integrity of Abimelech's intentions, this suggests that conscience and conscious intention, for all their limited grasp of any total situation, can interact at deep levels with the elements in that situation and with God. In this encounter between Abimelech and God, then, we have a remarkable picture of moral sensitivity and responsiveness on the part of a city-state king. Unlike the pharaoh of the Exodus, when God's word comes to Abimelech he responds in repentance and the fear of God (v. 8).

The dialogue between God and Abimelech is followed by a dialogue between Abimelech and Abraham. Abimelech's rhetorical questions (as such questions typically do) seek to elicit Abraham's own recognition and admission of the rightness of Abimelech's charge: "You have done to me things that ought not to be done" (v. 9). The final question puts its finger on the central issue: "What did you see [so the Hebrew], that you did this thing?" (v. 10). In Abimelech Abraham had "seen" a typical royal figure who would act in typical royal ways. He was of course not entirely wrong. Yet such a seeing, insofar as it was informed only by stereotypes and failed to allow for differences in individual kings, worked an injustice on this king. Human consciousness cannot penetrate to the full depth and width of the complex forces and agencies which surround one. Therefore human knowing cannot adequately take account of all the actual details of a given situation, but "sees" them in terms of typical past experiences and common understandings. This is especially true of the way different peoples and different social groups see and interact with each other, and particularly where such groups possess markedly different kinds and degrees of power. In such situations, one's fear of the other may lead to misperceptions which in fact may wrong the other.

Abraham excuses his actions because he "saw" no fear of God in this place (v. 11; contrast v. 8). Moreover, he lamely claims to have told only the truth (or, as he himself admits, a half-truth). Then he makes a pitch for Abimelech's sympathy, in his choice of words to describe his call: "When God caused me to wander from my father's house" (v. 13). The verb *ta'ah* refers basically to humans wandering about aimlessly (e.g., 21:14; 37:15) or sheep straying for want of a shepherd. Frequently it is a figure for error and sin (e.g., Isa. 53:6). In the causative form with a human subject it always refers to "leading astray." With God as subject it refers to God's judgments on oppressive "princes" (Ps. 107:40) or expresses bewilderment at God's unfathomable dealings with humankind (Job 12:24-25; and, very strangely, Isa. 63:15-17!). What is Abraham then saying? Is this merely a pitch for Abimelech's sympathy toward a poor itinerant? Or is he disclosing what it feels like to be called of God to a future in which one often feels lost and adrift? At such times, the fear of others can powerfully shape one's perceptions and actions toward them.

Abimelech's response is twofold. He restores Sarah to Abraham, along with material reparations, and he gives him free range in his territory, this last act (Gen. 20:15) echoing Abraham's generosity toward Lot in 13:8-9. Then Abimelech addresses Sarah directly, recognizing that she is in fact the one most deeply wronged. The last act is Abraham's intercession, through which God heals Abimelech and his house.

We may reflect on the whole episode along the following lines. Abimelech has unwittingly violated the objective structure of human relations, moving God to close all the wombs of his house but also to shut down any inclinations he might have toward Sarah. The dream is the point at which dis-closure begins to occur, a dis-closure which moves Abimelech to probe Abraham's hidden motives through a series of questions. These questions uncover Abraham's fear — not a fear of God, but a fear that there is no fear of God in this place. This fear closes Abraham off from Abimelech. The open admission of Abraham's fear is met with Abimelech's repentant acts of restoration and hospitality. Abraham then opens himself more fully to Abimelech by praying for this king whom he had "seen" as a threat, and God heals Abimelech's

70

house. In this way, all the various human and divine relations
which had been closed off from each other are now reopened.
Thus divine providence is disclosed to be at work, both in initiative
and in response, around and within the web of relations being
woven by the various stories making up the one story of the
world. It is a fitting prelude to the climax of the particular story
that began in 12:1-3, or rather in 11:30.

21:1-34

The narrative that began in 11:30 and 12:1-3 now comes to
complex closure, centering in turn on Sarah (21:1-7), Hagar (vv.
8-21), Abimelech (vv. 22-32), and finally on Abraham (vv. 33-
34). In the first three episodes Abraham is an auxiliary. In the
last episode the narrator focuses on him alone, taking up motifs
introduced in 12:6-8.

21:1-7   The opening lines, virtually poetic in their repetitive-
ness, reinforce the sense of satisfactory closure: "visited . . . as he
had said;/did . . . as he had promised." In Isa. 40–55 God is
First and Last, Beginning and End, One who promises and fulfills
(cf. Rev. 1:8). The "oneness" of God (Deut. 6:4) is spelled out
in Deuteronomy frequently in reference to the promises made to
the ancestors and soon to be made good in the entry into the
land. Strikingly, the opening lines here in Gen. 21 speak of God
visiting Sarah and doing to Sarah as promised. This underscores
her centrality in the story, made explicit in 17:19, 21; 18:9-15,
and now in retrospect implicit already in 12:1-3.

The son nevertheless is born "to Abraham," who names him
"Isaac" and circumcises (*mul*) him. This child is the fulfillment
of both Sarah's and Abraham's stories as individuals. Or rather,
as the unifying focus of their initially separate laughters (17:17;
18:12), Isaac is the sign in which their individual stories become
individual strands in one communal story. Thus, whereas in Exod.
2:22 Moses both names his son and gives the meaning of the
name, here Abraham does the naming (as in Gen. 16:15) and
Sarah gives the meaning: "God has made laughter for me." Her
laughter had begun in ironic disbelief and doubt. Yet even there,

71

the laughter had opened up a space within her settled despair. Now the laughter becomes a different kind of disbelief, as when one disbelieves for joy (cf. Luke 24:41) at something too good to be true which nevertheless has come true. The dreamlike character of the experience is captured in Ps. 126, with its movement from weeping to laughter. These two contrasting moods or modes of human existence mark the depths and the heights of the Psalter, the gravity of lament and the levity of praise. These contrasting moods also mark the journey from Exod. 2:23-25 to 15:1-18. Israel's foundational hymn of praise in Exod. 15:1-18, responding to Miriam's call to praise in 15:20-21, has its anticipation and root in Sarah's "God has given me laughter." In opening her womb Isaac has opened her soul to praise.

"Every one who hears will laugh with me" (Gen. 21:6). The laughter is hers, but not hers alone. Her laughter should cause joy in all who hear it (cf. Rom. 12:15). How wide is the circle of that joy? With Gen. 12:3b in mind (and cf. Ps. 126:2), we may suppose the circle to be as wide as human celebration can make it. For the moment, Sarah's soul opens to embrace all who will laugh with her.

"Who would have said to Abraham that Sarah would suckle children?" (Gen. 21:7). There is a verbal play here between "said" (Heb. *millel*) and "circumcised" (*mul*, v. 4; also *malal*). The play arises partly as sheer delight in the echoing play of language by which its main focus of meaning glances sideways to further dimensions of meaning. What might such a glance suggest here? The verb *millel*, "say, utter," and the noun *milla*, "word, speech, utterance," always have to do with wise utterance. Sarah celebrates a divine action that exceeds what human wisdom could have foreseen. In so doing she celebrates a deeper wisdom, whose laughter/play before God is a laughter/play in God's inhabited world and with the children of earth (cf. Prov. 8:30-31).

To name is to identify, to invoke, to define, and often to control. The divine self-naming in Exod. 3:13-15 identifies Yahweh, and enables Israel to call on Yahweh, but makes Yahweh present as one who cannot adequately be defined or therefore controlled. In laughter one breaks out of the confines of conventional expectation and understanding. Isaac, then, is a name that celebrates all of earth's children who respond to the creative and redemptive play of Yahweh in their midst.

21:8-21 Until he is weaned, Isaac knows his mother as the primary horizon of his life. His weaning feast marks his move into a wider circle. Within that wider circle, Sarah sees "the son of Hagar" (never named in this passage) "playing (*metsaheq*) with her son Isaac (*yitshaq*)" (restoring the last phrase with the help of the Greek). Oblivious as children will be to the complex histories and agendas of their parents, these two boys explore the delights of interaction in a world whose boundaries are as yet open horizons rather than borders guarded and controlled by settled adult opinion, proven adult knowledge, and narrowly purposed adult goals. For the boys, those boundaries are a threshold across which daily they move into wider regions of possibility through discoveries marked by laughter. That laughter is in fact the widening circle of Sarah's earlier laughter, the widening circle of the play of God with the creation. In their laughter, wisdom is justified by her children (Matt. 11:19, RSV mg).

Sarah does not see it that way. With an adult wisdom defined by clan experience, tradition, and observation, she sees Hagar's son as an alien threat standing inside the circle of her family's laughter. Is God's promise to her (Gen. 17 and 18) not enough for her? Is Abraham's commitment to the child of that promise not enough for her? Is it that Sarah feels she must act in concert with God and Abraham to secure the future of the promise? Or is she settling an old score? Her motives, however mixed, converge to expel Hagar's son from the circle of her laughter. (The Jewish and Christian communities of Sarah should be able to identify her agenda from within their own respective similarly defined and self-protective circles of concern; cf. John 9:22, 35; Gal. 4:21-31.)

The matter is displeasing to Abraham for the sake of his son Ishmael, for whom he has a responsibility and a concern Sarah cannot be expected to share. (Fathers too have their circles, and Ishmael stands properly within his.) With instructive irony God calls on Abraham not to be displeased because of the lad — and because of the slave woman. (God's circle is yet wider, embracing also Hagar.) Whatever Sarah says to him, he is to "hearken to her voice" (so the Hebrew; cf. Gen. 16:2 and commentary), for the twofold promise of 17:19-21 remains valid. (In being asked to entrust Ishmael to God and the wilderness, is Abraham being prepared here in a preliminary way for ch. 22? Compare 21:14 and 22:3.) Like Abraham in 20:13, Hagar wanders (*ta'ah*) in the wilderness of God's will (21:14).

Do the Sarah of vv. 8-10 and the Abraham of vv. 11-14 know of God's earlier promise to Hagar in the wilderness (ch. 16)? It is unlikely that Hagar has shared this with them. What positive relevance might her story have for them? Now, however, the promise to her comes to a severe test. The water used up, Hagar shelters the child in the shade of a bush and goes off "the distance of a bowshot." Why? So as not to witness the child's death? Or so that it will not hear the tone of desperation in her words, "let me not look upon the death of the child" (21:16)? (The distance of a bowshot would place her out of his hearing but keep him within range of her sight.) I take Hagar's words, together with her weeping, as a prayer that Ishmael's life may be spared.

Tellingly, while Hagar prays, it is to the child's own voice that God responds. In 16:11 Ishmael's name meant that God had heard her plight. In 17:20 it meant God had heard Abraham's. Now, though the lad's name is not mentioned, the meaning of his name underlies the angel's "fear not; for *God* has *heard* the voice of the lad where he is." (On "fear not," cf. 15:1 and commentary.) Ishmael's name connects him to God through his mother, through his father, and now in his own right. The weaning of parents from their children begins to come with the recognition that children have their own dealings directly with God, and that God's concern for them does not arise only in response to parental prayer, but also directly in response to the children themselves. That recognition does not mean the end of parental prayer; but it changes such prayer, from one of primary sheltering responsibility to one of auxiliary help.

God opens Hagar's eyes to see a well (cf. 22:13-14), echoing the spring of ch. 16. The promise of that earlier meeting is reiterated (21:18b) and then begins to be fulfilled (vv. 20-21). Hagar's son is at home in God's wilderness, Paran (cf. Deut.

33:2), where his mother provides him with a wife from Egypt. Thus the Hagar story as we have it ends at a well and a wife. These motifs signal the continuation of her story beyond the horizon of our immediate attention but within the horizon of God's providence. The two children who played together will meet once again, in an act that speaks of continuing ties between them, when they lay Abraham to rest alongside Sarah (Gen. 25:8-10).

21:22-32 As in ch. 20, the framing verses, 21:22a and 32b, identify this section as part of the story of Abimelech. In ch. 20 God's concern for Abraham and Sarah had been conveyed to Abimelech through a dream. Here God's concern for them becomes evident to him through their good fortune, as he says, "God is with you in all that you do." If these words refer in part to the birth of Isaac, then in some sense his comment is his way of laughing with Sarah (cf. vv. 6-7).

Yet Abimelech and Phicol are uneasy. They know Abraham to be capable of deceit in behalf of his own cause. Such a man who also enjoys God's favor is doubly dangerous. So they seek to stabilize relations with him. Since Abraham's well-being depends on his God, Abimelech first seeks a formal oath from him in the name of that God. (Abraham's formal oath would be, "May God do thus and so to me, and more also, if I deal falsely with you or with your offspring or with your posterity." Cf. 1 Sam. 3:17; 2 Kgs. 6:31.) Then, adopting Abraham's less formal language of Gen. 20:13 ("this is the *hesed* you must do me"), Abimelech says, "As I have done *hesed* with you, you will do also with me and with the land where you have sojourned."

The ethics of *hesed* is the ethics of loyalty between family and clan members. "Kindness" is the loyalty one shows to one's "kind" or kin. It is whatever response one owes to one's kin in a given situation. Such ethics roots in a compassion (*rahamim*) arising out of common ancestry (*rehem*, "womb"). In 20:14-16 Abimelech had acted with a generosity that echoed Abraham's dealings with his nephew (13:8-9), and with a regard for Sarah's name worthy of a kin. Unsure of Abraham, he now seeks a covenanting formal oath from him. It has been observed that covenant relations arise as a form of substitute kinship relations. That is, covenant relations formally extend kin ethics beyond the range of kin relations, implicitly exploring the possibility that different kinship communities may treat one another within the horizon of a common human kinship under God.

When Abraham complains of a well seized by Abimelech's servants, the shoe is now on the other foot. But, at great length and with some exasperation, Abimelech complains in return that Abraham once again has not been openly communicative. It is as though, not taking the offer of 20:15 at face value, Abraham has dug the well on the sly and kept quiet about it like a poacher on someone else's land. Another formal ceremony is called for to deal with both complaints. In a bilateral oath, Abraham claims the well as his and Abimelech acknowledges that claim.

The general need for oaths between humans is a symptom of the mutual fear and suspicion that so often leads to self-protective deceit. The oath itself is a means to the healing of such human relations, or at least a means of preventing such relations from falling deeper into mutual deception and betrayal. Where one's feelings and intentions are not available for public inspection, one's integrity can be pledged as security for the truth of what one vows to do. That integrity is pledged in the name of what is held as most sacred. Violation of such an oath destroys one's integrity and one's relation to what is most sacred. Where oaths cease to carry such sacred import, where they cease truly to be self-binding and become merely another cynical ploy in one's own cause, human relations become a hell on earth. That different communities, serving different gods, can honor the sanctity of each other's oaths is an implicit affirmation of one humanity that, however deeply diverse, lives and is held within one sacred horizon. Individuals and communities who honor and live by their own oaths and who trust one another's oaths within such a horizon live in hidden hope of the open truth of shared laughter. Within such a horizon, Abimelech takes leave of Abraham.

21:33-34 Sarah's giving birth, in 21:1-7 (like dry ground opening into a well of life — Prov. 30:15-16; Cant. 4:12, 16), is followed by three passages all centering in the well at Beer-sheba

(Gen. 21:8-21, 22-32, 33-34). The last passage concludes by connecting back to that birth, and indeed back to ch. 12. The Abraham who had earlier called upon God by altars or sacred trees (12:6-9; 13:18) now plants a tree and calls on Yahweh. With the birth of Isaac a new sacred tree grows in the land, and a new divine name appears on Abraham's lips. The Everlasting God stands behind the everlasting covenant (17:7, 13, 19) which has now been made good in Isaac, the tree securely rooted in the land promised as an everlasting possession (17:8). With this the saga of Abraham and Sarah themselves, which was begun in 11:30; 12:1-9, seems at last to be concluded, and we might expect the narrative to move on to the next generation. What began as a divine promise in the midst of barrenness ends as a divine fulfillment in the form of fruitfulness. In their case, the passage of time itself, by the way it moves to a rounded completeness, becomes an image of God's everlastingness; and the mark of that everlastingness is fruitfulness whether in the form of Isaac or the planted tree.

22:1-24

In the book of Job the divine silence is finally broken by Yahweh's address from out of the whirlwind (Job 38–41). Job responds in worship (42:1-6), but he does not tell us what it is in Yahweh's address that leads him to that response. How then can we be sure we interpret the spirit and meaning of his worship correctly? In such issues as Job deals with, it is as though we are brought to a point beyond which the text cannot control the interaction between the reader and the ultimate mystery. Finally the reader must become Job and make his or her own response. So it is with the present chapter. Commentators soon reach the point where, like Abraham's servants, they must stop and simply leave the reader with the text to "go yonder and worship." In that spirit, the following comments are offered diffidently.

22:1-14 At the beginning (Gen. 12:1), Yahweh had simply instructed Abraham, "Go. . . ." Now, before any instruction, God calls him by name, "Abraham." That name calls up all he has become and knows himself to be and to be hopeful of, including the future promised him (17:5). As such Abraham responds, "Here am I," placing himself completely at God's disposal. At the beginning God had instructed, "(a) Go . . . (b) to the land (c) that I will show you . . . (d) that I may make of you a great nation." Now God says, "Take *na* your son, your only son Isaac, whom you love, and (a) go (b) to the land of Moriah, (d) and offer him there as a burnt offering (c) upon one of the mountains of which I shall tell you." The pattern of address by now is familiar. But its content is horrifyingly unrecognizable. Can this be Yahweh speaking? (Only "God" [*elohim*] is spoken of through the first ten verses, and only with v. 11 does the name Yahweh reappear.) Yet there is the particle of persuasion, *na,* which Abram had used with Sarah (12:11, 13) and Sarah had used with him (16:2) (see commentary at both places). In a way that passes all understanding, God's request is to be heard — and to be trusted — as appropriate under the circumstances. Yet those circumstances are not indicated. It is as though the purposes of God in and through Abraham (12:3) call for this naked request to be nakedly trusted and obeyed.

The connection between this call to Abraham and the beginning of his vocation is underscored by the resumption of the theme of altar-building (22:9; cf. 12:7, 8; 13:18), as well perhaps as by the name "Moriah." The meaning of this name has been variously explained. In view of the oak of Moreh in 12:6 (see above) and the term *moreh,* "teacher," in Deut. 11:30; Job 36:22; Prov. 5:13; Isa. 30:20; and especially "teacher's hill" in Judg. 7:1, it may be that "Moriah" here is to be associated with the Hebrew root *hora,* "to teach," and means "Yahweh is my teacher." (Later identification of the mountain in Moriah with the temple site in Jerusalem [2 Chr. 3:1] might then be connected also with that temple as the source of Yahweh's *torah,* "teaching," for all peoples and nations, as in Isa. 2:2-5.) Such a meaning, connecting with Gen. 12:6, would also suggest the climactic character of this chapter as teaching the community of Abraham and Sarah what is at issue in their vocation amid the peoples. If according to 12:3 all families of the earth are invited to pray, "God bless us with children like Abraham and Sarah" (see also 21:6), according to ch. 22 they are invited to pray (if they dare), "God give us trust to obey like Abraham and Sarah."

What the chapter teaches in part is that when all "wandering" (see above on 20:13) seems to have ended in fulfillment (21:33-34), it begins again. In 12:1 Abram was called to leave his ancestral past for a new land. In that land his altars spoke of a promise that awaited him, in contrast to the Canaanite altars that spoke of established realities and of a future marked by the unchanging continuation of those established realities. Will Abraham's finally established reality in Isaac, symbolized in the tamarisk tree planted at Beer-sheba, now become indistinguishable from that of the Canaanites? The altar he is to build now (22:9) signifies his willingness to offer up that future to God, and so to relinquish his own control over it. The subversion of the patriarchal tradition of primogeniture, signalled for example in ch. 17, here comes to its climax.

The regular rhythm of threefold verbal patterns contributes to the laconic surface of a narrative taut with inexpressible feeling. God says, "take . . . go . . . and offer." The narrator tells us that early next morning Abraham "rose . . . saddled . . . and took," and that he "cut . . . arose . . . and went." On the third day he "lifted up . . . saw . . . and said." So far all the action has been God's or Abraham's, with Isaac and the servants only adjuncts. Now (for they are to "stay here") the servants are not even adjuncts. "As for me and the lad, we must go yonder, and we must worship, and we must return to you." These verbs are cohortatives, which typically express self-arousal or self-encouragement in an emphatic fixed determination and the personal interest in doing it (as in calls to worship; e.g., Ps. 95:1-2, 6). Also, they are plurals, drawing Isaac into conjoint action with his father. This conjoint action is then followed by Abraham's action: "He took . . . laid . . . and took." The wood goes to Isaac, for on the altar both must be consumed. The fire and the knife go to Abraham, for he must apply them. Then the verbs become plural again: "they went both of them together . . . they went both of them together . . . they came to the place."

This last sequence is punctuated by a piece of dialogue. Like God, Isaac addresses his father Abraham. But which of these latter

79

two words will he use? Unlike God Isaac says, "my father." So addressed, Abraham responds as he had to God, "here am I — my son." In a situation such as this, how does one both love God with all one's heart and soul and might, and love one's neighbor as oneself? Is not Abraham here torn between love of God and love of Isaac? Yet all he knows is that he is totally disposed toward both God and Isaac. Then, like a son being initiated into adult worship by assisting in it (cf. Exod. 12:26; 13:8; Deut. 6:20), Isaac asks, "Here is the fire and the wood; but where is the lamb?" Utterly disposed to God and to his son, Abraham frames his response with those two words: "*God* will provide (literally, "see to") himself a lamb for a burnt offering, my *son*." Between these two loyalties to God and to his son, Abraham can interpose only a providence which he cannot fathom but must trust. How can he bear to disguise from Isaac what he knows to be called for? Are Abraham's words offered in hope that, at the point of climactic action, when Isaac realizes that he is to be the offering, he may at least recall his father's words and understand his fate as his own terrible vocation? Does Abraham hope against hope for a way out of the impasse, a way that only God can provide?

The threefold pattern of verbs now gives way to a sevenfold pattern: "he built . . . arranged (RSV "laid in order") . . . bound . . . laid . . . put forth . . . took . . ." (Where is Isaac in all this? Is his conjoint action extinguished along with his voice? Or is his silence, like that of another lamb [Isa. 53:7], the mode of his own trusting participation in this rite? As in Job's response to God, what is unspoken here leaves the reader to answer for oneself.) The seventh verb is not a narrative past tense, describing what Abraham does, but shifts to an infinitive of intent — "to slay" — and then this intent is forestalled by the sound of Abraham's name (Gen. 22:10-11). Once again he responds, "Here am I."

This time the instruction of v. 2 is reversed, whereupon looking up and seeing a ram caught in the bushes, Abraham offers it up in the place of his son. Does this mean Isaac has not been sacrificed, as though this story memorializes for its readers the abolition of human sacrifice in favor of animal sacrifice? Yet Isaac has truly been sacrificed — truly given up and given over to God.

The life he will go on to live is now wholly God's, and Abraham no longer has any parental claim on it. The ram both takes Isaac's place and represents him in the sacrifice. That is the mystery, in this instance, of the divine providence. The teaching of this mountain in Moriah is that to live within the providence of God is to live within a horizon defined not by our "seeing to" but by God's provision ("pro-vision"). Yet at the same time, to live within that providence is to learn that the one thing God will not foresee is our response. God waits until we have acted before knowing our response (v. 12). If this has been Abraham's severest test of trust in God, it has been no less an occasion in which (as in the case of Job) God has trusted the human partner in the covenant. Such a portrayal of God is also part of the teaching of this story.

22:15-19 The second address from heaven integrates the events on the mountain in Moriah with the whole of the preceding narrative in chs. 12–21, by picking up key themes and drawing them together in a dense oath. The oath itself begins "Because you have done this" and ends "because you have obeyed (*shamaʿ,* "heard") my voice." Abraham has heard and responded to God's persuasive *na*. Now God swears an oath, which begins with the theme of blessing first heard in 12:2 and ends on its universal significance as in 12:3. By its connection with Abraham's obedience in 22:1-14, this oath underscores what sort of community God intends should prevail among the nations of the earth: It is a community based not on a parent's dynastic control of the future through one's children, but on covenanting trust in God's providence. In turn, if God's providence centers in such a trusting community, it encompasses all the families of the earth in its concern.

As in 15:17-21, the oath pledges the divine integrity as security for the fulfillment of the promise. Given the basis for the need of oaths between human parties (see above on 21:22-32), how are we to understand the portrayal of God as needing to swear an oath?

22:20-24 The narrative now re-establishes connections with Abraham's familial past, setting the stage for much of what will happen in the next several chapters. While in chs. 12–22 Abraham and Sarah have gone through such an epic passage from child-lessness to child-bearing, their close relatives back in Haran have had several children as a matter of course and in a fashion not unlike any other surrounding people. One might suppose, from this difference, that the biblical story flowing from Abraham and Sarah hereafter would have little in common with that of those relatives. Yet, as we shall see, it will be essential to draw a wife for Isaac from these relatives, and not from some other commu-nity. This suggests that in its own way the life story of these relatives who stayed in Haran has been no less a vocation than Abraham's in leaving that place.

A concluding image: The tree planted at Beer-sheba to honor the Everlasting God for the life of Isaac (21:33) symbolizes the restoration of the fruitfulness which is God's primal blessing on creation (1:1–2:3). At Moriah Abraham has been asked, in effect, to cut that tree down. Job, his own children dead, could cry out, "There is hope for a tree,/if it be cut down, that it will sprout again (*yahaliph*),/and that its shoots will not cease. . . ./At the scent of water it will bud,/and put forth branches like a young plant" (Job 14:7-9). If Job could believe that such a thing applied also to human death, he says, then in Sheol "all the days of my service I would wait, till my sprouting (*halipha*) would come. Thou wouldest call, and I would answer thee" (Job 14:14-15, author's translation). As the scent of water would cause the felled tree to sprout again, the sound of God's call would bring new life to dead Job. Both Gen. 22 and the book of Job lead us deep into the mystery of the Gardener who, according to John 15, prunes the fruit-bearing branch so that it may bear more fruit. This is a mystery which perhaps can be humanly plumbed only by the speaker at the Last Supper discourse, and perhaps also by Lazarus, who in the grave was given new power to hear and to respond to the call of Jesus to "come forth" (John 11:43).

23:1-20

With Gen. 22 the story of Abraham and Sarah has reached its climax, so that chs. 23 and 24 are transitional to the story of Isaac and Rebekah. In these chapters the movement from one generation to another is focused on the transition from Sarah to Rebekah. This is signalled in the topographic transition from a cave as a receptacle for the dead (23:19) to a well as a source of life-giving water (24:11). As we shall see, the cave and its grave are a sign of more than an ending. But first we may attend to the central scene, where Abraham negotiates with his Hittite hosts for a burial site.

The proceedings are highly stylized. Abraham and the Hittites engage in three verbal exchanges (direct speech: 23:3b-6, 7-11, 12-15), after which they exchange money and property (narrative: vv. 16-18). The verbal exchanges open with Abraham's request, and continue with the call to "hear" counter-proposals (*shamaʿ*, in vv. 6, 8, 11, 13, 15), until the negotiation is resolved when Abraham "hears" (*shamaʿ*, v. 16; RSV "agreed"). The importance of the verbal exchanges is underscored by the thrice-repeated phrase "in the hearing of" the citizenry (vv. 10, 13, 16), before the actual transfer of property takes place "in their sight" (v. 18, RSV "hearing"; cf. v. 11, RSV "presence"). Thus the transaction is sealed publicly and legally by their auditory and visual witness. Abraham, once only a "stranger and sojourner" among the Hittites (v. 4), now holds land in their midst, identified three times by name (Machpelah; vv. 9, 17, 19) and by function (Heb. *ahuzzat-qeber*, "burial possession"; vv. 4, 9, 20). Previously he had dug wells for his livestock in Abimelech's territory without telling him (21:25-32; see above), and earlier had deceived him in the matter of Sarah. In contrast, Abraham now acts entirely aboveboard with the Hittites.

The transaction advances the promissory theme announced to Abraham in 12:1 and reiterated in 12:7; 13:14-17; 17:8. His appropriation of the promise up to now has been largely symbolic, in the building of altars (12:7, 8; 13:18) and the planting of a tree (21:33). In 21:25-32 Abraham laid actual but secret claim to land by digging a well from which to draw earth's life-giving water. Now he publicly claims land by buying a cave in which to lay his dead in earth's bosom.

One may notice the possible connection between the oaks of Mamre in Hebron (13:18) and the field east of Mamre with all its trees (23:17), in which case the earlier altar at Mamre is now joined by the grave there as symbolic of the progress toward God's promise. Given the traditional practice of burying successive generations among the graves of their ancestors (that they may be "gathered to their ancestors"), Abraham by this step gives one more indication that his departure from Haran and Ur of the Chaldees is permanent. But while the thrice-repeated term *ahuzzah* here indicates a place of burial, generally in the Bible it refers to real estate as a dwelling place (e.g., 36:43; 47:11). Since in 17:8; 48:3-4 God promises the land to Abraham and to Jacob as "an everlasting possession," its occurrence three times in ch. 23, and again in 49:30; 50:13, takes on a foreshadowing connotation: The cave where the dead are laid to rest speaks of a time when the living will dwell in the land where God will give them rest from their enemies round about. Thus death is made to speak of life beyond itself.

This promissory theme is present also in the otherwise odd reference to "all the trees that were in the field" in which the cave was situated (23:17). Like wells, trees attest the capacity of earth to sustain life. A eunuch may describe himself as a "dry tree" (Isa. 56:3), while a dynasty-continuing child may be called a "shoot" or "branch" (Isa. 11:1; Jer. 23:5). So too, a barren woman may be likened to dry ground (Prov. 30:15-16; in Isa. 49:21 "barren" translates *galmud,* cognate with Arabic *jalmadatun,* "stony ground"), while a child-bearing woman may be called "a garden fountain, a well of living water,/and flowing streams from Lebanon" (Cant. 4:15; see above on Gen. 18:12). If the birth of Isaac moved Abraham to plant a tree in Beer-sheba (21:33), the field of trees in Machpelah draws the focus back to Sarah as, in her own way, a "mother of all living" (Gen. 3:20).

Though Abraham is the central actor in this chapter, it opens with a biographical notice of Sarah (23:1-2a) that should lead us to witness all the negotiations in the chapter as being on her behalf. Just as the trees around her grave speak of her barrenness become fruitful, so in her burial she is the first person actually to enter and find rest in the land. God had promised Abram, "you shall go to your fathers in peace" (15:15); and upon his death he will be "gathered to his people" (25:8). Gerhard von Rad comments on the latter passage, "The expression . . . is not correct here, to be sure, and is apparently used with a decidedly hackneyed meaning, for it presupposes the notion of an ancestral family grave" (*Genesis,* 257). But in fact the expression in 25:8 may there be given a distinctly fresh connotation. The similarity between 25:7 and 23:1 suggests that when Abraham dies he is indeed "gathered to his people," insofar as he is buried with Sarah the living font and the first to be buried of that people. If the expression conventionally refers to burial with one's ancestors, here it takes on an eschatological reference (see also Heb. 11:13). If, in time, those who die "in the Lord" are said to be gathered to Abraham's bosom (Luke 16:22), then by that very token they are gathered also to Sarah's. In her life and in her death, then, she images the One from whom and unto whom are all things (Rom. 11:36).

As a footnote to this chapter, the question arises as to how we are to understand for our own day God's promise of this land to the ancestors as an everlasting possession. Does this biblical promise give the physical descendants of Abraham and Sarah everlasting title to the specific territory described in, e.g., Gen. 13:14-17 or 15:18-21? Should Christians in any case understand these promises in purely heavenly terms, after the example of Heb. 11:16a? If the first view seems excessively literalistic, the second in its otherworldliness seems to lose sight of the this-worldly bearing of so much of the biblical message. Perhaps we can say that, at the least, this promise indicates God's intent (1) that the descendants of Abraham and Sarah are to have a *bona fide* place to live among the other peoples and nations of the earth and (2) that, likewise, all communities and peoples are entitled to such a place, so that no community is doomed to endless landlessness. To put this another way: if a place to live in this world is a sacramental pledge of a place to live in the next world (cf. John 14:1-3), no one should be deprived of such a pledge.

24:1-67

Following the double climax in Gen. 21 and 22, Abraham has buried Sarah and now draws near to his own death. It remains for him to put his affairs in order by engaging his chief servant in an oath concerning a wife for Isaac. The meaning of the symbolic act in vv. 2, 9 is not clear. Occurring only here and in 47:29, in both instances it comes at the end of a man's life, where he entrusts his wishes to another. Whatever its possible rootage in wider cultural practice (there is no known precise parallel), the symbolism may receive its biblical meaning as a peculiarly appropriate conclusion to the story of Abraham and Sarah which begins in their childlessness (11:30) and God's promise (12:1-3). Does the symbolic act combine notions reflected in the Latin word *testis,* which means both "testator" and "testicle"? And does this indicate the servant's acknowledgment of and submission to the potency and power of his master? Or does it indicate that, having his master's accumulated goods in his charge (24:2; the Hebrew of v. 10 reads literally, "with all the goods of his master in his hand"), he swears — by grasping in his hand the anatomical seat of his master's generative powers — to discharge his stewardship of them in accordance with his master's wishes? If in 21:22-31 relations between parties in the same generation are stabilized by an oath, here an oath stabilizes relations of continuity from one generation to another. Nothing will prevent the servant from disregarding the oath after the master's death, either by deserting the household or attempting to take it over forcibly. (After all, he had once stood to inherit his childless master [15:2-3], but such prospects have been dashed by Isaac's birth.) But to do so would be to destroy the master-servant relation, as well as the servant's own integrity pledged to Abraham by his oath.

Strikingly, the oath to ensure Abraham's particularist concerns (a wife not from "these people" but from "my kindred") is to be sworn, not in the name of "my father's God" (cf. 24:7, "my father's house," and, e.g., 26:24; 31:42), but in the all-encompassing name of "Yahweh, God of heaven and of the earth." Does Abraham thus echo in part the name by which Melchizedek had blessed God (14:19), and by which he himself had sworn not to be indebted to the king of Sodom (14:22)? In any case, we may note the twin themes of particular election and universal frame running through such passages as 12:1-3; 14:17-24; 17:18-21; 24:3-4.

The servant knows the oath will bind him to his master's wishes. But what if the prospective bride is not willing to bind herself to a future offered to her through a mere servant? Is the son to return to that land and marry into a kindred family there? Abraham assures him that the God who has sworn to him, "to your descendants I will give this land," will send an angel "before" the servant to give his mission success. But the servant's oath is only as binding as Yahweh's oath. If God cannot be trusted, then no purely personal agenda of Abraham's will really matter enough to persist in.

The scene in vv. 1-9 gives us our last close-up view of Abraham, as his last words frame him between two oaths — one from his servant and one from God. In the last analysis, then, the sort of human story that the name Abraham comes to stand for (see above on 12:1-3) rests on the power of oaths taken by God and by others. Abraham cannot unilaterally control the future through his loins, but must entrust that future both to divine and to human sworn faithfulness. Earlier the power of God was attested through the physical generativity in Abraham's loins and Sarah's womb. Now the power of God is attested — through a peculiarly appropriate rite of generative symbolism — as a moral and spiritual power that is felt in the claims of loyalty, felt in the value placed on integrity in response to those claims, and felt in the sense of identity gained in such integrity.

The well, as a source of water for household and for livestock, makes it a natural place for young men and women to meet one another. In the Bible, typically a future bride and groom meet at a well: e.g., Jacob and Rachel, Moses and Zipporah, and Jesus and the woman at the well (whose meeting is introduced in John 3:29-30 by John the Baptist as "friend of the bridegroom"!). In such a type scene, the water-giving well typifies the promise of fertility to the prospective couple.

In the present instance, of course, the servant serves as proxy for Isaac. Awaiting the women's arrival, he prays. Identifying the basis of his own "success" in God's steadfast love to Abraham, he fittingly addresses God as "Yahweh, God of my master Abraham" (Gen. 24:12; so also vv. 27, 42). Later he will refer often to God as prospering his way (vv. 21, 40, 42, 56); but in

v. 12 the RSV's "grant me success" translates a very interesting clause. The verbal root *qarah* means "encounter, meet, befall [by chance]," as when Ruth "just happened" to glean in Boaz's field (Ruth 2:3). In the present instance the clause literally says, "LORD, may you cause a chance encounter before me" (Gen. 24:12). What is the relation between God sending an angel before the servant (v. 7) and God making room before him for a chance encounter (v. 12)? In the present context, are these two ways of saying the same thing? And, given the conventional character of the first, does the second intimate something of the mystery of God's prevenient providence?

The language here is important. Sometimes we choose with a clear inner sense of what is right, or even of God's guidance. Sometimes the choice is as "wide open" as choosing between several attractive options (as in choosing between offered trees in 2:9a, 16). Since Scripture is often read as affirming a tight and explicitly directive divine providence, it is worth noting those passages that sponsor the sense that divine providence can work more loosely (one might say more self-confidently and trustingly), opening up a horizon of freedom for human choices that are made as one would choose a peach or a pear from a bowl of mixed fruit, the choice turning out in retrospect to have an uncanny sense of "rightness" about it. So the servant prays that this irreducibly "chance" choice (which could well have gone in another direction) may be taken up into the horizon of God's steadfast love for Abraham. Just as Abraham is entrusting his future into the hands of God and his servant, so the servant entrusts his actions to Abraham's God.

The quickness with which God answers the servant's prayer (24:15) is echoed in the quickness with which Rebekah responds to his request for water. The disjunctive syntax of v. 21 in Hebrew suggests that it does not follow the actions in vv. 18-21 but parallels them: "the man all the while gazing at her in silence to learn. . . ." His subsequent questions continue to convey to him the uncanny sense of rightness in his choice, and the chapter comes to its first climax with his act of worship in vv. 26-27. Fittingly, the earlier prayerful references to God's steadfast love (*hesed,* vv. 12, 14) give way to the fuller reference to God's "steadfast love and faithfulness" (*hesed*-and-*emet*, v. 27, as so often in the Bible).

Rebekah's similarly speedy report to her family issues in a likewise speedy invitation to share their hospitality — a hospitality, it would appear, that in Laban's case is quickened by the sight of the gifts the servant had given Rebekah after her hospitable response. But the servant will not accept the invitation until he has discharged his mission. We are treated now to a retelling of all that has happened. This is typical of ancient Near Eastern narratives, in which at times dozens of lines are repeated almost word for word (compare Job 1:6-12 with 2:1-7a). No doubt this occurs for the sheer love of a good story by hearers who delight in repetition rather than being bored with it. In the present instance another motive may be at work. The servant seeks to persuade his hearers that his mission is divinely as well as humanly mandated. Instead of simply asserting this, he tells the story from beginning to end, hoping that they will see the encounter at the well as he has seen it — as God's answer to his prayer.

The retelling comes to a climax that is reminiscent of the first climax in Gen. 24:26-27, but with two nice twists. This time, God's faithfulness to Abraham is referred to in shorter fashion (for RSV "had led me by the right way" in v. 48 we may translate, "had faithfully [*emet*] led me in the way"), while the phrase "steadfast love and faithfulness" (*hesed* and *emet*) is reserved for the appeal to Rebekah's family in v. 49 (RSV translates the phrase "loyally and truly"). The significance of this twist lies in the way the servant implicitly invites these kin of Abraham to act as Yahweh has acted and so to participate in the covenant bond between him and Yahweh. The God of heaven and earth has done all that God can do for Abraham and his servant. The rest is up to this family.

When the family has heard the servant's story, it is so self-evident that "the thing comes from Yahweh" that "we cannot speak to you bad or good." There is no room for a debate or independent process of reasoning concerning the pros and cons of the servant's case. God's claim on the family is direct and compelling; in its self-evidence it comes as a revelation. They recognize it as such and agree that Rebekah may go. This leads to the completion of the second climax in v. 52, with words that in vv. 26-27 preceded Abraham's blessing of God but here are delayed until after the response of the family. Thus, by the repetition of vv. 1-27 in vv. 34-49 the revelatory chain of events gets told twice, once by the narrator of the story and once by a character in the story. At the same time, the story gets heard twice, once by the reader and once by a character in the story. In this way, the reader who has heard the story twice is invited to share the response of the family in vv. 50-51. In this way, further, the horizons of narrator, characters, and reader — initially separated structurally and across increasing stretches of time and social location — now merge to encompass one story-formed community.

Finally the servant accepts the family's hospitality and then is invited to stay another ten days. He reminds them of the master whose agenda he serves (v. 56), and as in vv. 50-51 they accede to him. This time, however, Rebekah is called on to speak for herself. The importance of her response is implied in the reiteration of the possibility of her unwillingness in vv. 5, 8 and the softened and nuanced reiterations in vv. 39, 41. Her voluntary "I will go" — in Hebrew one word, *elek* — echoes Abraham's response in 12:4 (*wayyelek,* "and he went") after God's call to him to "go" (*lek*) in 12:1. Like Abraham, Rebekah leaves home and kindred for a strange land (though she does have kin to go to). Moreover, her lively hospitality to the servant at the well is as much an entertaining of angels unawares (cf. 24:7, 40) as Abraham's in 18:1-8. Thus Rebekah shows herself to be cut from the same cloth as Abraham. The call of Abraham may thus be said to be repeated in the second generation — not in Isaac, but in Rebekah!

The final scene is so affectingly suggestive that it is best left to the reader's discreetly veiled imagination. Two comments may be hazarded. First, the passage ends on a note that forms an inclusion with 23:1-2, in such a way as to suggest that the transition is as much from Sarah to Rebekah as from Abraham to Isaac. Second, the servant only now refers to Isaac as "my master." Throughout the chapter he has been totally loyal to Abraham, and now he places himself unreservedly under the one who has supplanted him as heir. Can anyone doubt that, for all the narrator's concern with transitions from Abraham to Isaac and from Sarah to Rebekah, the pivotal figure in this chapter is the servant? In our day many are suspicious of the language of servant stewardship, fearing it smacks of old patterns of hierarchical elitism, subservience, and systemic oppression. After all the pros and cons of such a social role are weighed and argued, one is left to reread the story and decide for oneself whether to say of such a stewardly role today, "The thing comes from Yahweh; we cannot say of it bad or good" (24:50).

A final note is in order concerning the thematically central and climactically placed expression "steadfast love and faithfulness" (vv. 27, 49). The passage that gives it its definitive biblical connotations which then reverberate softly through all its other occurrences may well be Exod. 34:6. That passage, conveying as it does God's forgiveness and restoration to Israel following the sin of the golden calf, is echoed often in subsequent biblical books, resurfacing in the NT (e.g., John 1:14, 17) and implicitly throughout Rom. 9–11 (compare Exod. 33:19; 34:6 with Rom. 9:15; 11:32). Yet for all the importance of this classical *locus*, it in turn depends on Gen. 24. As Paul knows regarding another issue in Rom. 11:28b, God's dealing with Israel in Exod. 32–34, as in Exod. 2:23–3:15, is based on the covenant with the ancestors of Genesis (see Exod. 32:13). Long before Israel stands in need of forgiveness, God's *hesed* and *emet* identify the basis of divine integrity toward these needy ancestors and, through them, toward all who would bless themselves by use of their name. To a religious tradition that has for a long time posed the problem of existence chiefly in terms of human sin and divine forgiveness, it is perhaps salutary to be reminded that the meaning of existence turns equally — if not more — on the question of divine faithfulness to a broken and needy world. It is in their positive witness to that question that the narratives of Gen. 12–50 inexhaustibly generate hope in generation after generation of readers.

25:1-18

With the exception of Gen. 14, the narrative since the beginning of ch. 12 has sustained a close-up focus on a few individuals portrayed through fully developed episodes. Now, between the end of the Abraham-Sarah story in chs. 23 and 24 and the beginning of the Isaac-Rebekah story in 25:19, it would appear at first that the narrator has simply placed a loose collection of materials not to be lost sight of, but in no particular order, with no great importance for the larger story and of little interest for the theological reader.

However, such a conclusion may be premature. By the inclusion of these summarizing materials the narrator reminds the reader that the human story is much wider, and much more diverse, than can be fully traced in the narrative. The close-up attention to individuals in chs. 12–24 — including people like Hagar, Abimelech, and the servant — kindles the imagination of the reader to appreciate that each of the individuals summarily named in the present passage lived a full life marked by all manner of vital concerns and diverse outcomes. Moreover, it shows that they too sought living space and maintained kindred connections, all under the aegis of "the God of heaven and earth" (24:3; 14:19, 22). Also, the absence of narrative line or dramatic movement in these materials inscribes in the biblical text the fact that, no matter how hard we may try to organize our knowledge into meaningful patterns, much that happens in the world will seem to us to be unconnected and to remain unintegrated. All we can do is summarize it by such names as we know, and remember that the full human story eludes our organizing control and even our awareness. However, the inclusion of such passages within the fully developed and goal-directed stories of Israel's ancestors invites us to believe that what eludes our own understanding and awareness may stand in the same intimate relation to God's purposes and presence as the ancestral stories (cf. the reminder in Amos 9:7). If one purpose in telling stories is to order human experience and show its possible meaning, the present passage suggests that biblical narrative is to be valued not only for its capacity to trace such order and meaning, but also for its realism in acknowledging what lives and moves beyond the sphere of our ordering and meaning, but not beyond the sphere of the God of heaven and earth. This is one of the many ways the biblical narrative contains safeguards against its use as an instrument of controlling (and oppressing) ideology against other peoples.

Gerhard von Rad writes, "Actually this section does detract somewhat from the uniqueness and extraordinariness of Isaac's procreation and birth" (*Genesis,* 256). Such a reading not only fails to appreciate the storyteller's art in including this material, but implies a theological devaluation of persons and people who do not "fit" the main story being presented. As indicated in the twin destinies of Ishmael and Isaac in Gen. 17:19-21 (see above), Abraham lives with one foot planted firmly in each son's subsequent story. He did not cease to have Ishmael-type children with the birth of Isaac. This, indeed, may be suggested by the juxtaposition of the materials relating to Keturah and her children (25:1-6) with the materials relating to Ishmael (vv. 12-18). Hebrews 11:13-16 has it that the ancestors of the faith "were strangers and exiles on the earth," and that "they desire a better country, that is, a heavenly one." But passages like Gen. 25:1-6 show these ancestors nevertheless fully living out their earthly lives, and not merely wrapping themselves in their desire like a cocoon and dreaming there of the butterflies they will one day become.

It remains to consider briefly the death and burial of Abraham. The narrator's report that "Isaac and Ishmael his sons buried him" takes one's breath away by its very matter-of-factness. Would one have expected this, after ch. 16, or 17, or 21? Yet in retrospect one remembers the passing mention of Isaac's visit to Beer-lahai-roi (24:62), and one notices that after his father's death he lives there for a time (25:11). It is again salutary to see the two story lines that were launched in 17:19-21 converge at Abraham's grave. Stories of the squabbling and worse that breaks out between rival groups of devotees at Christian holy sites in the Holy Land suggest that something could be learned by pondering 25:9 at length.

The form of the report of the burial is noteworthy. (a) He "was gathered to his people." (b) "Isaac and Ishmael his sons buried him in the cave of Machpelah. . . ." (c) "There Abraham was buried, with Sarah his wife." The juxtaposition of these three statements invites the conclusion drawn in the commentary on ch. 23: Sarah is the "people" to whom Abraham is gathered.

Subsequent generations will join them — in one sense (49:29-32; 50:13) or another (Luke 16:22). What of Ishmael? His death notice stands out in Gen. 25:17 for the way it echoes the death notice of Abraham: "he breathed his last and died, and was gathered to his people" (RSV here "kindred"). But who are Ishmael's people? Verse 18 tells us that he settled "over against all his brothers" (so Hebrew, as also in 16:12). This may mean that Ishmael dwelt toward Egypt, while Isaac dwelt in Canaan and the children of Keturah dwelt more eastward. Does this mean that Ishmael and Isaac came together one last time at Abraham's death and after that ceased to be connected in any sense, so that in their own deaths they were finally gathered to different peoples? Or is there some sense in which, in his own death and burial, Ishmael was gathered to Abraham as well as to Hagar? Our answer will depend on how we read the import of the ancestral stories, and of the biblical story as a whole.

25:19-34

Like the Abram-Sarai story, the Isaac-Rebekah story begins in barrenness. In the first story, the movement to fruitfulness was narrated over many chapters filled with trials and challenges to faith. In the second story, the movement is stated summarily (25:21), giving the impression that Isaac's faith consists simply in praying believingly and receiving an immediate positive answer. Yet v. 26 notes that the twins were born twenty years after the wedding, leaving the reader to wonder about a struggle of faith occurring entirely "off camera." Was it like Abraham's, or different in its trials? Such a gap in the narrative, by the room it makes for the imagination, allows the reader to believe that, like Isaac's, one's own pilgrimage in faith may be in the tradition of Abraham while differing in specific detail.

The children's movement within Rebekah (v. 22) becomes so vigorous, indeed so violent, that they threaten to crush one another. The verb here may be a form of the Hebrew verb "to run," which in the present form (a hithpolel) would give the meaning "to thrash against one another with the feet." The appropriateness of this meaning is that increasingly before birth infants flail and thrash about, especially with their feet. (Such a description of their prenatal activity sets the stage for the comment about Jacob's hand and Esau's heel in v. 26.) This activity becomes so violent as to give Rebekah intense concern. The precise meaning of her exclamation is unclear. If the Hebrew word *ken* is not taken to mean "thus," but "right, all right" (*ken*, from the root *kun*, "to be firm, stable, secure"), her cry can be translated, "if things are all right [in my womb], why am I like this?"

In such a concern over her pregnancy Rebekah inquires of Yahweh, who announces a destiny that has its roots already in her womb. (Cf. also Judg. 13:5, 7, 14; Ps. 22:9-10; 51:5; Jer. 1:5; Luke 1:41-44; John 3:3-5, all tracing vocation and character back to their roots in the prenatal situation.) Is this destiny foreordained by God? Do the twins struggle already in the womb because God has set them and their futures against each other? Or is their struggle an expression, not only of fetal vigor, but also of inherited drives and conflictual dynamics? One remembers that their uncle Laban has already been presented as a person "on the make" for economic advantage. Jacob, then, may be a "chip off the same block" as his uncle Laban, while Esau may take after an earlier ancestor who preferred hunting on the open range to herding and dwelling in tents (Gen. 25:27). Is God's announcement, then, an "election"? Or is it a sober and accurate prediction as to which of these two will in fact prevail by virtue of his own strength? Where in Jacob's story does it become clear that God has elected Jacob to inherit the promises to Abraham and Isaac? What is the relation between divine election and natural selection?

Jacob (*ya'aqob*) receives his name for grabbing his firstborn twin's heel (*'eqeb*) — as though unwilling to let up on the fetal wrestling even for a moment. Esau (*'esaw*) is named after the mantle of hair (*se'ar*) all over his body (in English one might call him Harry!), and later he is called Edom (*'edom*) because of the pottage that is red (*'adom*) like him (vv. 25, 30). Twins, they are by no means identical. Hairy Esau hunts as a man of the field, while Jacob is a tent dweller and a man characterized in Hebrew as *tam* — a word which in this context is unclear and variously translated and interpreted (e.g., KJV "plain"; RSV "quiet"; see further below). Isaac loves Esau for his meat. This is understandable enough. It is an economic boon, and a treat to the palate, that the firstborn should be a skillful hunter. But this only intensifies the conventional advantage of a firstborn over his siblings. Why does Rebekah love Jacob? Is it because of the annunciation to her, or because Jacob's father holds him in less regard, or both? In any case, this division of parental regard will only intensify their fetal conflict and in time draw the parents in on one side or the other of that conflict.

In their first fateful adult struggle, Esau/Edom sells his birthright for a serving of boiled lentils. Does Jacob know of the annunciation to his mother, or is he simply using his native wit in seizing a sudden opportunity to turn the ongoing struggle in his favor? In any case, it is clear that Esau is a nonreflective sort, given to action — one who likes to hunt, eat, and move on, as in the present instance: "he ate, he drank, he rose, he went his way, he despised his birthright." He lacks the patience for delayed satisfactions that is to be a quality of spirit characteristic of the new people that Yahweh is in process of fashioning.

But what is the significance of his name Esau and his hairyness? And in what sense is Jacob *tam*? Two other narrative contexts may help our interpretation, one biblical, one from Mesopotamia. (1) In the epic of Gilgamesh, the legendary king of Uruk in Babylonia, we read of Enkidu, a man of the steppe who is completely covered with body hair and who roams with the animals. Still in a state of nature, he seems hardly distinguishable from the animals. Only after seven days with a courtesan (sent from Uruk to lure him to the city to meet Gilgamesh) does the difference between Enkidu and the animals become clear; and only when he anoints his body with oil and puts on clothing in readiness for the city does he "become human" (Gilgamesh II.iii.25). (Shortly after he gets there, Enkidu and Gilgamesh engage in a titanic wrestling match!)

(2) The story of Enkidu displays intriguing connections with Gen. 2–3, where the first *adam* (the word in Hebrew resembles Esau's other name, Edom) is closely enough related to the animals to search for a mate among them. Only when the first woman appears does his own humanity become fully clear to him: "She

96

shall be called Woman (*ishshah*), because she was taken out of Man (*ish*)" (2:23). Previously called only *adam,* he here names himself *ish* after naming her *ishshah.* Shortly thereafter these two transgress the divine prohibition, fall into mutual recrimination, and the long tale of human alienation from God, the rest of creation, and one another is set in motion. This much seems clear: The God of the Garden story prefers the risk of human moral and spiritual deviance to the prospect of creaturely life spent simply in the gratifications of natural appetite, however good (2:9a, 16).

With these two narratives in mind, I propose the following difference between Esau and Jacob. Esau is the "natural" man. He is not morally inferior, for his life does not really move in the moral realm at all. He is simply a man of natural actions — literally, a "lone ranger" who lives by hunting and eating on the open range, and who survives from one day to the next. Jacob is not a "natural" man, but one poised before the complexities of human interaction with their opportunities for moral uprightness or deviance, spiritual integrity or alienation. Hebrew *tam* in this context then may mean, not "having integrity" (as it often does in the Bible), but what its cognate verb *tamam* sometimes points to — a state of completion (as in the building of the temple in 1 Kgs. 6:22). Esau was similar to the animals he hunted, like them living simply off his prey. Jacob was a fully differentiated human being — capable of moral and spiritual relations and actions, whatever their actual character positively or negatively. In this first adult action, of course, Jacob falls prey to the temptation to outwit his brother and to prey on his birthright.

If the community of Abraham and Sarah is called to be the beginning of a new people, Jacob signals the challenge facing Yahweh to redeem and transform what will threaten to subvert that whole vocation. This leads to a further observation, concerning the relation between the first and the third generation, Abraham and Jacob, in this sequence of founding ancestors. Abraham and Sarah were presented as a human couple in need of the healing of a natural deficiency — barrenness. To be sure, that deficiency was derivative in some sense from the sinfulness running through human existence since the garden; but nothing laid responsibility for their barrenness at their feet. Jacob is introduced at the outset as someone who is (like his uncle Laban) "on the make." How will such a sharp dealer become a name by which all families of the earth bless themselves? Or rather, what will the human scene become like, if all the families of the earth bless themselves in the name of such a character? One may note that the heritage of Abraham will pass through Isaac to Jacob because Jacob has gained that heritage through Esau's oath. That oath now establishes a human horizon within which Yahweh must operate, either by aborting the new beginning in Abraham or by redeeming it.

The relation between the first and third generations — and the different challenge facing divine action in the two instances — parallels what we see in the book of Exodus. In Exodus divine action is directed toward two different types of human crisis. In Exod. 1–24 Israel's plight is that it is innocently oppressed by the policies of imperial Egypt, and Yahweh's response (remembering the ancestors; 2:24) is to liberate innocent Israel from that oppression. In Exod. 32–34 Israel's plight is that it is in guilty violation of the covenant with Yahweh, and Yahweh's response (remembering the ancestors; 32:13) comes as forgiveness and covenant renewal. The two major forms of deliverance in the book of Exodus thus turn on God's earlier dealing with the ancestors. That earlier dealing, analogously, may be said to take two forms: the gradual education of Abraham in faith, and the gradual transformation of Jacob from the moral and spiritual deviance for which his name stands.

Such a perspective may help us to appreciate how God could elect a conniving Jacob over his older brother. Not only does this election overturn the patriarchal convention of primogeniture, but it also overturns the deep-seated human conviction that God must act to reward the good and to punish the wicked. In Jacob the good are warned, and the wicked are encouraged to see, that God is not primarily in the business of juridical rewards and punishments (though these may have an educative and disciplinary place in the total divine economy). God is in the business of redemption. That redemption will involve Jacob himself — and all his moral and spiritual kin — in the painful travail of new birth. (As we shall see, Esau too, in his own way, will be drawn into the sphere of divine redemptive action.)

26:1-33

Of the formulaic three, "Abraham, Isaac, and Jacob," Isaac seems to be painted in paler colors than the other two. Certainly his story takes up much less space. With the shift of focus from Gen. 25:21 to 25:22-34, throwing the dramatic interest from Isaac to the next generation, ch. 26 looks like a parenthetical summary of a life that does no more than faintly echo Abraham's. After the dramatic high point in ch. 22, Isaac appears to live out the rest of his days in a state of anticlimactic existential exhaustion, capable only of imitating elements in his father's life. Yet few people resemble Abraham in living the greater part of their lives toward their finest hour. The question is what meaning the rest of one's life may have when that hour seems to have come and gone early. Is there such a thing as a vocation to live out an apparent anticlimax faithfully? If so, Isaac may be its patron saint.

After the drama of 25:29-34, the narrative shifts back to Isaac with a scene that echoes 12:10 and 12:1-3. Faced with a famine, Isaac sets out southward like his father before him, until God stops him. Does this imply a belated critique of Abraham's move to Egypt, or does it indicate diversity of experience in the pilgrimage of faith? Abraham went to Egypt using his common sense, and God neither explicitly confirmed nor negated his decision. Isaac set out using his common sense reinforced by parental example, then was directed explicitly not to go. It is in the context of this difference from his father that God reiterates to Isaac words that echo the call of Abraham: He is to stay in "the land of which I shall tell you" (26:2). This echoes the end of 12:1, as 26:4b echoes 12:3, and the intervening words echo 15:5. Thus the narrator teaches a fundamental lesson concerning the character of living tradition: it combines continuity in meaning and purpose with elements of discontinuity in practice.

In God's address to Isaac we hear for the first time in the Bible the words "I will be with you." God next says them to Jacob in Paddan-aram, in telling him to return to the land of his fathers (31:3), and after that God says them to Moses who is to lead Israel out of Egypt to the Promised Land (Exod. 3:12). In the latter instance the words introduce the divine name, "I will be who I will be" (Exod. 3:14a), whose short form is "I will be" (v. 14b) and whose more common form is "Yahweh," who is then immediately identified again as "the God of your fathers, the God of Abraham, the God of Isaac, and the God of Jacob" (v. 15). In all three instances the promise to "be with you" comes in connection with the land. But while it bears on Jacob's and Moses' *journey to* that land, it bears on Isaac's *staying* there. That this rhetorical trace climaxing at the burning bush should begin, not with Abraham, but with Isaac, is a delicate hint that Isaac's relative colorlessness may be more in the eye of the reader than in the eye of Yahweh. Much is made of faith as a venturing forth into the unknown in the assurance of God's journeying presence on the way to a land of promise. Isaac reminds us that it is as much a venture of faith (and perhaps much harder) to stay where one is in the assurance of God's abiding presence amid unpromising circumstances.

God seeks through Isaac to fulfill the oath to Abraham. It is not uncommon to take God's covenant with Abraham as unilateral, so that all rests on God's promise and faithfulness and Abraham need do nothing but believe. Such an understanding is doubtful already on the basis of Gen. 12:1-5; 15:17, and is further questioned by 26:5. Fulfillment may indeed rest ultimately on God; but Abraham's response to that oath is also part of the ground of the future: "because Abraham obeyed my voice and kept my charge, my commandments, my statutes, and my laws."

Genesis 26:5 has all the marks of a late, perhaps Deuteronomistic editor. The question then is, Where in chs. 12–25 did that editor see Abraham doing all this? In Galatians Paul makes much of the pre-Sinai, pre-law faith of Abraham. Should we then dissociate Isaac from Sinai by neutralizing 26:5 through the recognition of its editorial character? Or should we take this verse as indicating that in the very journey of faith set out in chs. 12–25 we are to trace the inner spirit of response to God that, similarly, later moves Israel to observe Sinai's laws? Do the various specific steps in Abraham's life implicitly embody the same sort of day-by-day, situation-by-situation response to God that the various specific laws later call for? Is the editorial insertion so finely and smoothly stitched into the older epic narrative as to warn us that, though we may make appropriate theological distinctions between Abraham and Moses, we may drive no theological wedge between them? (Paul himself prefaces his treatment of Abraham in Rom. 3:31 with a "God forbid!" in which he rejects the notion of overthrowing the law and affirms rather its fulfillment.)

In Gen. 12:10–13:1 Abraham's move to Egypt led to the crisis over Sarah. Here, Isaac's obedient stay in Gerar leads to a similar crisis. Again he emulates his father. If his action illustrates how we stay in continuity with our past in part by repeating it, it illustrates also the problems that such continuity-by-repetition may bring. Isaac has learned nothing positive from his father's two experiences, but Abimelech seems to have done so, for this time he has stayed away from Rebekah. The Hebrew text in 26:8 reads *yitshaq metsaheq et ribqah* — "Isaac, 'Isaacing' ["playing," or "laughing"] with Rebekah." He is, we may say, "being himself" with her. But Isaac's fear has not enabled him to be himself — to play or interact openly — with Abimelech (the way he had played with Ishmael). In passing his wife off as his sister, he also passes himself off as someone he is not. If Isaac will not be open with Abimelech, how can Abimelech know him as Isaac — one to laugh with and thereby to join in Sarah's laughter (see above on 21:6)?

Abraham planted a tree in honor of Isaac's birth (21:33); now Isaac plants crops. In fact, though Isaac does not trust Abimelech, his obedience to Yahweh keeps him in a land of famine until his sowing brings forth "a hundredfold" (26:12a) and he prospers (vv. 12b-14a). Thereby he becomes the inspiration for Jesus' parable about parables (Mark 4:3-20). In that parable the "good soil" is an Isaac-like faith that is the human ground of things hoped for. Meanwhile, the movement from Gen. 26:6-11 to 26:12-14a echoes the movement from 12:10–13:1 to 13:2, while 26:14b echoes 13:7: Isaac resolves the hostility with Abimelech's men in the spirit of his father's separation from Lot, moving away to the valley of Gerar (26:17).

The conflict over the wells develops a theme broached in 21:25. Isaac begins by redigging his father's wells and restoring their names (26:18), then continues by digging fresh wells and naming them himself. This epitomizes Isaac as one who knows both how to live in continuity with a restored past and how to move forward into new territory. Though the first two new wells occasion new strife, the third does not; its name, Rehoboth, suggestive of "room" for everyone, celebrates a resolution reminiscent in its own way of the resolution between Abram and Lot in ch. 13. Nevertheless, Isaac moves on to Beer-sheba. Is it because this well is protected by the oath Abraham had Abimelech swear (21:29-31)? Or is it because Abraham had taken him there after the ordeal on Mt. Moriah and God's final reiteration of the promise (22:15-19)? In any case, Isaac too hears God's promise once again, along with "I am with you" (26:24). He seals his response with an altar and worship, pitches his tent (12:7-8), and digs another well.

The scene in 26:26-31 recapitulates 21:22-24, as Abimelech's mutual nonaggression pact with Abraham is repeated with Isaac. The repetition of this covenanting act in successive generations realistically traces the path along which hostile groups arrive at stable relations only by steps, reversals, and further steps. This time the place is named, not for the treaty, but for the newly dug well. Thus the various narrative references to Beer-sheba illustrate how diverse experiences endow a given name with diverse connotations, so that it comes to carry in itself a rich synopsis of a people's past. (This remains true whether we read the two passages in narrative sequence or as parallel and alternate acounts of the rise of the name.)

Beginning with words that echo 12:1-3, the chapter closes on a theme that echoes ch. 24 — the concern for wives in the next generation. The stark brevity of 26:34-35 in contrast to ch. 24 only intensifies the contrast between the social source of the wives in each case. The stage is set — or almost set — for Jacob to receive a wife, and he does so in a manner partly reminiscent of ch. 24. Yet that chapter, long as it is, does not prepare us for the much longer journey and return in chs. 28–35. The events in 27:1–28:9 gather the diverse human energies of Isaac and Rebekah, Esau and Jacob into a tangled knot of human cross-purposes transected by the divine purpose. These cross-purposes will go through a long and complex process before they can come to their manifold resolution in God's providence.

The compact rehearsal of Isaac's life in this chapter shows his vocation to be largely one of consolidating the trail Abraham has blazed by retracing many of its episodes. In so doing, however, he has not merely imitated them but has reenacted them with fresh nuance. In this connection one may note that the preposition "besides" in 26:1 (RSV) does not mean simply "in addition to," as though involving mere repetition. The Hebrew preposition *millebad*, formed from the noun *badad*, "separation," can here be translated "separate from" or "distinct from." The point is that, no matter how much one's situation may resemble that of another, there is an irreducible uniqueness about it. Despite all the precedents provided by others' parallel experiencs, the life of faith still consists in having to decide what one will do in one's own partly unique situation.

26:34–28:9

Jacob's gain of the birthright depended solely on whether Esau would sell it to him and then honor his oath after his father died. But Jacob can gain Isaac's blessing only from Isaac himself. It is this problem that precipitates the events in 27:1–28:5. Framed by references to Esau's wives (26:34-35; 28:6-9), this complex passage is composed of seven scenes each involving two family members. An eighth scene, fittingly falling outside this series, has Esau speaking only to himself of his hatred for Jacob.

Considered in terms of the family members involved in each, the seven scenes unfold in a twice-repeated pattern: (A) Esau-Isaac, 27:1-4; (B) Rebekah-Jacob, 27:5-17; (C) Jacob-Isaac, 27:18-29; (A') Esau-Isaac, 27:30-40; (B') Rebekah-Jacob, 27:42-45; (D) Rebekah-Isaac, 27:46; (C') Jacob-Isaac, 28:1-5. The significance of this pattern is that 25:28 had us think of two subgroups within this family of four, so we are prepared for scenes A and B, matching each parent with the favorite son. The third scene (C) cuts across this pattern of affinities, reinforcing its character as the scene of deception. In the first three-scene sequence, Rebekah works her strategy through Jacob and has no direct dealings with Isaac. However, after Isaac's awareness (in A') of Jacob's deception, it is necessary for Rebekah in scene D to intervene directly. Rather than attempt a dubious appeal to Isaac's sympathy for Jacob as the object of Esau's hatred, she appeals to his sympathy for her in the matter of the sons' wives. By this second strategy she gets him to send Jacob away with his renewed blessing, this time in the name of God Almighty (echoing ch. 17).

The whole chain of events opens with the observation that Isaac is blind. This will enable Jacob to deceive Isaac by means of his other four senses — touch (27:22-23), taste (v. 25), smell (v. 27), and hearing (vv. 18-24). In the first three deceptions Jacob offers sensory experience of what is not his own. In the fourth, he uses his own powers of speech to insist that the voice that sounds like Jacob's is in fact Esau's. Thus he turns his own voice into what appears to be someone else's. The speaking-hearing bond is unbroken between Jacob and his mother (cf., e.g., the repeated "hear [RSV "obey"] my word/voice," vv. 8, 13, 43). But such a bond of speaking and hearing between father and son is shattered by Jacob's deceptive speech, a betrayal possible only because of Isaac's blindness. Only after the deception is complete does Jacob "hear" father and mother (28:7).

The wordplay over the issues of blindness, hearing, and speech is reflected in part in 27:12: "Perhaps my father will feel me, and I shall seem to be mocking him." The Hebrew reads literally, "I shall be in his eyes as a mocker." The deception is intended to deprive Isaac even of that "sight" which he still possesses — the mental perception that can arise in his mind through the other four senses. The wordplay goes further. "Mocking him" translates Heb. *meta'tea'*, playing on (or a form of?) the verb *ta'ah*, "to err, wander, go astray." Jacob then is saying, "I shall be in his eyes as one leading astray" — a sighted man leading a blind man to stumble off the path. The wordplay also involves the preceding verse: *halaq*, literally "smooth," in the Bible usually refers to deceptive speech (e.g., Ps. 55:21), as when we refer to a "smooth talker." To be found out, Jacob fears, would be to incur a curse instead of a blessing — conveyed of course through speaking and hearing. So Jacob deceives by a combination of smooth words and hairy animal skins to hide his smoothness. The deception complete, he receives the blessing and goes on his way.

The truth comes as a profound shock to both Isaac (Gen. 27:33) and Esau (vv. 34-38). They both realize that, despite the deception, the blessing cannot be taken back. Some interpreters posit ancient dynamistic notions in which words, once spoken, released a power that could not be retracted. Others note that a blessing, like an oath, has a performative character: an oath is not only a statement, but the performance of an action in which the speaker intends the words to *convey* what they *describe*. One may ponder how oaths are understood in the contemporary world. Are they mere fossilized forms of speech once considered binding, but now requiring to be observed only if convenient or strategic, and breakable with impunity? If oaths in fact still bind those who utter them, does the violation of an oath still wreak a terrible price on the violator? If we enact and embody our moral and spiritual integrity when we take an oath, can that integrity survive when the oath is broken? Our appreciation of the force of blessing in this passage may turn on our own understanding and practice of oath-taking. Esau is a man of appetite and action, devoid of any moral and spiritual depth. Jacob is a "smoothie" in obtaining the blessing. Isaac, whatever else he may or may not be, is a man of his word. As such, he is the image of God whose promise, oath, and integrity give the divine blessing its efficacy.

Yet Esau in vv. 30-41 is no longer merely the lusty actor of old. Belatedly he has been jolted by his loss into awareness of a new dimension of existence, in which the inheritance that was of no concern to him now becomes of great concern. The jolt leaves him solitary in his hate. Now he himself enters a long process which, as we shall see, has a positive outcome for him. This is signalled already in the blessings the two receive.

Isaac blesses Jacob first with natural goods: of the dew of heaven (Heb. *mittal hashshamayim*), of the fatness of the earth (*mishmanney ha-arets*), and plenty of grain and wine. Then he blesses him with social blessings: peoples and nations will serve him, and he shall be lord over his brothers. This blessing secures to Jacob the right of primogeniture. Finally, Isaac confers a blessing derived from God's promise to Abraham in 12:3a. This also echoes 27:12, in such a way as to place Esau's hatred of Abraham's heir in v. 41 in an ominous light.

In response to Esau's anguished plea, Isaac blesses him likewise with natural goods. I follow RSV mg (and Jewish translators in JPS), translating the identical Hebrew phrases in the same way: "of the fatness of the earth (*mishmanney ha-arets*) shall your dwelling be, and of the dew of heaven (*mittal hashshamayim*) on high." If the nature blessing is shorter than Jacob's, this is because Jacob as now first heir receives a double blessing of goods. Then comes a blessing Jacob did not receive — "by your sword you shall live" — connecting with Esau's life as a hunter and reminiscent of the promise concerning Ishmael in 16:12a. This line is then seconded in a way that suggests limits on the use of that sword: "you shall serve your brother." Is this only a limitation? Or is it in its own way a blessing, in that curbing the reach of Esau's sword will lay the groundwork for his own positive future? One may compare the angel's charge to Hagar to return and subject herself to Sarai (16:9) — a constraint that will have a positive outcome. Esau's subjection (like Hagar's) is to be followed by Esau's freedom (like Ishmael's).

RSV "break loose" translates the verb *rud*, which occurs only here (27:40) and in Ps. 55:2 (RSV "I am overcome"). The noun *marod*, from the verb *rud*, likewise occurs only in Lam. 1:7; 3:19 (RSV "bitterness"); Isa. 58:7 (RSV "homeless"), in all three instances occurring alongside the noun *ani*, "affliction, poverty." These three passages, together with Ps. 55:2, suggest that in Gen. 27:40b we should hear a reference, not to breaking loose, but to a time of servitude crying out restlessly to God. Esau's eventual freedom will come, not by the sword, but at the hand of God who answers his cry. The blessing thus reinforces the earlier hint that Esau is awakening to new dimensions of what it means to be a human being. The final line of the blessing is not without its healing irony. Jacob deceived Isaac by, so to speak, putting Esau on his neck (v. 16) and thereby placed a yoke of submission on his brother's neck. Esau's eventual freedom, casting off that yoke, will undo that effect of the deception. So we see that, as in ch. 17, the passing of the older son's rights to the younger son does not simply leave the older son out in the cold.

One further detail leads to a final question. The detail lies in 27:20, where Jacob-as-Esau answers, "Yahweh your God has granted me success." Here, as in 24:12 (see above), RSV "success" translates *hiqrah,* "happen." Is Jacob cynically claiming God's sanction for a miraculous happenstance that he knows he and Rebekah have in fact engineered? Or does he speak ironically, intending Isaac to understand this answer in one sense, while in his own heart marvelling at the thought that God is blessing their efforts beyond their expectation? The deeper irony, of course, lies in the contrast between the two speakers in 24:12 and 27:20. In the former instance, God's steadfast love and faithfulness to Abraham is imaged in the servant's own integrity. In the latter instance, Jacob obscures God's character by his shameless attempt to implicate God in his deceit.

Where is God in this tangled knot of human agendas that work through both deceit and integrity? In 26:3 God had promised Isaac, "I will be *with* you." Are we to read the present series of events in that light, with the emphasis now, "I will be with *you*" rather than with the other three family members except as Isaac also blesses and responds to them? In regard to Isaac's blindness, we may note that a "horizon" (from the Greek verb *horao,* "to see") is the widest boundary of seeing or foreseeing. What if Isaac images God by working within a horizon constituted in part by the actions of others? In that case, does God's foreseeing (what Paul in Rom. 8:29 calls predestining, *pro-horizein,* literally "pre-horizoning") take into account and include the free actions of such as Rebekah and Jacob, and weave them into a finally redemptive outcome? Does God neither simply sanction nor simply reject human actions, but work within them to transform them toward the divine purposes?

Paul refers to the election of Jacob over Esau in Rom. 9:13, and follows with the divine words to Moses, "I will have mercy on whom I will have mercy" (v. 15). The exposition of these divine words in Rom. 9:18 might be taken to imply a mysterious divine providence in which the non-elect are simply let fall outside the circle of divine saving purpose. Yet in Rom. 11:32 Paul concludes that "God has consigned all to disobedience, that he may have mercy upon all." It is this conclusion that moves him to the great exclamation in Rom. 11:36, "For from him and through him and to him are all things." Esau and Jacob, who first wrestled within their mother's womb, in the present chapter struggle over the blessing, wrestling within the encompassing horizon of God's relentless patience, until (as we shall see) they both come to a new birth. In this way, these two ancestors exemplify in differing ways the affirmation that all things are not only from God, but also through God, and finally to God.

28:10-22

Jacob sets out from Beer-sheba, the site of God's promise to Isaac (Gen. 26:24). He comes to a certain "place." That this is a cult place (cf. 12:6) is suggested by the fact that sleeping with his head on "one of the stones of the place" is hardly a natural action. I take the stone to be a symbolic object used at a cult place to induce a revelatory dream. The strategy works. The dream comes in three vivid panels, each introduced by *hinneh*, "behold" (28:12 [RSV "that"], 12, 13). In the first panel he sees a ladder with its base in the earth and its top in the heavens. The latter phrase is reminiscent of Gen. 11:4, which reflects Mesopotamian imagery used in royal texts over a span of more than a thousand years. In that imagery Babylon, as the earthly center of divine rule of the cosmos, is founded in the depths of the earth and reaches into the heavens (cf. Ps. 78:69), and communication between gods and cosmos runs along this axis. In Gen. 11:4 the people build the city and tower for fear of being scattered from the land to which they have migrated, only to be scattered by God (v. 8). Here Jacob, fleeing from the land to which his grandfather has migrated, encounters God in a dream that promises he will return to the land.

The second panel shows angel messengers trafficking on the ladder. The sequence of their movement is important. The angels do not descend and ascend, implying messages from God to Jacob and responses from Jacob to God. Their ascending and descending suggests that communication is going up from Jacob and is being answered from heaven. This supports the idea that the stone under his head was a way of seeking contact with God. A much later night encounter with God, by the Jabbok, will disclose that Jacob has wrestled with God and humankind. In the case of humankind — specifically, in relation to Esau — that wrestling has gone on for a long time, since before birth. I suggest that the dream of ascending angels speaks of this lifelong wrestling in its Godward dimension, an activity so deep in Jacob — all during the time he wrestled with Esau — that he has not been aware of that activity until now. His lifelong waking struggle to "overtake" Esau has obscured until now the deepest reality of his soul, a continual crying out to God. It is the crisis of fleeing for his life into exile, into a land to which his father was not allowed to return, that presses him to the point where this deep unconscious wrestling with God finally surfaces and merges with his conscious prayer for help. But if the ascending angels speak of this lifelong wrestling with and crying out to God, the descending angels speak of a God who likewise all his life has been addressing Jacob deep within himself, with a message that only now finally breaks into his consciousness.

The third panel begins with God's self-identification — an important act in this Canaanite cult-center where so many gods appear to so many different worshippers. The identification is by proper name and by ancestral connection. Such a divine self-identification means that, though Jacob may be alienated from the land, his ancestral connection remains intact. In 27:28-29 Isaac's blessing on Jacob echoed some elements in the promises God had made to Abraham and to himself. God's promise to Jacob here gathers up even more elements from those promises. The relation between Isaac's blessing of Jacob and God's dream-promise to Jacob resembles the relation between the Aaronic priests and God in Num. 6:22-27. There, the Aaronic priest blesses the people according to a set form. As the priest puts the divine name upon the people, Yahweh says, "I will bless them." The blessing is not automatic, by some power inherent in the words themselves, nor does God dispense with the human agent. Similarly in Gen. 28 Isaac mediates the blessing in good faith, and God honors that agent through a direct divine blessing which later comes to consciousness through the dream.

The divine word to Jacob in vv. 13-15 is now itself punctuated in v. 15 with a "behold" that signals the central focus of that word. Whereas the first part of God's promise to Jacob repeats promises earlier made to his ancestors, the part following the "behold" is distinctive to him. This part of the promise comes into a very specific kind of life-situation. Whereas Abraham is the first to venture into a new land (12:1-4) and Isaac is the first to stay in that land in a time of famine (26:3), Jacob is the first to venture into exile, into a situation which threatens to negate all the future that the ancestral promise holds out to him. It is in such a context that God promises him,

> Behold, I am *with* you
>> and will keep you *wherever you go,*
>> and will bring you *back to this land;*
> for I will not *leave* you . . .

The last verb is *'azab,* "to let alone, leave, forsake, abandon." The promise addresses what I propose is Jacob's deepest fear, the fear of abandonment. Contemporary psychoanalytic students of human development identify the fear of abandonment as one of the earliest and deepest human fears. The infant needs the mother's constantly reappearing attention, to reassure it of the continuity of its own experience and identity, and to encourage it in its task of "going on being." For reasons beyond fathoming, some infants seem to be born secure and others to be born anxious. I propose that God's first word to Jacob, here in the night within the boundaries of this cult place, addresses an anxiety that has fueled his lifelong struggle with Esau since before birth. Or rather, the word that here breaks into Jacob's consciousness is the word of reassurance that God has been speaking to him in his depths from the very beginning, but which for some reason he has not been able to hear until now. That word or a similar word, it would appear, had come already to his mother in the annunciation of 25:23. Rebekah's preferential love for Jacob may have arisen in part out of the prenatal divine word to her. It may have come also out of a mother's special care and concern for an anxious child bent on securing its place in the world. One cannot be certain. The strands of human and divine interaction are at times distinguishable to humans, and at times distinguishable only to God; in the present case, they may be so closely interwoven as to be inseparable.

In the present instance, God meets Jacob's deepest fear with the reassuring promise of continual and unbroken divine presence, to keep him wherever he goes and to bring him back to his land of inheritance. One thinks again of the Priestly blessing in Num. 6 and its opening terms of blessing and keeping. (If the Priestly redaction of the Bible occurred in the exile or after the return, this experience may be said to be anticipated in Jacob's exile and return, so that the connection between Num. 6:24-26 and Gen. 28:15 is thematically profound.) One thinks also of Ps. 121 with its key word "keep" (a Psalmistic meditation on the Priestly blessing?), and especially its concluding verse. The ancestral texts of Genesis thus may be appreciated for the way in which their various narratives generate themes that later come to focal expression in liturgical and other forms of Israel's scriptural tradition. This is seen again in the promise, "I will not leave you until I have *done* that of which I have *spoken* to you." The faithful connection between divine speaking and doing becomes a prominent theme in the exilic prophet Deutero-Isaiah: Isa. 41:4, 25-27; 43:12; 44:7, 26; 46:11; 48:3; contrast 41:21-24. These reiterations come in response to the exiles' abandonment anxieties voiced in Isa. 40:27; 49:14.

Jacob's response on waking (Gen. 28:16-22) befits his first direct encounter with God. Wakened to the reality of God and the true character of the place, and filled with awe, Jacob now acts in the manner of his ancestors (12:6-8; 13:3-4, 18; 21:33; 26:25). He who had earlier gained the birthright by extracting an oath from Esau (25:33) now binds himself to God by offering an oath, on condition that God fulfills the divine promises of 28:15. Jacob does not merely repeat those promises as conditions; rather, he augments them in two specific ways (vv. 20-21). God's keeping is to include provision of food and clothing; and God's bringing home is to be concluded "in safety" (so translating *shalom* here, as in Isa. 41:3). (Shalom here may remind one of the very last term in the Priestly blessing of Num. 6, a term which describes the final outcome of the earlier term "keep" in that blessing.) On these conditions, Yahweh will become Jacob's own God, and Jacob will set up and maintain a cult to Yahweh at Bethel. So this "place" will stand as a witness to his descendants

111

of Yahweh's faithfulness to him going into exile, and of his own oath of loyalty to this God.

Writing of "Unpredictability and the Power of Promise" (*The Human Condition*, 243-47), Hannah Arendt identifies unpredictability as having a twofold basis: There is the "darkness of the human heart, . . . the basic unreliability of men who can never guarantee today who they will be tomorrow," and there is "the impossibility of foretelling the consequences of an act. . . ." She goes on, "The function of the faculty of promising is to master this twofold darkness of human affairs and is, as such, the only alternative to a mastery which relies on domination of one's self and rule over others." Tyrants, then, need not promise, since they strive to control the future by force. Or if they do promise, they need not hold to their promises except for strategic reasons. In the encounter between God and Jacob at Bethel, we see the beginning of the change in a person who out of existential anxiety has all his life attempted to dominate others in order to control his unknown future. Now he adopts a different approach to the future. He binds himself to a God he cannot control, trusting that God will be faithful to the promise God has freely made to him. The future is not thereby totally determined. It remains open to all manner of unforeseeable events. But whatever may happen, it will occur within the covenantal horizon of God's promise and Jacob's vow.

It remains only to note how the narrative has moved from mention of Beer-sheba in Gen. 26:33 to mention of Beer-sheba again in 28:10, these references bracketing the complex passage in 26:34–28:9 with its tangle of human agendas. The effect of this is to surround those tangled agendas with the divine promise at Beer-sheba to Isaac and then to Jacob. Thus again we are shown how divine providence works, making room for human freedom but surrounding (or keeping) it within the divine promises, and so not abandoning humankind to the consequences of that freedom when it is misused. The gift of freedom, in which one is "let alone" to act in one's own right, can itself be experienced as abandonment (cf. Mark 15:34!). In such cases, the resulting anxiety is a call for the deepest trust (cf. Luke 23:46); but it may express itself instead in Jacob-like strategies to secure one's own future. If, then, human anxiety has its roots in the terrible gift of a freedom that at times feels like abandonment, human faith has its roots in a divine keeping that, whether or not perceived in past experience, can begin at some point (however late in life) to be appropriated as a trustworthy promise.

29:1-35

As with the servant in Gen. 24, the narrator moves Jacob immediately to his point of arrival — again, a well. The details in 29:1-3 are intriguing: Why three flocks? Why the attention to the well's heavy stone cover? Why the singular expression at the beginning — literally, "Then Jacob lifted up his feet and went"? This parallels other more frequent usages such as lifting up one's eyes, hand, head, face, or heart. Clearly it connotes the beginning of an action. Does it connote also voluntary intention? If so, it signals the momentousness of Jacob's move. In 28:10 he was fleeing for his life from Esau. Now he is setting out on a different kind of journey that has its beginning in the events at Bethel.

In ch. 24 the first thing the servant did at the well was to pray for success, and Rebekah arrived before he was finished. Here, Jacob first talks with the shepherds, and Rachel arrives before they finish (29:6, 9). In contrast to Rebekah she comes, not at evening to draw water for the home, but at noon to water her sheep. Jacob's attempt to get rid of the shepherds, out of his immediate interest in Rachel, gives them opportunity to speak of the blocked well that must await all the flocks. Seeing her and Laban's sheep (cf. 24:30-31), Jacob's intensified interest moves him to unstop the well. In spite of the shepherds' statement in 29:8, he does not water all the flocks, but only Laban's. The irony is that here Jacob opens the well for Rachel's sheep only and not for the other three flocks, while later his other three women bear children and only Rachel's womb remains — for the longest time — unopened.

Why does Jacob weep (v. 11)? This reference to his emotions recalls Isaac's being comforted by Rebekah after Sarah's death (24:67). If the earlier comments about Jacob's being a lifelong sufferer from abandonment anxiety have any merit, this note signals a second stage in his eventual healing and transformation. The first came through his night encounter with God, and the second comes through this noontime encounter with another human being. Jacob is a long way from abandoning his problematical impatient "overtaking" strategies; but his weeping marks at least a second step.

Like Rebekah in 24:28-29, Rachel runs to tell Laban, who again is glad to welcome this kinsman into the family. After a month, he invites Jacob to negotiate a more permanent arrangement. Why does Jacob volunteer a seven-year servitude for Rachel, and how is it that this period seems like "a few days" to him? Is this the old impatient Jacob, or is he beginning to learn patience? The phrase "a few days" (29:20) involves an infrequent and peculiar use of the Hebrew word "one" (*ehad*) in the plural (*ahadim*). It is increasingly recognized that in 11:1 *debarim ahadim* does not mean "few words," but "words in common." The idiom seems to imply one-for-one correspondence, different people meaning the same things by the same words. (Similarly, in Ezek. 37:17 *ahadim* seems to imply such a match or correspondence between the sticks that they are as one stick; in Dan. 11:20 the phrase *yamim ahadim* [RSV "a few days"] follows earlier references to periods of "some years" in vv. 6, 8, suggesting that this king's period of power will last as many days as the corresponding years of the kings' power in vv. 6, 8.) In light of these usages, I propose that to Jacob the seven years seemed to him, not just as "a few days," but as "a corresponding number of days," that is, seven days. If the writer in 2 Pet. 3:8-9 can write of God's patience as one in which "a thousand years is as one day," then here Jacob is beginning to learn a patience in which he will begin to recover the divine image in himself.

The idiom *yamim ahadim,* "a corresponding number of days," may also have an additional connotation. We have already encountered its occurrence in Gen. 27:44, where Rebekah counsels Jacob to "stay with [Laban] *yamim ahadim,* until your brother's fury turns away." In 29:20, I propose, the idiom points to a correspondence between the length of Jacob's stay with Laban and the length of Esau's fury: "for as many days as it takes your brother's fury to turn away." This way of reading the text discloses a wonderful tension in Jacob's stay with Laban. At one and the same time that stay is under the aegis of Esau's hate for Jacob and under the aegis of Jacob's love for Rachel. During that time, as we shall see, Esau's hate is transformed into something else, while Jacob's love for Rachel is working a transformation on his impatience.

But Rachel is not the only agent of transformation. At the end of the seven years, he who had deceived his blind father now is deceived by his father-in-law in the darkness of the wedding night. Of course, Jacob's "righteous" indignation the next morning shows him to be unaware of having received a "reward" for his own deceptions; but the reader cannot miss the divine pedagogy in this first frustration of Jacob's grasping ambitions. By its contrast to the elections of Isaac and Jacob over their elder brothers, Laban's insistence on the rights of the older daughter helps the reader to appreciate this. In the end Jacob achieves his desire, and loves Rachel more than Leah.

The narrator leaves us in no doubt as to how Yahweh feels about the treatment of these two women. It is as though Jacob's preference for the younger sister is not to be taken as imaging Yahweh's election of the younger brother. Jacob's attention only to Rachel's sheep at the well, and his ignoring of the other three flocks, is inverted and turned back on his own head. Now Yahweh withholds from Rachel the power to conceive, and grants it to the other three women. As for Leah, her fertility in contrast to Rachel's barrenness does not lead her to echo Hagar's attitude toward Sarai in a similar situation. In her four naming speeches, Leah focuses only on her relation with Jacob and with Yahweh. The content and sequence of these namings are noteworthy:

	Relation to Jacob	Relation to God
Reuben	He will now love me	Yahweh has seen (*ra'ah*) me
Simeon	I am hated	Yahweh has heard (*shama'*)
Levi	He will now be joined (*lawah*) to me	—————
Judah	—————	I will praise Yahweh

The first two names bear on Leah's relation to both Jacob and

God, and play on the verb in the motive (or "because") clause. In the third instance the name bears only on her relation to Jacob. Here, the name plays on the verb in the main clause, while the motive clause suggests that Leah is thinking of the three sons as a three-strand cord joining or binding Jacob to her. But in the fourth instance, she makes no reference to Jacob (giving up on him?) and addresses herself only to God. Her husband may be a disappointment to her and an occasion of affliction, but God has seen Leah, and heard her (cf. 16:11; Exod. 2:23-25; 3:7-8), and has become her praise (cf. Exod. 15:1-18).

Whatever the disparity of the two wives in Jacob's eyes, they are unified in the eyes of the women of later Israel, who see them as *together* building up the house of Israel. These later women join the names of Rachel and Leah together as a means of blessing Naomi's daughter-in-law Ruth (Ruth 4:11). Granted, in this blessing the younger Rachel's name precedes the older Leah's; yet it is Leah's fourth son, Judah, to whom Tamar (an outsider like Ruth) will bear the ancestor of David. Thus, the disparities of election do not persist indefinitely.

30:1-24

Whatever Leah's attitude toward Rachel, the latter is clearly jealous of her older sister. Rachel's cry to Jacob is not just emotional exaggeration. RSV "I shall die" may also be translated, "I am dead." If Jacob does not give her children, that means she is barren and generatively dead. (Cf. Isa. 56:3 [the eunuch as a dead tree]; Prov. 30:16 [the barren woman like Sheol]; Rom. 4:17; also Rom. 4:19, where Sarah's womb is described by the Greek term *nekrosis*, "deadness"; similarly Heb. 11:12, where Abraham is described as *nenekromenou*, "having died.") Jacob angrily retorts, "Am I in the place of God?" If he is not generatively dead (cf. again Heb. 11:12), still it is God who is the ultimate giver of life. We may suspect that Jacob's anger masks and redirects his frustration at not having children by his favorite wife, and thereby his frustration at again being thwarted in his aims. Rachel falls back on the custom to which Sarai had resorted, that through Bilhah "even I may be built up."

116

Rachel takes the first son, Dan, as a sign that God has heard her, adjudicated her struggle with Leah, and decided in her favor — for Leah by now is no longer bearing (Gen. 29:35). The second son's name, Naphtali, shows that Rachel's primary concern is to compete with Leah. Thus she resembles Jacob in his struggle with his older brother. If the two brothers wrestled *in* the womb, the two sisters wrestle *by means of* the womb. Not to be outdone, Leah resorts to the same strategy. When Zilpah bears her two sons, Leah's names for them — "good fortune" and "happiness" — disclose the same mood reflected in the name of her own fourth son Judah.

The two sons by Zilpah so counter the two sons by Bilhah that Rachel is pressed to another stratagem. But for this she must seek Leah's help. Unlike her brusque demand of Jacob in 30:1, Rachel's request in v. 14 comes with the *na* of logical persuasion or appeal. After the negotiation for the mandrakes (love or fertility potions), Leah bears two more sons. The first (her fifth son) she names as her "reward" for having given her maid to Jacob. While each of the first five sons has been named in relation to God or to Jacob, the sixth son, Zebulun, is named in relation to both God and Jacob, by a play on two different verbs that share some similar sounds. On the one hand, Zebulun gives Leah hope that Jacob will "honor" (*zabal*) her; on the other hand, he signals to her that God has "endowed" (*zabad*) her with a good "dowry" (*zebed*). With their similar note of reward, these last two sons give Leah a sense of final satisfaction: Then God graces her with a seventh child — a girl! But why is Dinah's name not interpreted? Is it because she is female and therefore, even though a seventh child, insignificant? Or is it because Rachel has already interpreted the name (Dinah is from the same Hebrew root as Dan in v. 6), so that Leah needs only to apply the feminine form of that name to her last child to show her conviction that with this daughter God has now judged in her favor?

But just as Yahweh had responded to Jacob's preference for Rachel by opening Leah's womb, now Yahweh responds to Leah's sense of triumph by remembering Rachel. It should be noted that, in the Bible, God's remembering is never merely an inert and interior cognitive recall of something or someone in the past.

Always it is the beginning of God's action on behalf of the one remembered. Apart from God's remembering, one's life would fade into oblivion and nonbeing (Ps. 88:5); but to be remembered by God is to be carried forward into the future (e.g., Gen. 8:1; Exod. 2:24; Job 14:13-15!). As God has heard Leah (Gen. 29:33; 30:17), so God now hears Rachel (v. 22). In addition to her appeals to Jacob, her offer to him of Bilhah, and her negotiations with Leah for the mandrakes, has Rachel also prayed directly to God for help? Or have her three "wrestlings" with Jacob and Leah been, at the same time and at a very deep level within her, wrestlings in prayer with God? In the latter case, Rachel is very much Jacob's counterpart.

What Jacob could not do (though he had been able to roll the stone from the well-mouth), God now does, opening Rachel's womb. She imitates Leah's action in v. 20 by giving her son a name with a double significance. In regard to the past, the name Joseph (*yoseph*) means that God has taken away (*asaph*) her reproach. In regard to the future, the same name is a prayer that God may add (*yasaph*) another son.

The struggle of these two women will continue later, in the unsettled relations between various Israelite tribes and then, after the death of Solomon, in the changing relations between the kingdoms of Israel and Judah. In the face of these ongoing ambiguous relations, one wonders whether the unification of the sisters in Ruth 4:11-12 does not arise as a wistful hope from a strife-weary storyteller. Long experience of social strife may tempt one to believe that the motives that drive people into conflict and that move them to uneasy calculated truces are more realistic than the aspirations for harmony embodied in such texts as Ruth 4:11-12 and Gen. 12:3. Yet even partisan energies can contain positive potential. For example, Rachel's partisan cry to Jacob in 30:1 seems to have carried positive connotations for Jeremiah, long after the north-south rivalry was ended by the fall of Samaria in 722 B.C. Descended from Rachel's youngest son (Jer. 1:1), Jeremiah not only wrestles with God for the soul of Judah and Jerusalem during the last fateful years of the southern kingdom, but also wrestles over the fate of his exiled northern kin who are descended from Rachel. In Jer. 31:15-22 Jeremiah hears God's answer as a response to Rachel weeping in Ramah (apparently her burial place). The echo of Gen. 30:1 in Jer. 31:15 emerges in the following translations of these two texts:

"Give me children! If not (*ayin*), I am dead."

She refuses to be comforted for her children,
    because they are not (*ayin*).

To Jeremiah, Rachel dead in Ramah and Rachel "dead" before Jacob are one Rachel, so that her earlier prayer for children who never have been becomes now a prayer for children who are no longer. If the editors of the Psalter could associate their communal petitions for God's mercy and deliverance with Moses' intercession at Sinai and Paran (compare Ps. 90 with Exod. 32:11-14; Num. 14:13-19), so likewise Jeremiah finds his own concern for his northern kinfolk arising as a contemporary form of the travail of his maternal ancestor Rachel. Conversely, in God's answer to Rachel in Gen. 30 the prophet hears a divine word for his own day. Needless to say, in her lifetime Rachel was consciously concerned only with the lack of offspring to match those of her rival sister. If Jeremiah heard her prayers for children as intercessions for vanished descendants generations later, we have here a biblical example of what some interpreters have referred to as the *sensus plenior* of a text, the "fuller sense" which it may gain with the passage of time. Such an example encourages the contemporary reader to nest one's own prayer concerns in the cries and prayers of the great biblical characters, and so to position oneself to hear an answer for today through God's answer to the men and women of old.

30:25–31:21

If 29:31–30:24 has traced the struggle between the two sisters over increase through children, 30:25–31:21 traces a parallel struggle between Jacob and the sisters' father over increase through possessions. The first clause in 30:25 is not only a time-indicator, for Joseph's birth may suggest to Jacob that it is time to return home. His mother had told him to stay away for as many days as it would take Esau's fury to subside. At Bethel God had promised to go with Jacob and to bring him home. Given his love for Rachel over Leah, Jacob may have interpreted Rachel's barrenness and the fertility of the other three as God's displeasure with him. In that case, Joseph's birth comes as a sign of divine favor, so that Jacob may now think of returning home safely (cf. 28:21). He asks Laban to release him from all obligations so that he may leave. (One may compare the address of Moses to his father-in-law in Exod. 4:18, and to Pharaoh in 5:1, and the different responses in these instances.)

Laban's response opens, literally, "If I have found favor in your sight" (Gen. 30:27) — a common way of making a proposal it is hoped will meet with the hearer's approval. Jacob does not take up the proposal, but only expands on Laban's admission of being blessed on Jacob's account. Laban repeats the proposal. Jacob agrees to stay, but on condition that he be allowed to determine what he shall receive — namely, the clearly marked livestock — so that when Laban comes to look into his wages his "honesty" (RSV for *tsedaqah*) will answer for him. Or *tsedaqah* may refer here to Jacob's "prosperity" (as it does in, e.g., Prov. 8:18; Joel 2:23). Laban agrees, then sets out once again to deceive. The sequel, in Gen. 30:37-43, is strange, to say the least. Many take it as reflecting ancient superstitions mingled with rudimentary notions of selective stock breeding. That may be so — or something else may be going on here that the narrator will disclose later (see below); a statement in 30:43 will pick up and extend the narrator's remarks made earlier at 13:2; 26:13.

This observation leads directly into 31:1. Analogous to Rachel's jealousy of Leah, Laban's sons resent Jacob's prosperity and he hears of it. Also he notices a change in Laban's bearing toward him. The Hebrew of v. 2 reads literally, "Jacob saw the face of Laban, that it was not with him as in times past." (The same Hebrew idiom occurs in v. 5, "it [the face of Laban] was not toward him. . . ." The stage begins to be set for a contrasting face in 33:10.) Laban's disfavor warns Jacob that it is time to leave. The reference to land and kindred in 31:3 echoes 12:1; 26:3; 28:15. The divine presence working hiddenly ever since

Bethel thus resurfaces in Jacob's consciousness. If Laban is no longer "with" him (31:2), God is with him (v. 5). Jacob's "you know" to Laban's daughters (v. 6), coming after his twofold "you know" to Laban (30:26, 29), marks his speech in this whole passage with a note of formality, almost of oath-taking, as though Jacob is drawing near to a watershed in his life and wants everyone to be clear where he stands.

Jacob now rehearses for his wives the result of his stock-breeding activities (31:8-9). As he tells it, this result is in fact God's restoration to him of what is rightfully his (RSV "taken away" in vv. 9, 16 translates a verb which means "to rescue by snatching away"). But then Jacob goes on to tell them something that the narrator had not previously reported to the reader: He had a dream concerning the stock-breeding (vv. 10-12). Apparently his actions with the rods in 30:37-43 followed the dream, by way of testing it (like Gideon's fleece in Judg. 6:36-40). In that case, Jacob's report in Gen. 31:9 shows God's fulfillment of the dream. Finally he relates God's call to return, in a way that draws the deep connection with ch. 28 even more clearly into the open.

The decision facing Jacob's wives is like the decision that lay before Rebekah (24:58). She had said simply, "I will go," for she had left with Laban's blessing. Given Laban's present attitude (he has cheated not only Jacob but his daughters also), their longer and more formal announcement has almost the character of performative language, cutting their ties with him through an act of speech, as in a formal declaration of divorce.

With this, Jacob and his wives set out directly from their rendezvous in the field (31:4). Did Rachel slip back to Laban's house for his household gods (v. 19)? Or had the wives already suspected what Jacob had to say to them, and brought these figures with them when they joined him in the field? Given their likely significance as fertility or ancestral images, and given her recourse to various stratagems already in 30:1-24, Rachel's motives are clear enough. And given Jacob's testimony in 31:5-12, and the wives' own response in v. 16, Rachel's understanding of her own action is straightforward The verb *ganab* in v. 19 can mean "to steal" and also "to steal away," that is, to slip away unnoticed (in either case, "to act by stealth"). Which sense does the narrator intend us to hear? Or are we to hear both senses? The very next verse says, literally, that "Jacob 'stole the heart (or "mind," or "understanding"; RSV "outwitted") of' Laban the Aramean, in that he did not tell him that he intended to flee." Here the reference is surely to slipping away unnoticed, since this time Jacob is not stealing anything that is not his. Or is an action hidden from a former associate a form of stealing, a taking away of a former common understanding? The verb in vv. 19, 20 resonates back to 30:33. Given how often in the Bible this verb indicates action carried out at night or "under cover," we see that Jacob is still to a considerable degree the "shady" person he was already in the womb; and Rachel by her action shows herself to be his right hand. Does her stealth set in motion a nemesis, a fate, that in time will overtake her and leave Jacob with only Benjamin, the son of his right hand?

31:22-55

The climactic interaction between Jacob and Laban opens with a chase (31:22-23) and closes with a peaceful leave-taking (v. 55). Within this chase and leave-taking the narrator presents God's dream-warning to Laban (v. 24) and the covenant between Laban and Jacob in the name of God (vv. 45-54). Between the dream-warning and the covenant come Laban's passionate speech and Jacob's pacifying response (vv. 25-32), and Jacob's passionate speech and Laban's pacifying response (vv. 36-44). At the very center, the narrator focuses our attention on Laban, Rachel, and the household gods (vv. 33-35) — as though the outcome of the whole interaction turns on this central scene.

Jacob's journey east and his sojourn there since 28:10 have been played out against the background of the servant's journey east in ch. 24. Now, the climactic interaction with Laban (beginning in 30:25) corresponds to 24:54-61 in the following ways: "Send me back (*shallehuni*)" (24:54) . . . "let me go (*shallehuni*) that I may go (*we'eleka*) to my master" (24:56), corresponds to "send me away (*shalleheni*), that I may go (*we'eleka*)" (30:25) . . . "let me go (*we'eleka*)" (30:26). Also, Laban's blessing of

Rebekah (24:60), followed by "the servant . . . went his way (*wayyelak*)" (24:61), corresponds to Laban's blessing of his grand-children and daughters (31:55), followed by "Jacob went on his way" (*halak*) (32:1). These narrative echoes underline the way in which human interactions in one generation pattern themselves partly on interactions in a previous generation without repeating them exactly. As another example of this, we may consider the way Jacob's interaction with Laban involves deceit or at least disguised actions, yet ends in blessing. Compare this interaction with what transpires in 26:34–28:9.

The chase (31:22-23) recalls the chase in 14:13-16 (cf. espe-cially 14:15; 31:26) and in 16:7. But the dream-visitation (31:24) forestalls a similar outcome. The words of God to Laban, "take heed that you say not a word to Jacob, either good or bad," echo those Laban himself had long ago spoken to Abraham's servant, "we cannot speak to you bad or good" (24:50-51). It is as though Laban's own words, long since sunk so far in his deep memory as to have been forgotten, are now stirred up within him in a similar situation to become God's word to him in that situation. Once again we see how God's word arises in intimate connection with a person's past experience, inseparable from it yet not simply equated with it.

The two sets of exchanges between Laban and Jacob — 31:25-30/31-32, and vv. 36-42/43-44 — show these two pressing con-flicting claims against each other, each in a spirit of outraged justice. Granted that both Laban and Jacob are complex and grasping characters, one cannot help but be so affected by their arguments as to be drawn into sympathy with each of them in turn. Whose claim is right? Laban's first words to Jacob (v. 26) echo Jacob's words to him in 29:25. Twice Laban uses the word *ganab*, in 31:26 meaning "to steal" (RSV "cheat"), in v. 27 meaning "to slip away stealthily." His "you have done foolishly" (v. 28) points to a violation of kinship ethos (cf. 29:26) that normally would place Jacob at his mercy; for 31:29 reads literally, "It is in the god of my hand to do you harm." (Laban here seems to refer to his own personal or family god — not necessarily the same God that Abraham and his descendants worship.) But the God of Jacob's father has stayed that hand. Nevertheless, Laban asks, why has Jacob stolen his gods? Jacob's answer to vv. 26-28 echoes Abraham's answer to Abimelech (20:11); as for the gods (31:30b), Jacob swears by the life of whoever has taken them that he does not have them. The turning of Jacob's habitual deceit back on his own head, which began with Rachel in 29:21-30, here through her theft and concealment reaches its tragic climax, as he unwittingly places her life in jeopardy by his oath. (The verb *ganab* occurs in 30:33; 31:19, 20, 26, 27, 30, and, for the seventh time, 32.)

If Jephthah's daughter was the innocent victim of her father's rash oath (Judg. 11:29-40), Rachel here mirrors Jacob through her own deceitful ruse. What should we think of Rachel hiding these fertility or ancestral figurines under her claim to be in "the way of women" (Gen. 31:35)? Is Laban to think she would never dream of bringing such sacred symbols into such proximity with what in that culture would be considered her state of ritual impurity? Is she in fact in such a state, or is she only claiming to be? Does her action so compromise her with God as to leave her a less than innocent victim of Jacob's vow? Yet her deceit spares her life, and that of Benjamin and all his descendants. Search as we might, how shall we find answers to such questions? Saul/Paul, the Benjaminite who wrote Rom. 9–11, confessed that there are depths to human conflicted interaction and God's redemptive dealings with it all that are unfathomable (Rom. 11:33-36).

Jacob now lays his case before the assembled kin, "that they may decide (*hokiah*) between us two" (Gen. 31:37). His passionate speech ends where Laban's did (v. 29), with reference to his own ancestral god (v. 42). He appeals to the God who "saw" his affliction and who "decided (*hokiah*; RSV "rebuked you") last night." (Also, if Laban can appeal to "the god of my hand" [v. 29], Jacob can appeal to God's vindication of "the labor of my hands" [v. 42].) Laban does not wait for the assembled kin to decide the issue; for he already knows from his dream that Jacob is right. Their past dealings cannot be changed. So he proposes a covenant to stabilize future relations with Jacob (see Hannah Arendt's remarks, quoted above, on 28:20-22).

The covenant ceremony is striking for the fact that the action is given primarily to Jacob and the speaking primarily to Laban.

124

Jacob's stone pillar is reminiscent of 28:18. The act of gathering stones, making a heap, and eating before it may serve to implicate his kin in the terms of the covenant. Only then does Laban name the heap, in his own Aramaic language, Jegar-sahadutha, "the heap of witness," after which Jacob gives it a Hebrew name, Galeed, which means the same thing. Laban then takes up Jacob's own Hebrew terms to spell out his agreement as to the significance of the covenant markers: The heap will be a witness between them; and the pillar will be a "watchpost" (RSV mg) signifying that God will watch (literally, keep a watchful eye on) covenant-violating behavior when they are hidden (*nissater*; RSV "absent") from one another. It is as though the painstaking care and openness with which their covenant is made, by contrast with the way the two have repeatedly deceived one another in word and action, are to put an end to all that deceit.

The covenant is to be a mutual nonaggression pact (31:52), with one unilateral clause binding Jacob to safeguard the domestic interests of Laban's daughters (v. 50). Like the bilingual naming (v. 47), Laban's appeal to heaven is bilateral, as he invokes the respective family gods: "the God of Abraham and the God of Nahor — may they [so the Hebrew!] judge between us." Then Laban adds, "the God of their father," that is, the God of Terah. (As brothers who were separated when Abraham left Haran for Canaan [11:27-31], it would appear that Abraham and Nahor were later remembered as founders of different clans each with its ancestral god.)

In response, Jacob swears by the Fear of his father Isaac. The specific focus in his appeal to God reflects God's interaction with him in 28:11-22, and in particular Jacob's conditional vow that Yahweh, "the God of Abraham your father and *the God of Isaac*" (28:13; cf. 31:42; 32:9), would become his own God. The God of Isaac is the same God as the God of Abraham, but with a special nuance. The God of Isaac is Abraham's God, who elected Isaac rather than Ishmael to continue the particular vocation begun in 12:1-3. When Jacob here swears by the God of Isaac, then, he is swearing by the electing God in whose name Isaac blessed him (rather than Esau) with the blessings of 27:28-29; 28:3-4. This means that, in taking leave of Laban to return home,

Jacob here swears an oath that becomes integrally bound up with the oath he had sworn to God in 28:20-22. It is as he lives by these two oaths — one to God and one to Laban in the name of God — that Jacob will become in fact the *ish tam,* the "man of integrity," he was said to be in principle in 25:27. (On the word *tam,* "integrity," as applied to Jacob, see above on 25:27).

In ch. 14 the formalities between Abraham and Melchizedek were under the aegis of (Yahweh) God Most High, maker of heaven and earth. Here they are under the aegis of the respective ancestral gods of Jacob and Laban, and beyond that, the God of their one common ancestor Terah. Thus, in ch. 31 as in ch. 14, the narrative both recognizes a genuine plurality of religious traditions and communities, and presses behind them to a level at which that pluralism is nested in a divine unity. Does the feast in 31:54 again include only Jacob's kin as referred to in v. 46? Or does it embrace also Laban and his entourage, who through the covenant may now be considered proper kin? The long and tangled dealings between Laban and Jacob come to a resolution signalled in Laban's farewell kiss and blessing upon his daughters and their offspring.

Looking back over chs. 12–31, with an eye to the interweaving of divine elective action and human character, one may conclude that the family with which God chose to work was a "mixed bag." However Abraham may act toward Pharaoh and Abimelech, his relations to his own kin are straightforward. Similarly, granted Sarai's treatment of Hagar, in comparison with Rebekah and Rachel she otherwise acts straightforwardly; and Isaac — again except for Abimelech — is so straightforward as to be gullible. In contrast to Ishmael and Esau (who in this respect more nearly resemble their fathers), Laban, Rebekah, Jacob, and Rachel all display deep-seated tendencies to deceive even their closest kin. (Cf. Hos. 11:12, which, before summarizing Jacob's life in 12:2-6, charges his descendants in the northern kingdom with lies and deceit.) It is as though these four take after Nahor's side rather than Abraham's side of Terah's descendants. But God does not simply elect one side over the other, for the narrative weaves both sides of the ancestral character — straightforwardness and deviousness — into the elective story of Jacob. If Abraham's name is to be a means by which all families of the earth may bless themselves — and thus redeem the fragmentation of the human community at the tower of Babel — the family of Terah must itself be delivered of its internal disputes and problems. True kin — "my bone and my flesh" (Gen. 29:14; cf. 2:23) — should have no need of deceit, in transparent openness to one another (cf. Gen. 2:25). Where that openness is not possible, covenants with their sworn oaths come as a covering for human frailty and sin.

But if words of blessing (in 12:3 or in 31:55) can achieve or signal human reconciliation, what are we to make of Jacob's self-curse in 31:32 and its terrible legacy for Rachel (who is not even buried with the other ancestors)? Who wishes to live with a worldview — which is to say, who wishes to live in a world — in which such rash oaths can be thought to have such consequences? But then, shall we choose rather to live in a world where words have lost all positive as well as negative performative and binding power — a world where words gradually become only shrill empty noises hurled at each other by parties bent on direct warring action?

32:1-21

The theme in chs. 29–30, involving three fertile and one initially barren woman, was signalled in part by the three flocks in 29:2 and then, separately, Rachel's flock in 29:6, 9. (It may be noted that her name *rahel* means "ewe," like that Hebrew word in 31:38.) The angels (or "messengers"; *mal'akim*) in 32:1-2 may similarly signal a theme in chs. 32–33, as they move Jacob to name the place Mahanaim, "two armies." Does he see this twofold angelic army as being on his side or against him? In either case, Jacob sends messengers (*mal'akim*) to Esau with a deferential message, as from a servant to a lord (32:3). Is this merely the old tricky Jacob? Or is he here paying respect to Esau's biological seniority? His hasty reference to his possessions — as though he might offer tribute to Esau — is a clear if implicit bid for his brother's favor. But the messengers bring back an ominous report: Esau is coming with hundreds of men — a virtual army. Is God, then, on Esau's side against him, and has Jacob misread what he thought was God's word for him to return? Does the angelic message concerning two armies lie behind his move then to divide his entourage into two companies (Heb. *mahanot,* "companies," is from the same root as the place name Mahanaim)?

Jacob's prayer (vv. 9-12) is a model of persuasive rhetoric, worthy of comparison with the prayers of Moses in Exod. 32:11-13; Num. 14:13-19. Jacob opens and closes his petition by reference to the ancestors (the wording in Gen. 32:12 shows that he quotes God's promise to Abraham in 22:17 rather than the promise to Jacob in 28:14). Within these references to the ancestors, he appeals twice to God's promise to do him good. Then, nested within that twofold appeal, he makes his central petition, "deliver me, *na,* from the hand of Esau, for I fear him, lest he come and slay me — women and children" (so the Hebrew). Jacob declares himself unworthy of all God's steadfast love and all God's faithfulness (cf. 24:27). Is he just using the rhetoric he thinks will work with God? If he is sincere, this is a Jacob we have not seen before.

Having prayed, Jacob acts, in preparing a *minhah* (RSV "present") for his brother. The term can mean "gift" or "tribute," depending on the context. The repeated reference to "your servant Jacob" and "my lord Esau" may suggest to Esau that Jacob is offering tribute to an acknowledged superior. Two details are noteworthy: (1) The verb *ehar,* "hang back," in 32:4 (RSV "stayed") is echoed in the twofold "behind us" *(ahar)* in vv. 18, 20. (2) The word *peney,* "face" (or "*fore*-part"), occurs frequently in vv. 13-21: "be*fore* me" (v. 16), "be*fore* you" (v. 17), "be*fore* him" (v. 21); and especially in v. 20, the core of the passage: "I may appease his *face* (*panayw*) with the *minhah* that goes be*fore* me, and afterwards I shall see his *face;* perhaps he will lift up my *face*" (author's translation). The sevenfold occurrence of *peney,* "face, fore," contrasts with the threefold ocurrence of the word *ehar/ahar,* "hang back, behind," dramatizing Jacob's struggle with the issues of concealment and openness between himself and others. The sevenfold "face" also prepares for the double climax in 32:30; 33:10.

We may now draw the following details together: (1) The repeated reference to the *minhah* — a word that after the covenant at Sinai is often used to refer to offerings in the cult. (2) The use of the verb *kipper,* "appease, propitiate" — also used often, after Sinai, to refer to cultic atonement (as on Yom Kippur, the Day of Atonement). (3) Seeing God *face* to *face* at *Peni*el (32:30), and seeing Esau's reconciled face as God's face (33:10). Cf. the issues in Exod. 3:6; 19:21; 24:10, 11(!); 33:18, 20. (4) All God's steadfast love and all God's faithfulness — as in Gen. 24:27 and Exod. 34:6-7. These elements suggest that there is a "type/antitype" correlation between Jacob's pivotal experiences at Jabbok/Peniel and the cultic provision for atonement and forgiveness in Israel since Sinai. In Exodus and in Deuteronomy (cf. Rom. 11:28) the promises to the ancestors are the basis for God's forgiveness to subsequent generations. Here at Jabbok/Peniel we see Jacob, himself an ancestor, already making an appeal for reconciliation on the same basis.

Jacob here (as in Hos. 12:2-6) is Israel in miniature, as Esau is Edom in miniature. In Genesis these two figures interact as individuals, yet they also stand for the interaction of the two peoples who descend from them. In this way, the ancestral narratives in Gen. 12–50 frequently get at the heart of complex communal and collective issues by presenting them in the form of individual interactions. This enables us to apply the ancestral stories more easily to ourselves as individuals; but we should not overlook what these stories have to say to us about our interactions as a people with other peoples.

32:22-32

The central issue for Jacob is inscribed in the name given him at birth, "heel-grabber, supplanter." The centrality of this night by the Jabbok for his life is signalled by the fact that after it he receives a new name. Abraham and Sarah's new names in ch. 17 signified their new stature under God's promise. Babylon received a new meaning in 11:1-9, by inversion of its consonantal elements, *bbl* to *bll* (= "confusion"). The present passage plays repeatedly on Jacob's name: (1) Jabbok echoes it by inversion of two consonants: *y'qb* to *ybq*. (2) The nocturnal struggle is indicated by a verb occurring only here, *abaq* (32:24), and strikingly

reminds us of 25:22. (3) Jacob's hip is dislocated, or displaced
— *yqʿ*, a verb that elsewhere always refers to alienation between
parties.

What has Jacob's old name to do with the stream, the wrestling,
and the dislocation, and what is the relation of his old name to
his new name? The key may lie in the identity of the one with
whom he wrestles — an identity the stranger or alien refuses to
disclose directly. From the explanation of the new name (32:28b),
this figure may be divine, or human, or both. The combination
of darkness, a river, wrestling all night, and a new name at daybreak
implies that at Jabbok Jacob "enters the womb a second time"
(John 3:4) to undergo rebirth. It is as though the solution of
Jacob's identity and character must begin as early as the problem.
One may compare such radical negative images as Ps. 51:5; Isa.
48:8 (literally, "from the womb you were called a rebel") and
equally radical positive images in Jer. 1:5; Ps. 22:9-10 (literally,
"from my mother's womb you have been my God" — a claim to
prenatal trust); Isa. 46:3-4. The existential and theological question is, Which is the foundational statement concerning a human
being: sin? Or a potential for basic trust, which only later gives
way to anxiety and sin? Genesis 2 and 3 posit a situation of original
goodness in creation as a whole, including humankind, and a
subsequent (but only subsequent) calamity that obscures but
cannot obliterate the divine image.

Such OT passages suggest that we should not be surprised to
meet the same issues in the life of Jacob — the ancestor who gave
his name (indeed, both names!) to the people of the biblical
covenant. The Anglican rite of baptism at one time included a
bidding prayer with these clauses: ". . . seeing that God willeth
all men to be saved from the fault and corruption of *the nature
which they inherit,* as well as from the actual sins which they
commit, . . . [may God] grant unto this child that which *by nature*
he/she cannot have" (italics added). In such a bidding the inherited nature, which cannot receive all that God has to give, is
not human nature as God created it, but human "second nature"
as distorted by sin. However one understands older doctrines of
sinfulness by inheritance, or "original sin," contemporary psy-
chologists help us to see how the human psyche can inherit flaws

(as well as sound virtues!) from parents and earlier generations and then build a whole life around those flaws, making them one's own until living in accordance with them becomes "second nature." The case of Jacob is a prime example.

The striking thing about this story is that, if Jacob is simply a supplanter and needs nothing else but radical transformation (or new birth), why is he not defeated by his opponent? Why does his new name enshrine the fact that *he* has prevailed? Again, if Jacob has indeed prevailed, why does his name not remain Jacob? All this implies that "Israel" is the true name of one who has been struggling since before birth and finally has won out.

The name "Jacob" then implies that the persona we have been seeing through much of the story to this point is a false mask of the true person. Insofar as his parents named him after something that was indeed the case about him, but was not the deepest truth in him, they misnamed him. Then he "bought into" that name, living out the "script" that his own existential anxieties and his parents' perceptions colluded in writing for him. The ascending angels of 28:12 related to Jacob as still in the deepest sense in the image of God. They acted as true God-given energies of the person God created him to be, all along at great depth crying to heaven and there being heard (cf. Matt. 18:5-6, 10), even while the waking Jacob was busy with strategies to bend heaven and earth to his anxiety-driven will. The alien by the Jabbok may not only be God, Esau, Isaac, and Laban, but may also refer to the fact that he has been alienated from his own true self. If in respect to his false self Jacob has needed transformation, in respect to his deepest self as created in God's image he has needed liberation.

At birth Jacob had grabbed Esau by the heel and eventually had overtaken him. Now at (another) daybreak this figure touches him on the thigh and dislocates it — as Jacob had displaced Esau — so that he may displace no longer. In this act we see Jacob's false self displaced. God names him for who he most deeply is and has been since the beginning. The name is new to him only in that for the first time he knows himself as God has known him (cf. 1 Cor. 13:12).

Contemporary psychoanalysts speak of the need to return to the point — however early — at which one underwent a life-crippling trauma, to face the fear of annihilation that was unbearable then, and in the safe presence of the therapist finally to undergo that trauma in a way that restores basic trust. Jacob is a parade example. Questions as to "who sinned, this man or his parents" (John 9:2) may be unanswerable. Yet, given the pattern of character in Laban, Rebekah, Jacob, and Rachel, in contrast to Abraham, Sarah, Isaac, and Leah, one may suspect that Jacob's character is an ambiguous inheritance and that for much of his life he has bought into the negative side.

In this connection, one wonders about the significance of the "Jabbok." The place name derives from Heb. *baqaq*, "to empty," from the gurgling noise of emptying water. (The verb, always with negative connotations, means "emptied out" [Isa. 19:3], "lay waste" [24:1], "utterly laid waste" [24:3], "stripped" [Nah. 2:3], "make void" [Jer. 19:7], "empty" [51:2].) The "stream" itself is a *nahal,* a wadi, running and gurgling briefly after rain until it runs dry and waits for the next rain — unlike the "living water" of an artesian well or perennial stream (cf. Jer. 15:18). This stream with its name is a perfect image of the situation with Abram-Sarai and Isaac-Rebekah, not to mention Jacob-Rachel. What psychic scars arise within a family that over the generations repeatedly must live in anxious hope of children (e.g., Gen. 30:1) and has one, if at all, only after a long wait? Already in the womb Jacob may have sensitively received such deep anxieties from his parents and grandparents. Now, the play on the names *ya'qob/yab-boq* signals his return to the "place" of original trauma — a place that for a long time was barren and only after twenty years became fertile. There he finally meets the God who gives all life and bears it from womb to old age (Isa. 46:3-4). In that meeting Jacob finally comes face to face also with his own true self as Israel. This is what will free him to come clean with Esau — and not hang back hiding — when day breaks.

33:1-20

The Jacob who has hung back behind his appeasing "gift," on seeing Esau's approach with the armed band now goes be*fore* (literally, "in the face of") his entourage, ordering it from the most expendable (beginning with himself) to the most precious. His sevenfold bowing embodies a well-known form of address by an inferior to a superior. Esau's response is moving, as is the sudden shift in verbal subject from singular to plural: Esau runs, he embraces Jacob, he falls on his neck, he kisses him — and they weep. Does Esau's embrace and kiss trigger a shameful memory in Jacob — of how he had disguised his neck to feel like Esau (Gen. 27:16) when he kissed his father (vv. 26-27) — and then erase the shame?

When Esau asks the question Jacob had anticipated (33:5; 32:17), Jacob's first word sounds the note of favor he hopes will mark Esau's attitude to him: "The children with whom Yahweh has favored (*hanan*) your servant" (author's translation). The formal ritual, repeated three times (33:6-7), underscores Jacob's self-designation as "your servant." When Esau asks the meaning of the "company" he had previously "met" (v. 8; 32:17), does he wish to hear the answer from Jacob himself, and not just from his servants? Jacob's response — "to find favor (*hen*) in the sight of my lord" — both continues the deferential address and seeks in Esau the attitude he has just spoken of finding in God (see also Jacob's initial message to Esau, 32:5).

Esau brushes aside the deferential address to him with his own address to "my brother," and declines the "gift" because "I have much" (*yesh-li rab*). Jacob's response comes as the heart of the occasion:

a   No, *na'*, if, *na'*, I have found favor (*hen*) in your sight,
b   then take my present (*minhah*) from my hand;
c   for truly I have seen your face like seeing the face of God,
c' with such favor (*hen*) have you been pleased (*ratsah*) with me.
b' Take, *na'*, my blessing (*berakah*) that is brought to you,
a' for God has favored (*hanan*) me and I have everything (*yesh-li-kol*). (author's translation)

The overtones of cultic offering noted above in 32:13-21a continue in these lines, especially in light of the themes of the divine face and the divine name in Exod. 33–34. (Cf. Exod. 33:19, "I will be gracious [*hanan*] to whom I will be gracious, and will show mercy on whom I will show mercy"; 34:6, "Yahweh, Yahweh, a God merciful and gracious [*hannun*].") These connotations will sound again in the Priestly blessing whose central benediction is "Yahweh shine his face upon you and be gracious (*hanan*) to you" (Num. 6:25). The verb *ratsah* several times indicates God's acceptance of a sacrifice and the person offering it.

This cultic parallel helps us to appreciate the significance of Esau's final acceptance of the gift. Is it, after all, a purchase of his favor? No more so, I suggest, than cultic sacrifice is a purchase of God's favor, for that sacrifice is a divinely given way to come to God and receive God's favor. There is a deep wisdom here, in which Jacob's penitent self-abasement is followed by Esau's acceptance of Jacob's gift, which becomes a blessing. Esau's acceptance of Jacob's gift and Jacob's blessing of Esau are a combined sign of Jacob's full restoration to a bilateral relation. Esau, who at one time had traded away his inheritance to satisfy an immediate hunger, can now say, "I have much"; and he who for so long had grasped at everything in sight can now say, "I have everything." They are at peace.

The climactic exchange falls away quickly then into Esau's invitation, Jacob's demurral, Esau's offer of safe escort, Jacob's further demurral, and their separation — Esau to Seir, Jacob to Succoth. Do we see here yet another deception — a sign of a not yet fully resolved fear? That may be. Or it may be that Jacob has arrived at a wisdom at which impulsive Esau, for all his own transformation, has not yet arrived. In some cases reconciliation may lead, not to cohabitation, but to separation on good terms. If that is the case here, then this separation echoes that of Abraham and Lot in Gen. 13:7-17. Jacob's arrival at Shechem "safely" signals God's faithful answer to Jacob's prayer in 28:21. At that time Jacob had promised that for such faithfulness, Yahweh, "the God of Abraham . . . and the God of Isaac" (28:13), would become his own God (v. 21). Though it will be a while yet before Jacob arrives at Bethel to make good his vow of cult and tithes (28:22; 35:1-4), he does not delay to erect an altar and call it

El-Elohe-Israel. The naming has a twofold significance. It identifies who his own personal God is from now on; and it seals Jacob's acceptance of his own identity, Israel, as given in the naming at Jabbok.

A final reflection can be offered on this conclusion to the saga of Esau and Jacob. At the outset, I have suggested, the difference between Esau and Jacob lay partly in Jacob's capacity for moral and spiritual response (whether positive or negative), whereas Esau seemed lacking in that capacity, preoccupied in a life of direct action driven by bodily needs and devoid of reflection or of the temporal imagination we call patience. The narrative subsequently has traced Jacob's transformation in stages with which the reader can enter into sympathetic identification, climaxing at Jabbok. By what stages, and through what factors, has Esau come to be the person we see in this chapter — the person whom to see is (for Jacob) like seeing the face of God? The narrator does not tell us. In our passion for finding "canonical" models of legitimate experience of God, we are here given a model known only to God. Jacob's experience of transformation is a possibility for those who need it. Esau's experience may serve to remind us that Jacob's experience is not a necessity to be imposed on those with whom God has transforming dealings in a way known only to God (cf. Deut. 29:29; John 10:16; 21:21-22). Thus Esau joins the Ishmael of Gen. 17:20. They in turn will be joined by Jethro the priest of Midian who, having no experience of Red Sea deliverance, nor Sinai covenant, nor entry into the Promised Land, yet presides at a cult in celebration of Yahweh (Exod. 18:10-12) and remains (v. 27) a lifetime resident in that wilderness where Yahweh is most truly at home.

34:1-31

This passage weaves together several familiar narrative themes, in each instance giving them a fresh and problematical turn. (1) It explores further the possibility and conditions of relations between the community of the ancestor and the host society. (2) It provides a twist on the three earlier episodes in which women are vulnerable to the sexual interest of the dominant power of the region. (3) It raises the issue of extra-clan marriage, in contrast to the intra-clan marriages of the ancestors. The passage is filled with conflicting emotions that pretend to seek unity and end in violence. In this last respect, it comes in stark contrast to Gen. 33 with its reconciliation between brothers long at enmity.

Furthermore, with this chapter the action begins to pass to the next generation. The primary actors are Shechem and Dinah's brothers. Hamor and Jacob, while still enjoying full parental authority, act only in response to their sons' initiatives. If the story of Jacob is of a deeply divided person who has finally "come to himself" (32:28) and has begun to use that name for himself (33:20), this passage raises in an ominous way the question as to how effectively this newly affirmed identity will pass on to his descendants. The sons appear to accept the new identity — or at least the new name (34:7). Yet their actions suggest that they are what the narrator calls them — sons of Jacob (vv. 7, 13, 25, 27).

The driving energies of the primary actors are *eros* and *eris,* passion and strife, energies that stand in sharp contrast to the way the passage opens. Dinah sets out to see the women of the land. This introduces a new dimension of possibility into the story. Until now, relations between the ancestral community and host societies have been traced through the interactions of the men. What may happen when the women of the two societies get together? Shechem's rape aborts that prospect (except perhaps in our imagination). Given the power-relations between the sexes, the rape is tragically no surprise. What is unexpected is Shechem's subsequent love for Dinah (vv. 3, 8, 19; contrast 2 Sam. 13:14-15). A moment ago he had forced her; now he appeals to her. "Speak tenderly" (Gen. 34:3) translates an idiom literally meaning "speak upon the heart." It implies a sensitive use of language to change another's deep and strongly felt conviction or disposition (Gen. 50:21; Judg. 19:3; Ruth 2:13; 1 Sam. 1:13; 2 Sam. 19:7; 2 Chr. 30:22; 32:6; Isa. 40:2; Hos. 2:14). The contexts of this idiom's use illustrate how words may seek to assuage a guilty conscience, reassure an anxious spirit, or placate a sense of moral outrage.

Dinah's brothers are outraged (Gen. 34:7, 13, 31) at the "folly" perpetrated against the honor of the family. (After "wrought" in

v. 7, RSV "in" may be translated "against"; this verb and prep-osition in Hebrew usually signify action *against* someone.) As-suring the brothers of his new feeling for her, Shechem proposes to make her his wife in the community where he holds an honored position (vv. 4, 8-12, 19). He even has his father propose a general relation of intermarriage and economic interdependence.

The sons of Jacob object that intermarriage with the uncir-cumcised would be a disgrace (v. 14). The word "disgrace" of course identifies their keen sense of having been dishonored by Shechem's action. But it serves also to imply against the She-chemites that their daughters' proper marital relations with the Shechemites would be as much a folly, defilement, and prostitu-tion (vv. 7, 13, 31) as Dinah's rape. Their deceitful proposal (vv. 15-17) may mask a plan that only Simeon and Levi later carry out. Or it may disguise an intent simply to throw cold water on the proposal by asking too high a price. (Why would a stronger and more established people willingly adopt the ritual identity of this small group of newcomers?) Perhaps the brothers hope simply to cool Shechem's ardor so they can safely go their way, supposedly free from any desire for revenge (v. 17).

If that is their intention, it backfires. Shechem accepts their condition. But now, how is he to sell the idea to his fellow city-dwellers, who have no interest in Dinah, and can hardly be expected to want to undergo the rite of this insignificant family? He appeals to their economic interest (vv. 21-23). If he means this, the proposal to the sons of Israel in vv. 8-12 becomes misleading. Or he may be misleading his city-folk to gain their agreement. The sordidness of the situation mounts on both sides. Do Dinah's brothers now find themselves in a situation they had not bargained for, and do they disagree among themselves over what to do? Is this why only two of them slip off and carry out the general massacre?

The whole passage is riddled with betrayal. Innocence is betrayed into the hands of ruthless appetite. When this appetite moderates into something that under normal circumstances one might sympathize with (the desire for marriage), that moderated feeling is then served by strategies of deceit. The sacral institutions of marriage and circumcision are debased into weapons in the struggle for revenge and goods. Simeon and Levi come upon the city "unawares" (v. 25). The last-mentioned term translates *betah*, "trust," here used adverbially. The men of Shechem were trusting in the benign intentions of the sons of Jacob; and that trust Simeon and Levi abruptly betrayed. Thus, the passage unblinkingly portrays the tangle of intersocietal relations where the energies of passion and anger override ethical sensibilities, and where the ritual arrangements that channel passion and define social boundaries and covenants are cynically debased. If there is little or nothing to admire in Shechem and his fellows, the actions of Jacob's sons are no less objectionable. However justified their feeling may be, they will only bring down a terrible retribution on their heads (v. 30). Jacob's perspective here may be partly prudential. But he may also see in his sons disheartening signs of his old self, so that his rebuke of them is an implicit self-judgment. His view of the rape of Dinah is no different from theirs (vv. 5, 13, 27). Yet his silence (RSV "held his peace" in v. 5, as in Isa. 42:14, translates the verb *harash*, "keep silent") may reflect a temperamental and behavioral change in him since Jabbok.

In reflecting on the story of Sodom and Gomorrah, I raised the possibility that the narrator's view of the multiple rape in Judg. 19 is signalled by the single detail in v. 27 concerning the concubine's hands. Is there any clue in this chapter as to the narrator's view? Or does the narrator remain completely silent, like Dinah and Leah — and God? In a book concerned with the foundations of a new community through barren marriages that become fertile, the chapter is a study in the rape of justice. What will it take to redeem marriage and circumcision (or, for Christians, baptism), both of them ordinances of union and of inclusion, from their use as weapons in struggles for power and wealth? That is to say, what will it take for the children of Jacob to become the children of Israel?

35:1–36:43

If the double climax of the Abraham story comes in Gen. 21 and 22 with the birth and the offering of Isaac, the double climax of the Jacob story comes with the transformation at the Jabbok and the reconciliation with Esau. With Abraham, the climax is followed by two transitional episodes, the burial of Sarah and a wife for Isaac (chs. 23 and 24). After that, summary details are followed by Abraham's death and burial. With Jacob, the climax is followed by several sorts of concluding information in the present two chapters. But whereas Abraham's death and burial preceded the Isaac narrative, Jacob's death and burial (along with his final blessing — what may be his most significant act) are delayed until almost the end of Genesis. This delay follows the precedent of Isaac's death and burial notice, which is delayed to the end of ch. 35, after the summary list of Jacob's children and just before the much fuller list of Isaac's posterity through Esau.

35:1-4 Is the divine instruction in v. 1 given to prod Jacob into fulfilling his vow made at Bethel in 28:20-22? Or does it come as a sign that what is about to happen there comes not merely in fulfillment of a human vow but also in response to a divine word? The latter is suggested by the fact that in ancient Near Eastern tradition major cult places often are built in response to divine directives. Bethel's importance for Israelite tradition is signalled by what happens in Jacob's response: foreshadowing Moses' actions in Exod. 19, Jacob calls his whole entourage to acts of ritual purification.

Most noteworthy is the call to put away the foreign gods. Readers instructed by Sinai may misconstrue it as an exhortation to abandon prohibited practices. However, prior to Sinai no such prohibition existed. As Abraham's interaction with Melchizedek reminds us, and as is implicit in the conditional character of Jacob's vow in Gen. 28, in the ancestral period the relation to deity was defined much more permissively. (One might take Josh. 24:2, 14 as descriptive rather than critical of ancestral practice.) The importance of the present passage lies in its portrayal of a movement toward exclusive cultic loyalty, out of a voluntary individual oath that was then divinely sanctioned. The way Jacob in Gen. 35:3 exactly echoes and then nuances the words of God in v. 1, and the way his word and God's bracket Jacob's call to preparation in v. 2, suggest that this call is based on Jacob's own restatement of what God has just said to him:

v. 1 (a) who *appeared* to you
       (b) *when you fled* from your brother Esau
v. 3 (a') who *answered* me in the day of my distress
       (b') and *has been with me* wherever I have gone.

God in (a) tells what God did; Jacob in (a') tells why God did it. God in (b) tells of Jacob's flight into exile; Jacob in (b') tells of God's care during that exile. These shifts in nuance suggest that the call to put away the foreign gods comes not by divine demand, but as Jacob's own voluntary response to what God has done for him. This response is similar to such free confessions as Exod. 15:11; 18:10-11; 19:8. The entourage's action reads, in Hebrew, "They gave to Jacob all the foreign gods *in their hand.* . . ." The reference to hand and to ear (Gen. 35:4) may connote their power of action and hearing, both of which they thus bind over to the God of Bethel (cf. Exod. 29:20).

35:5-8   Why the "terror from God" along the way to Bethel? One may think of the terror of the peoples on hearing of the Red Sea deliverance (Exod. 15:15-16) and during the Jordan crossing (Josh. 5:1), or of Exod. 23:20-33 with its promise to send terror before the people and its prohibition of other gods. Again, the similarity between these passages should not obscure the fact that Jacob's experience foreshadows Sinai rather than conforming to its explicit injunctions. (Here, as elsewhere in the ancestral narratives, divine-human relations and interactions foreshadow the divine-human relations that are formally structured in the Sinai covenant. While it is important to recognize that the latter covenant inaugurates a new stage in divine-human relations, it is important also to remember that these new relations fundamentally resemble, continue, and further develop the relations that already existed between God and the ancestors.) Genesis 35:5 provides yet further evidence that God is bringing Jacob "safely" back to Bethel (28:21; 33:18).

The burial of Rebekah's wet nurse under an oak below Bethel (35:8) is as tantalizingly unexplained as the hiding of the gods under the oak near Shechem. Even more tantalizing is the fact that the burial of the wet nurse leads to a naming of the oak, while the hiding of the gods does not lead to a naming of that oak. Why this difference? Again, given the commonness of wet nurses in the ancient world, why does the narrator trouble to mention Rebekah's nurse at all, in 24:59 and again here? Her importance may be related to recurrent problems of insufficient breast milk in the mother (especially one who has twins). Another term for foster mother is *omenet* — one who gives unfailing support and care — from the root *amen*, "reliable, faithful." (Unlike a "deceitful brook, and waters that fail" [Jer. 15:18], a perennial stream may be named *amanah* [2 Kgs. 5:12].) This nurse apparently supplied Jacob with the unfailing supply of milk that Rebekah could not. As thus standing in for the mother, she became the primal earthly sign of God's unfailing presence and provision through all Jacob's wanderings. This would explain the mention of her death precisely at this point, following Gen. 35:1-4 and 5-7, which bring to a faithful conclusion the promises of ch. 28. This would also account for the name Oak of Weeping, after Jacob's deep filial feeling for her (cf. 24:67). The oak over her burial was named, unlike the oaks over the foreign gods, because it was with her rather than those figurines that God's faithful presence came to be experienced.

35:9-15 At 13:3-4 I reflected on how revisiting memorable sites serves to knit past and present together. A similar function here takes on a nuance specific to Jacob. At Bethel in ch. 28 Jacob knew himself only as Jacob fleeing from a brother he had twice duped. Since then he has been given a new name and an identity that is more truly his. But those who have gone through some form of Jacob's experience know well how the encounter with places and people from one's past can powerfully pull one into past self-understandings (Mark 6:1-5). So God repeats the new name "Israel" at Bethel, where earlier the ascending angels had already attested his deepest but as yet unnamed character. Jacob's acts in Gen. 35:14-15 repeat his acts in ch. 28, as his contribution to this event that weaves his true identity back into his old life. Thus the past becomes healed in interaction with the present.

God's promise to Jacob in 35:11-12 has echoed at several points the promise to Abraham in ch. 17. Now we come in 35:16-20 to the birth of a son who will become the direct ancestor of Israel's first king, Saul, and of Saul/Paul, apostle of Messiah Jesus. Along the way Rachel goes into hard labor. When her labor is at its hardest, the midwife encourages her with a word that we have heard at 15:1 (Abraham's childlessness); 21:17 (Hagar's fear for Ishmael); and 26:24 (Isaac's concern for his posterity in the face of Abimelech). It is a word that will be echoed many times in the Bible. (In its Greek translation — *tharsei*, "be of good cheer" — this word occurs in John 16:33 at the end of Jesus' Last Discourse, before his prayer and shortly after his image of the woman sorrowing in childbirth but whose sorrow turns into joy.)

Elsewhere in the OT a woman crying out in birth travail is a standard image for soldiers facing defeat in battle. Obstetricians observe that at the extreme point of a hard labor it is not uncommon for the mother to experience a sudden dramatic drop in energy and morale, and that the midwife's encouragement then is strategic. (According to Grantley Dick-Read, *Childbirth Without Fear* [New York: Harper, 1944], in England the midwife may announce that it is time for a cup of tea!) Rachel's only cry comes in the naming of the child. But is that cry one of joy, or of sorrow, or both? The pivotal word *oni* can be derived from a root *on*, "weary toil, trouble, sorrow, wickedness," or another root *on*, "vigor, wealth, strength" (as in Gen. 49:3). Does she name the boy after the fact that she is dying, or after her ability to conceive and bear, given in response to her prayer in naming Joseph (30:24, "may Yahweh add to me another son")? Perhaps she means both.

What does Jacob hear in her naming? He may (correctly or incorrectly) hear a cry of sorrow and quickly change it to a more positive note. Or he may (correctly or incorrectly) hear a cry of triumph and name the child to identify Rachel as truly his own "right hand" (Benjamin) — as though her vigor in prevailing with God and with humankind (Leah?) has been his own chief strength. At Rachel's dying, are they separated through misunderstanding or united one last time through understanding? The text does not say, leaving us to ponder the matter. In any case, it is striking that this singular occasion of double-naming follows the reiteration of God's renaming of Jacob in 35:10. If Rachel in death does not join the other ancestors at Machpelah, her memorial may be not only the pillar marking her grave but also the name of her second child.

35:22-29   Firstborn Reuben now attempts to force the transition to the next generation, by an act that is a clear bid to seize leadership of the family. Coming right after the birth of Benjamin, his act may mean he fears that Jacob intends this youngest son to be his chief heir. As in 34:5, Reuben's action provokes no comment from Jacob. The narrator simply proceeds to a summary listing of the twelve sons of Jacob, grouped by mothers. The concluding notice (vv. 27-29) brings Jacob back to Isaac, whom he had tricked into blessing him. When Isaac dies, the sons who come to bury him are listed in the order of their birth (contrast 25:9).

36:1-43   Chapter 36 opens with the formula, *elleh toledot,* "these are the generations of. . . ." As Frank M. Cross observes, this formula occurs five times before Terah and five times in chs. 12–50 (*Canaanite Myth and Hebrew Epic,* 302). It also occurs five times introducing genealogies (*) and five times introducing narrative sections (†):

2:4a	These are the generations of the heavens and the earth	(†)
5:1	This is the book of the generations of Adam	(*)
6:9	These are the generations of Noah	(†)
10:1	These are the generations of the sons of Noah	(*)
11:10	These are the generations of the sons of Shem	(*)
	. . . .	
11:27	These are the generations of Terah	(†)
25:12	These are the generations of Ishmael	(*)
25:19	These are the generations of Isaac	(†)
36:1	These are the generations of Esau (see also 36:9)	(*)
37:2	These are the generations of Jacob	(†)

It occurs also at Sinai, in Num. 3:1: "These are the generations of Aaron and Moses (*)."

Several things may be said about this device for structuring Genesis. (1) The formula comes from the Priestly editor of the whole tradition. (2) The formula structures the Genesis narrative into two major sections: universal history as a story of sin, judgment, and renewed sin (Gen. 1:1–11:26); and the history of Terah's descendants as a story of the redemption of humankind working through election of a particular people (11:26–50:26). (3) The formula spans the narrative from its grounding in creation and the universal human commission to its climax at Sinai where Israel is elected out of all God's earth to be a priestly kingdom and a holy nation (Exod. 19:3-6). (4) Prior to Terah, the first four occurrences of the formula are universal in compass while the fifth singles out one human line among others. Yet even while it does this, the other human lines are also carefully noted. We see here already the double emphasis on universal inclusion and particular election present also in Gen. 17:19-21. (5) Within the story of redemptive election through Terah's descendants, the formula occurs in conformity to the double emphasis in ch. 10 and in 17:19-21 (see above). Through two generations of Abraham's descendants, Ishmael/Isaac and Esau/Jacob, the formula spans both elected younger brother and nonelected older brother. Given that after Esau and Jacob any further elective distinctions occur only within Israel (see below on 38:27-30), the last four occurrences of the formula in Genesis imply that the communities of Ishmael and Esau, though not elected to Israel's specific vocation, remain firmly held within the providential horizon of the Creator of heaven and earth (2:4a; 14:19, 22; 24:3).

(6) One may reconsider the usual matter-of-fact distinction between the two uses of the formula, as introducing genealogies and narratives. Though translations introduce this interpretive distinction into the text, the reader of the Hebrew text encounters the same word *toledot* each time, a noun from the verb *yalad*, "to bear, bring forth." Two points may be made about this. First, the distinction between "genealogy" and "narrative" is a surface distinction only, a distinction between a list or sequence of names and a sequence of events involving named persons. In a so-called genealogy, each name stands for a life narrative, involving birth, a life process filled with events, and a death and burial, after which

that name is remembered as a unique heartbeat in the ongoing pulse and rhythm of the story of that people. The reader who has the patience and the imagination to linger over each name in a genealogy, out of respect for its untold story, will gain a wider and deeper appreciation for the richness of the streams of life followed by the diverse "generations of heaven and earth." Chapter 36 is a case in point. What human experience or aspiration is hidden, for example, in the name Reuel, "friend of God" (v. 4)? What of the delightful note in v. 24 which we come upon unexpectedly, the way a desert traveller might come upon an oasis? Do these represent a host of experiences of which time would fail the narrator to tell (Heb. 11:32)? When we note how Gen. 36:6-8 echo 13:5-17, and how Esau's action echoes Abraham's, are we not led to unfathomable wonderings about the relation between the universal providence and the providential elections of the biblical God?

The second point is that the term *toledot* may invite us to a particular view of the story of heaven and earth — quite unlike the Babylonian creation story with its creation founded in cosmic battle. The biblical Creator has endowed the earth with the capacity to "bring forth vegetation." Each kind of vegetation is to have its own reproductive seed built into it (1:11-12). This is to be true also for animal life (1:22), and for human life as well (1:28). When the *toledot* formula introduces both genealogies and narratives, this suggests a "generative" view of universal history — that events grow out of previous events as their seed, and that communities may live out of a rich sense of their past as empowering them toward a promising future. When they come to a point where their past seems barren and their future hopeless, and they resort to military might to force their way into the future (as a sort of rape), their judgment is fittingly imaged in terms of the death of vegetation (Isa. 40:6-8, 23-24; 41:2, 15-16; 43:17). Is the elective story then a testimony to how the good God of a good creation works within history in its ambiguity of good and evil, to bring that history through to final unambiguous fruition for the whole creation (Isa. 42:3-4; 53:2)? Such a vision of the historical process will in time produce the apocalyptic vision with which the Christian Bible ends — in a garden with a bride and groom beside the fountain of the water of life, offered to all who are thirsty (Rev. 21:1-6; 22:17; cf. Isa. 55:1-13; John 4:7-15).

(7) The final comment on the formula follows from the puzzling fact that there is no heading, "These are the generations of Abraham." Given the stylistic care and the theological nuance with which the Priestly editor has distributed this formula in Genesis, the omission cannot be accidental. It may be that this formula is not used with Abraham because he is the father not only of a particular people but also of a wider multitude. The same Priestly source that structures Genesis in part through the *toledot* formulas states unequivocally in Gen. 17:4-5:

> You shall be the father of a multitude of nations
> > (*ab-hamon goyim*).
> No longer shall your name be Abram (*ab-ram*),
> but your name shall be Abraham (*ab-raham*);
> for I have made you the father of a multitude of nations
> > (*ab-hamon goyim*).

What is the scope of this multitude? The book of Revelation affirms that it is "a great *multitude* that no one could count" (Rev. 7:9, NRSV), made up of those who follow the Lamb who "will guide them to springs of living water" (v. 17). This apocalyptic vision conforms to Paul's statement in Gal. 3:27-29. In the terms of Genesis, the final multitude will be made up of all who bless themselves by Abraham (Gen. 12:3). Given that the *toledot* formula is first used in 2:4a to introduce Adam and Eve in the garden, and given that Abraham is presented as the beginning of a new humanity, the Priestly editor of Genesis may avoid supplying Abraham with a specific genealogy in hope that the "multitude of nations" will finally encompass all the generations of humankind.

This at any rate seems to be the way the American poet Robert Frost has read the Genesis story. His poem, "The Generations of Men," views a reunion of tenth-generation descendants at the site of the original home of their ancestors within the frame of the story of Abraham and Sarah. Standing before the hole in the ground that was the basement and now is the only trace of the ancestral home, one descendant says to another, "This is the pit from which we Starks were digged" — echoing Isa. 51:1-3. In Isaiah the "pit" was barren but became fertile like Eden. In Frost's poem the meeting of the man and the woman beside the basement hole gives it the significance of the wells beside which the servant met Rebekah and Jacob met Rachel. By framing the specific ancestry of this Stark family within the biblical story of Abraham and Sarah, and yet calling the poem "The Generations of Men," Frost appears to see in Abraham's story a potentially universal significance. Indeed, his whole poem is an invitation to his readers to listen to the biblical story for its resourcefulness in equipping subsequent generations for their own futures. But, as the poem goes on to show, they must know how not simply to impose their own meanings on the biblical story, but to listen carefully for what it has to say.

37:1-36

With the *toledot* formula, the Priestly narrator announces the beginning of the story of the next generation. The question is, Who will succeed to the leadership? Reuben, Simeon, and Levi have all come under their father's disfavor. A generation earlier Isaac had loved Esau, but through connivance another son had gained the inheritance; so there is no assurance that the sons of Jacob's favored wife have an inside track. Then what of Judah? Thus the questions might be supposed to go on inside the sons' heads.

The narrator's spotlight falls on Joseph — much younger than the ten, but still a man. When the brothers busy themselves shepherding, he is with the sons of the two concubines. This is odd. One suspects that Leah's sons resent him as oldest son of the favorite wife, and will have nothing to do with him. The phrase "an ill (or "evil") report of them" (Gen. 37:2) is usually taken to refer to what Joseph tells his father about his brothers. Much has been written about him as a spoiled brat and tattletale whose delusions of grandeur must undergo severe refining and tempering before he becomes a fit instrument of God. This is not the understanding of Joseph that will be developed here. The only evidence that he might be a brat is the phrase "an evil report of them," so it calls for our close attention.

The English phrase here, like the Hebrew phrase it translates, can mean either "his evil report about them" or "their evil speech about him." The noun *dibbah*, from the verb *dabab*, refers to quiet or muffled speech, as in the whispering of gossipers or plotters. In Ps. 31:13; Jer. 20:10 *dibbah* occurs in the same phrase as here. In those two places an innocent person tells God about "the whispering of many," that is, the whispering plots of many against him. In the psalm these enemies are "my neighbors" (31:11). In Jer. 20:10 they are "my familiar friends" (cf. Jer. 11:21; 1:1). This, I take it, exactly parallels the situation in Gen. 37:2. Our first picture of Joseph, then, is of an individual surrounded like Jeremiah or the innocent psalmist by those who wish him evil. This picture is repeated with deepening gravity for several episodes, before Joseph's saving reversal comes. Thus we see that Joseph's words to his brothers in 50:20, "you meant evil against me," touch on their negative attitudes toward him beginning at least as early as 37:2, and possibly even earlier (see further on 41:46, 50-52).

(The two primary moods of address to God in the Psalter are complaint and praise. Taken as a whole, the Psalter traces the movement from the first mood to the second. These two moods, and the movement from the first to the second, are traced also in the book of Exodus, from Exod. 2:23-25 to 15:1-18, 21. In my analysis the Joseph story itself already traces the same movement. Once again, then, individual ancestral experiences foreshadow the experiences of their descendants as individuals and as a people. There is this difference. In Exodus and in Jer. 20:13 God is praised for deliverance from the hand of evildoers. In the Joseph story God is celebrated for delivering the evildoers as well (Gen. 50:15-21). Perhaps it is only such an inclusive deliverance that can finally allow the last Psalm to say, in its final bidding, "let everything that breathes praise Yahweh."

The syntax of Gen. 37:3 indicates that it does not follow temporally from v. 2, but comes as a parenthetical explanation for the brothers' attitude toward Joseph. In that case, it is easiest to take the end of v. 4 as saying the same thing as the end of v. 2:

148

The brothers' talk to him and to each other about him is not peaceable *(leshalom)*, but hostile and ominous. All this is for nothing Joseph has done, but because of the robe that daily reminds them of their father's favor toward "the son of his old age." (Is not Benjamin the son of Jacob's old age? We may have here a sign of traditions imperfectly harmonized in editing. Or Benjamin may be left out of the picture because he is still a wee tot, and the narrator is establishing the character of the relations between the grown sons, of whom Joseph is distinctly the youngest.)

What triggers Joseph's dreams? The robe (*ketonet*) is of a special sort indicated by the puzzling word *passim* ("many colored"? "long sleeved"? "spangled"?). Whatever it is, a *ketonet passim* is also what kings' daughters wear (2 Sam. 13:18). Joseph's robe may give expression to Jacob's half-conscious or unconscious intentions for him. Like his father's intentions, the robe may stir Joseph's imagination to dream along similar lines. (One may compare how Abraham's call in Gen. 12:1-3 takes up earlier intentions of his father Terah. See above on 12:4-9.) In that case, we see once again how God works and speaks in and through the dynamics of human relations and aspirations. The brothers take Joseph's dream report as his upstart claim on the inheritance, through a boast of greater virility and economic power, and a grandiose claim to "cosmic" stature. What will become clear only later (for Joseph is not yet an interpreter of dreams) is that the first dream speaks of his role in economic plenty while the second speaks of him as a master of times and seasons (cf. Gen. 1:14-19) — times of plenty and times of want. (Ironically, it is this first son of a mother who came into her fertile vigor only after a long barren season who is called in these dreams to provide sustenance for the sons of vigorous Leah in a time of earth's barrenness.)

Jacob, who struggled with his brother over the inheritance, now perceives even his favorite son as entering into the current struggle. For all his love of him Jacob rebukes Joseph. Does Jacob regret the robe he gave him? Does he feel guilty for having elicited such grandiosity through his favor? Yet, recollecting what was said to him at Jabbok about having struggled with God and humans and prevailing, does Jacob hesitate simply to discount

Joseph? He keeps his thoughts to himself, and he keeps the dream sayings in mind. Following his silences in 34:5; 35:22, this is the third indication that a new Jacob is emerging.

In spite of the brothers' animosity, Jacob now asks Joseph to inquire after their welfare (*shalom*, 37:14) — they who cannot speak well (*leshalom*) of him. The irony is that Joseph's inquiry into their well-being takes him to the brink of death, which turns into a place where he can preserve them alive (50:20). He sets out, and a man finds him "wandering" in the fields. The verb *ta'ah*, as in 20:13; 21:14, portrays Joseph as lost or uncertain of his way. Why does this scene intervene between 37:14 and v. 18? Coming on the brink of Joseph's exile from hostile brothers, it may echo Jacob's encounter with God at Bethel in his flight from Esau. In that case, the man who directs him is an "angel unawares," an anonymous token of God's hidden presence with Joseph on a journey deeper and deeper into danger.

The stream of negative consciousness against Joseph has run stronger and stronger, through vv. 2, 4, 5 and 8 (where "yet more" [*yosiphu*] plays on his name), 11, to vv. 18-20. Why does Reuben intervene? Perhaps he hopes by protecting the boy to reinstate himself in his father's eyes (cf. 42:22). Yet Reuben has no objection to a little judicious humiliation.

While they eat they see an Ishmaelite caravan pass by with a rich cargo that will fetch a fine price in Egypt. Clearly these cousins are doing well for themselves, as we are given a brief glimpse of Ishmael's descendants spoken of in 17:20; 21:13, 20-21. Envying what must appear to a hard-working shepherd as an easier and more profitable trade, Judah is stirred to think they can "kill two birds with one stone" — get rid of Joseph and make a windfall profit. (His appeal to his brothers' brotherly feeling for Joseph [37:27] may be simply to get them to agree to his profit-making proposal; but it may also be genuine, betraying a trace of family feeling for Joseph. In such tangled human relations, motives are often mixed.) The sudden appearance of Midianite traders, and then, after all, the sale to the Ishmaelites, is usually taken as an example of imperfectly harmonized variants of the Joseph story. That may be. But the text as it stands may imply that Judah looked around for the best price, which in the end he got from his richly laden cousins. (A fine irony: Joseph the outcast is sold into Egypt by way of outcast Ishmael.)

Reuben, finding Joseph gone (*eynennu*, "he was not"), unwittingly anticipates Rachel's cry in Jer. 31:15. But her cry is for her sons, while Reuben's cry is for himself. Rather than reinstate himself with Jacob as firstborn, by protecting Joseph, Reuben will now be even worse off for not doing so. The deception with the robe dipped in blood completely fools the Jacob who himself had fooled his father for the blessing. The blood on the robe seems to spell the end of all that the robe, and Joseph's dreams, had promised. Jacob's grief is so deep that he refuses all efforts to comfort him. The motif recurs in Ps. 77:2; Jer. 15:18 (contrast 6:14; 8:11); 31:15. Whether Jacob and Rachel were united or separated in the double naming of their second son, they are united in this grief. (Was Jeremiah so familiar with the Joseph story that the eventual healing of Jacob's grief over supposedly dead Joseph [cf. 42:38; 44:27-31; 45:25-28; 46:29-30] helped to sponsor his own prophecy of return in Jer. 31:16-17?) In his words, "I shall go down to my son mourning all the way to Sheol" (Gen. 37:35, author's translation), Jacob's grief reaches toward an eschatological horizon that will mark either a final comfort or a confirmation of grief as the final end of any deep love. The happy irony is that he will indeed "go down" to his son, who at that very moment is going down to Egypt to "prepare a place" for everyone.

38:1-30

The abrupt intrusion of the Judah-Tamar episode delays the development of the Joseph story and so heightens its suspense. But the episode has its own connections with what has gone before. The plot in ch. 37 turned implicitly on the question of inheritance from Jacob, and the ironies in the present story revolve on that question. Several related thematic threads spun since ch. 12 are given a new twist, and then left dangling, to be picked up at later points in the saga of Jacob's descendants.

Judah "goes down" from his brothers to Adullam, a place meaning "retreat, refuge," perhaps suggesting his desire to get away for a time from family politics. Two details are noteworthy about this mention of Adullam. First, it is otherwise associated only with David, who also will twice "go down" to it, in flight from Saul (1 Sam. 22:1) and for other reasons later (2 Sam. 23:13). Second, this chapter which opens with reference to Adullam ends with the birth notice of an ancestor of David. These two details, each in its own way making connections with the David story, suggest that this chapter connects immediate issues of clan leadership to such royal promises as Gen. 17:6, 16 (see below on 49:10).

But that is to get ahead of the story. Judah's marriage to the daughter of a Canaanite evokes memories of Esau's two Canaanite wives (26:34-35; 28:8-9), raising the possibility that Judah has disqualified himself. Three sons are born in short order to this fruitful marriage: Er (from *'ur,* "rouse oneself, awake"), Onan (from *on,* "vigor, prosperity"), and Shelah ("quietness, ease, prosperity"). Why the notice that the last was born at Chezib? This place name, from the verb *kazab,* "to lie, deceive," probably identifies a wadi that runs only when it rains and dries up in time of drought. (The "deceitful brook" in Jer. 15:18 is *akzab,* and the "waters that fail" are literally "waters that are not faithful.") So too, it is in connection with Shelah that Judah will lie to Tamar (Gen. 38:11).

The narrative moves quickly to the matter of provision for a next generation, as Judah gets firstborn Er a wife, Tamar ("date-palm"). (Coincidentally, the next Tamar we read about is a daughter of David [2 Sam. 13:1, 2] — she who wore a robe similar to Joseph's!) But Er dies at God's hand without issue, and Judah counsels Onan to raise up offspring to Er by Tamar. (Once again we note that an element in the covenant law stemming from Sinai [Deut. 25:5-10] codifies an ancestral practice.) This practice presupposes primogeniture as a cornerstone of patriarchy. By a delicious irony, the concern for primogeniture here sets the stage for another instance in which that cornerstone will be ignored and the future of the house of Judah built on a different foundation. (Cf. Ps. 118:22, celebrating a king in the line of David who himself was chosen over his older brothers [1 Sam. 16].)

Onan is motivated by the fact that any children he has by

Tamar will destroy his own chance to inherit from his father. But he too dies at God's hand. If Shelah dies likewise, Judah will be without heirs, and any inheritance he may gain from Jacob will lose all lasting significance. So he misleads Tamar into waiting until Shelah is grown up (Gen. 38:11). (In Ruth 1:12b-13a Naomi inadvertently echoes Judah's words to Tamar, but without deceit.) The connotations of the place name Chezib now begin to emerge: Two husbands have failed Tamar, one like a dry wadi and one through deceit; and Judah's deceit means the third son will fail her too.

The next deceit belongs to Tamar. At sheep-shearing time she disguises herself and sits by the entrance to Enaim (literally, "twin wells"). Such a meeting with a man at a well in connection with sheep-herding arouses the reader's anticipation over issues of marriage, procreation, and inheritance. Meanwhile Judah, having finished grieving for his wife, takes her for a harlot (*zonah*) and contracts for her favor. Tamar leads him skillfully into her trap to gain custody of his insignia of identity and authority (and inheritance?). The transaction consummated, they go their way. Returning to reclaim his pledge, and not finding her, Judah couches his inquiries in terms that show how he wants his hearers to think of his previous action. Now he does not call her a harlot, but a *qedeshah*, a "holy one" (Gen. 38:21). (RSV ignores the shift; RSV mg "cult prostitute" is anachronistic. It is only after Sinai [cf. Hosea] that the ancient Near Eastern fertility customs involving a *qedeshah* come — however rightly — to be considered a prostitution of right sexual relations.) Judah, who has sought this woman's favor simply out of his sexual appetite, wants others now to think he has been with her for sacral purposes having to do with procreation. The nice irony is that Tamar — acting not as a *zonah* but more in the spirit of a *qedeshah* — in fact conceives.

But while he disguises his purely appetitive act by the term *qedeshah* (which occurs three times), Tamar's visible pregnancy is taken as a sign of harlotry (*zonah*, likewise occurring three times in all). Which version of her act will prevail? Is she a harlot or a holy one? Judah's judgment is swift and merciless. As swiftly, Tamar produces her trump card (today they might be his credit cards). Though she relinquishes control of the insignia, Tamar's

153

repeated statements to Judah by way of her messengers ensure that everyone will know of the affair. Thus the chain of deceit ends in truth. Three times she is taken for a harlot; three times she is taken as a "holy one"; finally, Judah utters a judgment that shocks conventional ethical and religious sensibilities — "she is more righteous than I."

This story reminds us that "righteousness" (*tsedaqah*) in the Bible has to do primarily with acts of faithful loyalty that give life to the community. However much the ethics of the post-Sinai community may rightly be embodied in covenantal laws, royal decrees, wise sayings, and priestly *torah*, such later embodiments of Israel's ethics have their rootage in the ethics of family and clan loyalty — what elsewhere in Genesis, and generally, is called *hesed*.

The final scene confirms the significance of the place name Enaim. She who met her man at twin wells in connection with shepherding now is doubly fruitful and bears twins. The event recalls the birth of Jacob and Esau, but with a twist. Whereas Jacob followed Esau, grasping his heel, here the firstborn crosses the finish line with only a hand, but then falls back and is surpassed by the younger brother. The scarlet thread is meant to leave no doubt as to who is legally firstborn. But the narrative thread from ch. 12 onward puts the legal status of the firstborn in doubt, and that doubt is later confirmed by the connection between the secondborn and David disclosed at the end of the book of Ruth.

In ch. 16 the action began with Sarah but passed to Hagar as the central figure. Here the action begins with Judah but passes to Tamar, whose integral place among the ancestors is shown in several ways. First, the themes of procreation, marriage, well, and sheep mark her as the third woman in a succession of scenes starting with Rebekah and Rachel and later moving on to Zipporah in Exod. 2:15-22. Second, her move from childlessness to children marks Tamar as fourth in a succession of women that reaches back to Sarah. Third, she echoes aspects of the deceit practiced in different ways by Rebekah, Jacob, Laban, and Rachel. But by the way her subversion of Judah's deceit is called righteous, Tamar's action is not simply likened to theirs, but plays a more intriguing role in the divine providence.

154

Fourth, Tamar will join Rachel and Leah as a trio of names used to bless Boaz's bride (Ruth 4:12). Fifth, the formula "these are the generations of" will occur for the last time in the OT in Ruth 4:18, introducing the genealogy that will end (so far as the OT is concerned) in David. If the Priestly editor has distributed this formula so as to sustain a double emphasis on both universal scope and particular election (see above on ch. 36), the formula in Ruth will bring that emphasis to bear on the Davidic throne, where themes of the election of David and Zion, and of universal providence, take on new currency. (Note esp. Ps. 72, whose concluding words [v. 17] echo Gen. 12:3: "May his name endure forever,/his fame continue as long as the sun!/May men bless themselves by him,/all nations call him blessed.")

Tamar is the first of the four women — all foreigners by birth — to figure in Matt. 1:3. We may note too that Matt. 1:1 employs the old Priestly formula. Apparently modelled on Gen. 5:1, it may imply — as Luke's genealogy does in another way — that Jesus is not only son of David and son of Abraham, but also son of humankind. Is it partly for this reason that Jesus' lineage in Matthew includes ancestors from both inside and outside elect Israel?

The notice in Matt. 1:3 may not exhaust Tamar's presence in the NT. When the Sadducees pose Jesus a question, in the form of a story designed to expose the problematics of resurrection, they begin from the provision for levirate marriage (Mark 12:18-23). The appeal is to Moses in Deut. 25:5-10; but their words, "and raise up seed unto his brother" (KJV), in fact more closely echo Judah's words in Gen. 38:8. This is highly ironic. The Sadducees are strict students of the *torah* and reject the Pharisees' belief in resurrection on the grounds that the *torah* does not teach it. Yet their inadvertent use of Judah's words rather than those of Moses points away from Sinai and to the ancestors, and specifically to Tamar. By this unintended allusion they undercut the force of their own story of barrenness. Unlike the woman with seven husbands, but like Sarah, Rachel, and Rebekah, Tamar has eventually given birth. When Jesus retorts that they know neither the Scriptures nor the power of God, and then refers to God as the God of the ancestors, he apparently sees in God's gift of children to the barren ancestors — so "raising up" children to them, as Gen. 38:8 puts it — a foreshadowing of God's power to raise up the dead to new life. In her own way, then, Tamar is drawn into the NT testimony concerning the Resurrection.

This may be the case also in John 4. The meeting of the woman at the well is to be read in narrative sequence with Gen. 24; 29; Exod. 2:15-22; and — in respect to one detail — especially with Gen. 38. Tamar has "gone to the well" twice with husbands Er and Onan, each time coming away thirsty (Prov. 30:15-16). The Samaritan woman has "gone to the well" five times with a husband and come away thirsty. But — as this episode's conformity to the familiar type-scene should tell us — her insatiable thirst is not a sexual appetite as such. Her fivefold marriage is best understood as reflecting her *torah*-observant persistence (Deut. 25:5-10) in seeking to raise up a child to her first husband. The relevance of Deuteronomy in John 4 is implied in the woman's allusion to a "coming" prophet-messiah (Deut. 18:15) and in Jesus' reference to the debate about the right place to worship God (Deut. 12:5 and often). Has she followed the example of Tamar, in resorting to a man not her husband? In any case, the parallel between the two women is striking. But her current man is only number six in her life. Everything in the imagery of John 4 points to Jesus — the seventh man — as the one who will satisfy her thirst. Tamar's meeting with Judah at Enaim has made her an ancestor of the Messiah. At Jacob's well (at noon — as in Gen. 29:7!) the Samaritan woman meets the Messiah. The "children" born of this meeting are those who believe and so become "children of God" (John 4:39-42; cf. 1:11-13; and note the themes in 3:1-15, 27-30). Thus, out of her belly now flow rivers of living water (John 7:38, KJV, following the Greek *koilia*, "belly, womb," as in John 3:4). Since, in John, belief issues in eternal life, the echo of Tamar in John 4 joins the echo of Tamar in Mark 12, in bearing witness to God's faithful persistence (or "righteousness") which finally is sealed by the gift of life that only one who is greater than Jacob can give (John 4:12-14; contrast Gen. 30:2).

39:1-23

Joseph's descent to Egypt evokes three other sojourns away from the land of promise: Abram's (Gen. 12), the servant's (ch. 24), and Jacob's (chs. 28–33). But the theme this time is more ominously shaded. The verb *yarad*, "go down" (39:1), refers of course to travel from Canaan to Egypt. But it can also refer to death as a going down to "the Pit" or Sheol (e.g., Isa. 5:14; Ps. 22:29). The incident at the pit and Jacob's lament in Gen. 37:35 give Joseph's descent this added connotation. Like Jonah (Jonah 1:3 [twice], 5; 2:6a, Hebrew), Joseph descends ever lower into the depths. Yet at each stage God is with him (Gen. 37:15-17; 39:2, 21), to prosper his way as the way of Abraham's servant had prospered (*hitsliah*, 24:21, 40, 42, 56; 39:2 [RSV "became a successful man"], 3, 23). As a servant, whatever Joseph does turns Potiphar a benefit (cf. 30:27). Faithful over a little, Joseph is now entrusted with much (Luke 16:10; 19:17; Matt. 25:23; cf. 1 Cor. 4:1-2). Genesis 39:4b (literally, "and all he had he put in his hand") echoes 24:10 (see above).

Potiphar so trusts Joseph with his household that "he did not know apart from him anything except the bread he ate" (39:6, Hebrew). All decisions were in Joseph's hands, except for Pharaoh's food. The narrator notes Joseph's attractive appearance — as does Potiphar's wife. The question for Joseph is whether she is included in what Potiphar has left in his charge. Joseph's response to the wife echoes the narrator's words in vv. 4 and 6, with a potentially tempting addition (marked off with †): "Lo, my lord does not know what is in his house apart from me, and all he has he has put in my hand; †he is not greater in this house than I am†; and he has not kept back anything except you, because you are his wife" (vv. 8-9, author's translation). This word-for-word echo juxtaposes "bread" and "wife" in a way that, as we shall see, engages issues at the very heart of stewardship. The addition might signal a temptation to avail himself of the master's privileges. But for Joseph, stewardship is a responsibility that ultimately is received from God, even where one is a bought slave and the master is an Egyptian. He would not consider a move on Potiphar's wife justified by the injustice of his situation.

The wife sets her trap. When Joseph flees it, she keeps his garment. (His clothes keep getting him in trouble!) She complains to her servants of the man Pharaoh has brought in "to insult us." On Potiphar's return, she shows him the garment and repeats her story, for her husband's benefit shifting the focus to "insult *me*." Joseph lands in the king's prison, where, however, God is with him in steadfast love (*hesed*, as in 24:12, 27, 49; the word attributes to God the fundamental character that within a clan moves one member to act loyally in behalf of another member, as called for by the situation). Again, his behavior (undergirded by God's *hesed*) wins Joseph a position of trust in the prison. Like Potiphar, the prison keeper "did not (need to) oversee anything that was in his hand, because Yahweh was with him" (39:23, Hebrew). Once faithful over much, Joseph knows how to be faithful over what in conventional eyes would seem to be very little indeed!

There is an old saying that Scripture is its own interpreter. Recently, scholars have shown in some detail how later Scriptures have arisen as interpretations or commentaries on earlier traditions. If Scripture at such points teaches us how to interpret Scripture, we should pause long enough to let Ps. 105:16-22 teach us how to read the Joseph story.

Whereas in Gen. 12:10; 26:1 the narrator simply announces famine, without theological commentary, in Gen. 41:25-32 the famine is revealed as something God "is about to do." So too, in Ps. 105:16 God "summoned a famine on the land." Then the psalmist adds a line that characterizes God's action more specifically: "and broke every staff of bread." Since breaking a staff is an idiom for defeat of an enemy, the psalmist apparently intends in the word "summoned" the overtones of the divine warrior's rally of the forces of nature as God's army against the enemy (cf. the Exodus plagues against Egypt; also Exod. 15:8, 10, 12; Judg. 5:20; Hab. 3, esp. v. 5; also Wisd. 5:17-23). The famine summoned against Canaan, then, follows directly upon Gen. 39:12-15, where God "rebuked kings" on behalf of the ancestors (Ps. 105:14). We have seen in Gen. 12–34 that the ancestors' host countries have not always been hospitable to them, and that God has had to intervene on their behalf. Psalm 105:16 understands the famine in Canaan, then, not simply as a natural calamity, but as part of God's providential intervention to protect the ancestors from the powers of Canaan.

But it is not only the powers of Canaan who are hostile, for Joseph's brothers have become hostile to him (as already in Gen. 37:2). They sell Joseph into Egypt, and their guilty consciences later will testify that this was their act (42:21). But Ps. 105:17 (like Gen. 50:20) sees in their selling God's sending — a divine providence that makes room for human freedom and draws the evil results of that freedom into the horizon of God's transforming and saving actions.

Joseph's feet are hurt with fetters (Ps. 105:18). The verb *'innah* here refers not only to the physical pain of the material fetters, but also to his inner pain through these constraints on his mobility, freedom, and power of action. In the next line *nephesh* (RSV "neck") can mean "throat, appetite, desire, emotion, breath, life-force, self." Thus the *nephesh* as the life-force or soul is positively a "lust for life," an appetite for experience that feeds on and grows by (or is embittered and poisoned by) experience. (The Sumerian pictogram adopted to represent the cognate Akkadian word *napishtu* is a human head with markings on the throat.) In recent years the line has been read as Joseph's neck entering into irons. But for this we should expect *tsawwa'r*, "neck" (cf. Gen. 27:40; Deut. 28:48 [a yoke of iron!]; Isa. 10:27; 52:2; and often in Jer. 27–28 [a yoke of iron in 28:13]; 30:8). Psalm 105:18b no doubt presupposes an iron neck-collar; but *nephesh* as "soul" continues the note of affliction sounded in the previous verb *'innah*. Just as the foot irons afflict him inwardly, the neck iron "enters into" his *nephesh*. In one of his so-called Terrible Sonnets, Gerard Manley Hopkins cries out, "I am gall, I am heartburn: God's most deep decree/Bitter would have me taste: my taste was me." In his bondage Joseph tastes the full bitterness and irony of his plight. He has dreamed high dreams; and his fettered slavery is iron in his soul.

The psalmist continues in Ps. 105:19: "Until the time that his saying came to pass,/the word of Yahweh tested (*tsaraph*) him." The verb *tsaraph* literally means "smelt, refine." Playing on the reference to iron in v. 18, it expounds the humanly imposed afflictions in that verse as God's mysterious transforming work in the depths of Joseph's soul. Once again, what is meant against him for evil, God takes up and means for good (Gen. 50:20). In Gen. 37:9 Joseph had dreamed of the sun, moon, and stars — those rulers of times and seasons, days and years (Gen. 1:14-19). This dream had foreshadowed his capacity to give the sort of economic and social leadership that calls for knowing when things are to be done. By its reference to "time" (Hebrew, KJV), Ps. 105:19 shows that Joseph became a master of time by first experiencing God's mysterious times for his own life.

At the right time, the king sent and released Joseph (Ps. 105:20a), reversing the action of those who had sold him into slavery (v. 17b). If v. 20a balances v. 17b, v. 20b may also balance v. 17a (the two verses displaying the pattern ABB′A′). In that case, just as God worked through the brothers who sold Joseph into slavery (v. 17), so the divine and true "ruler of the peoples" works through the human king to set Joseph free (v. 20). In liberation as in affliction, Joseph is learning about times from the lord of times. When he himself becomes a lord and ruler (v. 21), he is equipped to instruct (or bind) princes and to teach wisdom to Pharaoh's elders (v. 22). (In Exod. 1:8-10 a pharaoh who "does not know" Joseph or his wisdom says to his court, "let us deal wisely" with the Hebrews [Hebrew, KJV].)

Joseph *instructs* the Egyptian princes at his pleasure (Ps. 105:22a, RSV). The verb is *asar*, "tie, bind, imprison," and RSV "pleasure" translates *nephesh*. Thus v. 22 picks up themes in v. 18, where God worked to refine Joseph, and applies them to the way Joseph teaches the elders of Egypt out of his own painful experience. His *nephesh*, his "lust for life," has learned to delay and channel its appetites in service to the divine lord of time and ruler of the peoples. These lessons he now teaches the Egyptian elders, a teaching that will "bind" their own "lust for life" so that they do not use their positions of power simply for their own ends and appetites.

Thus, Ps. 105:16-22 sees in the Joseph story (and passes on to us) a succinct instruction in the wisdom by which the divine "ruler of the peoples" would guide the human rulers of this world. The key to this wisdom is honest stewardship: how to place one's own appetites under God's authority and discipline, when one has been put in charge of someone else's affairs. The relevance for political economy is pointed up in two later stories where rulers do not observe this discipline and wisdom. David's affair with Bathsheba has its obvious personal dimension; but as a symptom of the abuse of royal power, the affair bears directly on matters of state. It is not coincidental that Nathan characterizes the root dynamic as a "wayfarer's" appetite and its satisfaction (2 Sam. 12:4) — an image of the sudden coming and fulfillment of sexual desire. The other story also turns on appetite. The corruption of the northern (Israelite) monarchy is typified in Ahab's desire to eat from a garden bought from Naboth — or sulkingly not eat at all (1 Kgs. 21:1-5). The political and economic relevance of fasting is that it disciplines God-given appetites. The fast called by Jezebel cynically debases the purpose of a fast, in that her fast serves an appetite (hers and Ahab's) that it should serve to bridle. In both of these instances, the problem is a king who does not truly recognize that his appetites are under the discipline of a higher authority. It is no accident, then, that the beginning of the story of Joseph in Egypt focuses on the appetites of the king of Egypt (Gen. 39:6) and of Potiphar's wife (vv. 7, 12), and on Joseph's refusal to indulge his own appetite.

The picture of Joseph's industrious stewardship under the alien power of Egypt may be compared to Jesus' teaching on steward-ship in Matt. 25:23 = Luke 19:17. Jesus contrasts a third steward, who holds the talent in inactive trust for a master viewed as severe, with the first two stewards who perform their trust to their master's profit, whatever their view of him. Apparently stewards are not justified in betraying their stewardship just because their master is harsh. Jesus' teaching becomes even more pointed in Luke 16:11: "If then you have not been faithful in the unrighteous mammon, who will entrust to you the true riches?" "If you have not been faithful in that which is another's, who will give you that which is your own?" (v. 12). I would have supposed that one becomes an honest steward of another's goods out of one's own sense of what it is to be an owner. Jesus' words imply that we become trustworthy with what is "our own" by proving to be trustworthy with "what is not our own."

In that case, Joseph is the parade example. His early dreams gave the clue to what was "his own." Like Jacob, his true self lay deep within him where he imaged God. That true self manifested itself in dreams of a vocation to economic leadership based on a commanding sense of times and seasons. But he entered into what was "his own" through a schooling in what was not his own. (There is a lesson here for current advocates of a spirituality of self-realization.) What enabled Joseph to endure this schooling, without resorting to the devious strategies his father Jacob had adopted as a "supplanter"? Was it because, deeper than any bitter taste his experience could place on his tongue, deep in his *nephesh* — his appetite for life — he had tasted and seen that Yahweh was good (Ps. 34:8) and could be trusted? If Jacob was a divided soul from the womb (cf. Ps. 51, esp. v. 5) and later became (in William James's phrase) a "twice-born" person, Joseph may have been "once-born," one of those rare persons in whom the divine image remains to a remarkable degree unobscured. The clue to such a person may lie in Ps. 22, especially vv. 9-10:

a   Thou art he who took me from the belly (*beten*);
b   thou didst entrust me upon my mother's breasts (*shadayim*).
b'   Upon thee was I cast from the womb (*rehem*),
a'   from my mother's belly (*beten*) thou hast been my God. (author's translation)

Like this psalmist, Joseph from the very beginning may have experienced his mother's womb (*rehem*) as God's compassion (*rahamim*), and his mother's reliable breasts (*shadayim*) as the reliability of *Shadday* (RSV "Almighty"; cf. Gen. 49:22-26). From Rachel, then, or from Rebekah's wet nurse, or from both, Joseph had received what some psychoanalysts now call "good enough mothering," of the sort that enabled him to "taste and see that Yahweh is good"; and this would have helped to forestall his inheritance of the negative clan psychodynamics manifest in Laban, Rebekah, and his father Jacob. (What, then, of those children who do not receive "good enough mothering" — or fathering? Their plight is serious indeed. Such is the fatefulness of the freedom God gives humankind. Yet Isa. 49:14-16 affirms that experience of God's compassion and nurture is not confined to positive mothering experiences.)

40:1-23

Potiphar's titles, "officer" (*saris*) and "captain of the guard" (*"sar tabbahim*), are literally "eunuch" and "chief slaughterer, cook, guard" (Gen. 37:35; 39:1). The terms refer to the fact that the royal guard had certain skills (if not duties) in common with the royal slaughterers, while royal officials generally were often rendered immune from temptation to abuse their stewardship in serving their own appetites, or in seeking to usurp the throne and establish their own dynasty. Though Potiphar, as married, would not literally be a eunuch, and though we cannot tell about the butler and baker (each called a *saris*), to bear the title among other officials who were eunuchs would be a salutary reminder to bridle one's appetites. The point here is that the butler and baker as well as the dream imagery continue the thematics of food and appetite from ch. 39. One may assume that their sin was to displease the king's appetite (cf. 39:6b).

We learn belatedly (40:20) that the two dreamed three days before the king's birthday. Given their awareness of the date, and the general climate of anticipation before the birthday of one considered a child of the gods, the themes of the dreams — the food and the three-day time lapse — are not surprising. Pharaoh apparently already had in mind to display his royal/divine will in a certain dramatic way; and unwittingly (as when one is listening at night to a local radio broadcast whose wavelength is suddenly invaded by a shortwave signal from half a continent away) the butler and baker in their sleep tune in on the king's thoughts. (They were, after all, trained to anticipate his whims and changing tastes.) All this we readers may propose after the fact. But, as any psychoanalyst knows, it was not so easy for the dreamers at the time to interpret their own dream symbolism.

Joseph's response is salutary. He neither claims power to interpret nor shrugs off the dreams as an unfathomable divine mystery. He who must wonder what his own dreams might yet mean, and who might be forgiven for giving up on dreams as meaningless shadows, affirms that dreams belong to God and offers to hear these two. Revelation concerning the future then comes through Joseph's divinely given ability to interpret formative factors in the present situation that express themselves in the symbolism of dreams.

The dreams have to do with food and time — the two subjects of Joseph's own two dreams. In short order he gives their meaning. In his new-found gift of dream interpretation, is Joseph beginning to draw near the realization of his own dreams? If so, the irony is that his only concern is to return to the land from which he was stolen (v. 15), a sign that as yet he doesn't understand his dreams. (One could say, "he interpreted the dreams of others; his own dreams he cannot interpret.") He urges the butler (v. 14) to

(a) "remember me, (b) when it is well with you,
    (c) and do *hesed* with me, *na'*,
(a') and remember me to Pharaoh, (b') and get me out
    of this house." (author's translation)

The connection between memory and *hesed* (RSV "kindness" — what one owes one's own "kind" in a given situation) draws attention to the fact that a fundamental aspect of *hesed* is memory of past relations. Ethics, like group ethos, lives into the future out of shared memory. To forget *hesed* is to become disconnected from one's meaningful past and thereby to abandon oneself to an uprooted future.

The day comes for all Egypt to celebrate the king's divine birth and stature. What better way for him to demonstrate this than by an act that manifests his power of life and death, in restoring one servant and executing another? Yet even if the servants' offenses may have deserved some punishment, the king seems to have totally forgotten what the baker once was to him and did for him. By executing him the king shows that he has the power and the right to shape the future in disregard of all past ties and relations. Such royal power does not embody the *hesed* of God (compare Deut. 32:39; Hos. 6:1; 1 Sam. 2:6-10; and Gen. 24:27;

164

Exod. 2:23-25; 3:6, 13-15; 32:7-10, 11-14; 34:6; cf. also Gen. 39:21). Likewise the butler, restored to the service of this pharaoh, forgets the *hesed* he had promised to Joseph (40:23).

41:1-57

Two years later, Pharaoh dreams twice in one night. The cows coming out of the Nile speak of the fact that "Egypt is the gift of the Nile." Its annual flood fertilizes the river plain to produce food for livestock and humans. Pharaoh first resorts to his court experts — his sages and his magicians. At the point where everyone is baffled, the butler "remembers" his faults (41:9). It is as though the similarity of Pharaoh's dream-bafflement to the butler's own in prison jars loose in his memory Joseph's word, "remember me to Pharaoh." Yet what the butler says is, "I remember my faults today." His conscience is the upsurge into his consciousness of a deep memory by which he has remained unconsciously connected with his past. Thus conscience is the sign of reawakening *hesed*.

Hurried in and told of the dreams, and of his reputation as a dream interpreter, Joseph again disclaims any personal powers. Only God can answer (v. 16). This he says to a king who is held to be divine but who cannot divine his own dreams! As soon as Joseph hears the dreams he gives the interpretation (v. 25). The doubling means the thing is fixed by God and will shortly come to pass. When Joseph proposes a state policy, Pharaoh not only sees its wisdom but sees in him the wisdom to implement it. Similarly to his actions with Potiphar and the jailer (39:4-6, 22-23), Pharaoh places Joseph in charge of everything save the throne (41:40). The signet ring, gold chain, and especially the garments of fine linen placed on him signal the end of Joseph's troubles (contrast the tunic in ch. 37 and the robe in ch. 39).

With an Egyptian name and two sons by an Egyptian priest's daughter, Joseph begins a new life. The firstborn signifies that finally he can forget the hardships of youth in his father's house. The second signifies the fact that his years of affliction in Egypt have given way to fruitfulness. It is as though for Joseph to remember would be to keep in mind the pain of a past which no longer means anything to him — as though some things are simply better given up on and forgotten. Yet what of his dreams that spoke of his brothers and parents bowing to him? Joseph seems to consign both his family and his own youthful dream-self to the "land of forgetfulness" (Ps. 88:12), that is, the realm of the dead. What then will happen to his capacity for *hesed*? (The psalmist in Ps. 88:11 identifies the land of forgetfulness as marking the limit of God's *hesed*.) Jacob, too, no doubt has long since ceased to keep the dream-sayings in mind (Gen. 37:11) — but that is because he believes Joseph dead. Yet if Joseph and Jacob forget, the outcome of the story will show that God in *hesed* continues to keep them in remembrance.

A further note on "times." The three days and the seven years of the officers' and Pharaoh's dreams are typical indicators of a shorter or longer duration. Joseph's own life displays the following times: (1) Sold into Egypt at seventeen (37:2) and at thirty entering Pharaoh's service (41:46), his span of "affliction" (v. 52) was fourteen years (twice seven). (In Hebrew reckoning, year seventeen counts as one, eighteen as two, etc., to thirty as fourteen.) (2) If Pharaoh dreamed when Joseph was thirty, two years after the baker's and butler's dreams, the latter dreams occurred when Joseph was twenty-eight (four sevens). (3) Counting backwards from age seventeen when he was sold into Egypt (seventeen as one, sixteen as two, etc.), fourteen years of "hardship" (v. 51) would begin in Joseph's fourth year — a typical age for weaning. If 21:7-8 is a guide (see above), it would be after weaning that Joseph would move out from the circle of his mother's care and protection and begin to interact significantly with his father and his older siblings. There, his father's special favor toward him would become more evident, and the brothers' hostility (rather than the play as in 21:9) would set in.

These figures show that Joseph experienced nothing but trouble for two periods of twice seven years: from the end of his breast-feeding to his going into Egypt, and from then to his rise in Pharaoh's service. Has this experience in any way equipped Joseph to interpret the time symbolism in the dreams of the two officers and Pharaoh? I suggest that through deep immersion in the temporal pulse and shape of his own life Joseph has learned

166

— not consciously, but by an obscure God-taught intuition — how to read the time-marked dreams of others. This immersion, I suggest, is anchored in bodily memories of rhythmic satisfied feeding and care, memories that provide a lens for him to interpret the food imagery in the two pairs of dreams, those of the baker and butler, and those of Pharaoh. Such a deeply connected wisdom would be another sign of one who is not a divided self like his father, but profoundly whole. Is wisdom in fact just this — a profound sense of the connectedness and the proper relations of all things in God's good time?

42:1-38

In three earlier transitions to a new generation, the prospective mother had been met at a well: Rebekah, Rachel, and — in her own way — Tamar. The transition to Joseph was signalled by the Priestly formula at Gen. 37:2. But the ironies that abound in the Joseph story are perhaps nowhere so vivid as in the play on the well motif in his instance, a play which is recognized only in retrospect after one sees it leading to a wife. The motif is not so much introduced as hinted at in ch. 37, in the reference to a pit that "was empty, there was no water in it" (37:24). The hint is drawn out in the three narratives just considered: (1) Joseph's descent into a dungeon; (2) Joseph in the dungeon; (3) Joseph's ascent to Pharaoh's side. In ch. 39 he finally meets a woman, but she is not his future wife. Potiphar's wife embodies the enticing woman of Prov. 7:6-27 (even to the latter's Egyptian bed linens and her absent husband; vv. 16, 19)! Though Joseph in his youthful wisdom declines her, he still goes down into a dungeon (cf. Prov. 7:27; 9:18). Only with his ascent to Pharaoh's side does he finally meet his wife, having avoided the strange woman (Prov. 7) through the hidden offices of lady wisdom (Prov. 8–9). (Since the story of Joseph has many of the marks of a wisdom tale, the presence of these latter themes is not surprising.)

The wife of Potiphar and the daughter of the priest of On mark off Gen. 39–41 as the first part of the story of Joseph in Egypt. The shift of scene back to Canaan in ch. 42 introduces the second part, which will end with Jacob and family going down to Egypt. As Judah had held back his youngest, Shelah, from Tamar (ch. 38), so Jacob sends the ten brothers to Egypt but holds back Benjamin. Their bowing before Joseph (42:6) begins to fulfill Joseph's two dreams. As if recalling the pain of his former hardships among them, he greets his own kind like strangers — hardly an example of *hesed!* The key word in Joseph's retort is revealing: "you are spies, you have come to see the nakedness (*'erwa;* RSV "weakness") of the land" (v. 9). In the Bible "nakedness" always refers to sexual organs, whose exposure outside of sanctioned intimacy is a shame. In his youth Joseph had innocently disclosed his dreams that went to the heart of his identity and vocation — and the brothers had poured shame upon him (cf. Jesus at Nazareth and at Caesarea Philippi; Matt. 13:53-58; 16:13-20). Now Joseph feels the renewed sting of that old wound as the brothers' spying on the nakedness of his adopted land. Brushing aside their denial, he repeats the charge, and after their further denial he puts them to a test.

First he swears twice, not by God but by Pharaoh ("by the life of Pharaoh"; Gen. 42:15-16) — as if to underscore that his brothers are at the mercy of a foreign ruler who in his power of life and death may not recognize the claims of their God. Only after three days does Joseph encourage them by saying that he fears God (v. 18) and by proposing that one brother be held hostage while the others return for Benjamin. Perhaps it is this first faint sign of *hesed* that pricks them in their depths, where they still are connected to Joseph in bonds of brotherhood, and where their guilt has all along resided as a hidden memory of Joseph's unheeded cries and pleas for mercy, that day from the pit (v. 21). Only now, as they themselves are in a dungeon at his hands (v. 17), do his cries first come to the brothers' awareness, since back at the pit their hatred had rendered them deaf. Martin Heidegger has said that guilt is the silent call of being to itself. As with the butler in belatedly remembering Joseph (41:9; cf. 40:14), the brothers' guilt is good guilt, in that it calls them back to their true being.

Does Joseph only now learn of Reuben's life-saving act, back at the pit? He weeps and chooses, not firstborn Reuben, but Simeon to stay behind — further signs of Joseph's awakening to family memory and past experience. Then he secretly returns their money in their sacks. Their terrified "What is this that God has done to us?" (42:28) sets up a dramatic irony, in that their newly aroused guilt brings them to a state of religious anxiety that will not be fully resolved until 50:19-20. (The irony is that God is indeed doing strange things to them, but not with the negative intent that their guilt makes them read into the situation.) Returning home, the brothers report all to Jacob, taking care to reverse the order of their words to Joseph (v. 13), so that with Jacob they might pass quickly over Joseph and end on Benjamin (v. 32). But their words only move Jacob to lament (v. 36). Reuben quickly offers his own two sons as hostages — he who had earlier tried to take over from Jacob (35:22). But Jacob refuses, echoing the words he had used on hearing of Joseph's departure (42:38; 37:35). This last blow would kill him.

43:1-34

Jacob gives Simeon up for lost, and hopes for an end to the famine, but instead it grows worse. When he would send the sons for more grain, they point out Joseph's oath (43:3, literally, "he bore solemn witness against us"). Their words in vv. 3-5 echo in substance and in enveloping structure Joseph's words in 42:14-16. The twofold "you shall not see my face" sounds like a threat; but in view of 42:24; 45:1, 12, 28; 46:30 (and cf. 33:10), the threat may mask a hope and a promise. When Jacob (still in part the deceiver) utters the wish that they had not spoken the full truth (43:6), their response (v. 7) may be a fabrication to persuade him. Or it may disclose words of Joseph not reported in ch. 42. Or it may reflect an overtone in his words that they only now become aware of.

Where Reuben had failed, Judah now succeeds, perhaps because the worsening famine now threatens everyone, and perhaps in part because of Judah's willingness to offer himself as surety (43:9b). His "let me bear the blame for ever" indicates the desperate and terrible extremes of self-curse to which people can go when speaking out of deep concern in a critical situation. One cannot help thinking of a similar self-curse in Matt. 27:25, where "the people" say, "His blood be on us and on our children," meaning that they take full responsibility for Jesus' death, in the conviction that he justly deserves to die. God's response to such a self-curse is indicated by Matt. 1:21; 26:28. (The first passage already informs the Christian reader that Jesus "will save his people [the Jews] from their sins," and the second passage, even more specifically, emphasizes that the very blood or death for which his people have taken responsibility is "poured out for many for the forgiveness of sins." The "many" here — as in, e.g., Isa. 53:12, "the sin of many" — does not mean "less than all," but everyone, considered as a great multitude.) When people bless, God will honor the blessing — even Isaac's blessing of Jacob. But a curse involves decisions over life and death that are reserved to God alone (Deut. 32:39). God's redemptive action on behalf of the people of Jacob (and so on behalf of all those who bless themselves in Abraham's name — Gen. 12:3) can work even through the brothers' intentions against Joseph (50:20) and through Reuben's well-intentioned but misguided self-curse. Likewise, this same God in *hesed* seals a covenant in the blood of Jesus which will work redemption for the people of Jacob and on behalf of all those who bless themselves in Jesus as Abraham's seed — working even through the well-intentioned but misguided self-curse of Matt. 27:25.

Jacob gives in (Gen. 43:11). His closing words in v. 14 show that he has no realistic hope; yet his mood seems to be, "who knows?" (cf. Jonah 3:9; Esth. 4:14). As when he offered a gift to appease Esau (Gen. 33), Jacob sends a present, a *"zimrah* of the land" (43:11), delicious sweetmeats, of the sort a doting father might give a favorite son. Then he appeals to El Shaddai ("God Almighty," v. 14) to grant Judah compassion (*rahamim,* from the same root as *rehem,* "womb"). In his later blessing of Joseph, Shaddai is the name under which Jacob will call on God to give the blessings of breasts (*shadayim*) and womb (*rehem*) (49:25; cf. 17:1-6, 15-16; 28:3; 35:11; 48:3-4). Here, fearing that he will be bereaved of children, Jacob appeals for compassion to the God of breast and womb.

The scene in 43:16-17, 24-25 echoes the hospitality seen in 18:1-8, even to the time of day. However, the brothers' guilty consciences lead them to interpret the hospitality negatively. The words "seek occasion against us" (43:18) translate a verb meaning literally "roll around back upon us" and illustrate how guilty fears of retribution blind people to the possibility of grace. (Thus, a guilty conscience is an imperfect lens through which to interpret others' actions, leading one often to attribute negative motives and intentions to them.) To such guilty fears the servant, acting for Joseph, says *shalom* and "Fear not!" (v. 23) and then tends to the brothers' first needs. The servant explains the money in their sacks as an act of God. Of course he and the reader know that it is an act of Joseph (42:25), but the brothers do not know this, and they are left to add this to their sense of God working in strange ways (cf. 42:21, 28). Yet was it not ultimately an act of God (cf. 50:20)? How otherwise shall we explain what it was that moved Joseph to put the money there and not simply to repay them evil for evil, out of the still fresh, resentful pain that moved him to speak roughly to them not long before (42:7)? The source of his compassion is the compassion of Shaddai, whom Jacob invoked in 43:14.

In Joseph's presence, the brothers fulfill his dreams a second time (v. 26). Again, Joseph's own first word is *shalom* (RSV "well"). They bow a third time (cf. Jacob's seven in 33:3). Recognizing Benjamin — or hardly recognizing this young man whom he had last seen as an infant — Joseph is moved from speech about him to address him directly: "God have mercy on you, my son!" (author's translation). (The verb *hanan* is the same verb used by the brothers in 42:21, "when he besought us" — literally, "when he begged us for mercy.") What moves Joseph to address Benjamin as "my son," and what causes his compassion (*rahamim*, not RSV "heart") to grow warm? Is it that, when Rachel died, and with Rebekah's nurse already dead, Joseph had tried to "mother" his infant brother, and now he is stirred at the level of such a deep memory? Is it that, remembering his own treatment at the hands of the other ten brothers for fourteen or so years, Joseph is overwhelmed with feeling for what Benjamin also may have had to go through? Is Joseph's compassion a result of Jacob's prayer that "the man" in Egypt might show compassion (43:14)?

Then Joseph "controls" himself. (The verb *apaq*, like the noun *apiq*, "channel," refers to waters confined in a streambed. It occurs again in Isa. 63:15 of Yahweh restraining the divine compassion [*rahamim*].) Unrestrained, Joseph's compassion would issue in behavior to which he cannot give himself at this point (cf. Isa. 42:14; 54:7-8). So, channelling his feelings into an expression of formal hospitality, he calls for food.

(The narrator's observation in Gen. 43:32 introduces a dramatic irony that endures in a different form to our own day. Later Torah-based food laws will erect a fundamental division between Jews and Gentiles. Later still, the Jewish and gentile followers of Jesus will practice open table fellowship in his name. They will understand him in his death to have "broken down the dividing wall" erected between Jews and Gentiles by the food laws of the Torah [Eph. 2:11-16]. Yet their open table fellowship, by the way it offends the conscience of Torah-observant Jews, will only result in the strengthening of that wall. Paul will address the issue at Rome by reference to Jesus as serving both communities [Rom. 14:1–15:13]. Paul's reference to Christ as "servant" [*diakonon*, Rom. 15:8] may be an allusion to Christ as an attendant at table, like the deacons of Acts 6 appointed to care for "the daily distribution" [*diakonia*] of food between Hebrews and Hellenists. To bring all this back to Genesis, Joseph himself may be said to have become "a servant [in Egypt] for the sake of the circumcised, to show God's truthfulness in confirming the promises given to the ancestors" [Rom. 15:8, author's translation]. Similarly, it may be said that Pharaoh and the Egyptians, in their treatment of Joseph and his family from Gen. 45:16 to the climax in 50:4-11, glorify the God of the Hebrews who has shown mercy to the Hebrews [Rom. 15:9]. If in Gen. 43:32-34 Joseph and his "separated brethren" still eat separately from one another, and in 50:15-21 they are fully reconciled, what may this whole narrative teach us concerning current and future relations between Christians and their elder brothers and sisters the Jews? Insofar as Abraham and his descendants are relative newcomers among the nations of Gen. 10, perhaps we should think of Gentiles as the jealous elder brothers, and of Jews as the elected younger brother Joseph!)

172

The notice about the seating arrangements, of course, heightens another dramatic irony to which the narrator, Joseph, and the reader are privy. The brothers in their ignorance find Joseph's knowledge of them amazing. We know that their host is preparing to surprise them with grace, a grace that even now cannot restrain itself from favoring Benjamin fivefold. In the end, the brothers drink and become "well drunk" (*shakar*, 43:34). This word often refers to drunkenness, in many instances negatively, at times associated with exposure of one's nakedness (as in the case of Noah) or with deadly plots in the guise of hospitality (Hos. 7:3-7). But being "well drunk" is not universally condemned in the Bible. Like sexual relations, it is a blessing within sanctioned contexts (e.g., John 2:10). Such drinking (like the nakedness of Gen. 2:25) is a sign of vulnerable openness between intimates. In such drinking, everyone's guard comes down and everyone becomes elated together (Prov. 31:6-9; Ps. 104:15). So understood, the brothers' drinking is a sign that they feel secure enough with Joseph to entrust themselves to his hospitality. (As a sad afterthought, one may contrast the scene in Gen. 34:24-29, where the Shechemites entrust themelves in their nakedness to Jacob's sons, and then that trust is betrayed.)

44:1–45:28

This second return of the money is surely another hint of Joseph's gracious intentions, following on his fivefold favor to Benjamin at dinner (43:34). Yet Joseph shortly sends the steward after his brothers (cf. Exod. 14:5-8). It is as though he is acting in the grip of compassion one moment and continuing deep hurt in the next, not knowing what his mind is or how to sort out his feelings toward his brothers. The instruction in Gen. 44:5, like the oath by the life of Pharaoh in 42:15, may betray a desire to terrify them with a sense of their vulnerability to Joseph's powers. When the servant overtakes them, the brothers respond (44:7) with a Hebrew idiom of which "far be it" is too weak a translation. It is an oath — "a defilement on your servants" — if they have done such a thing. (Its force may be compared to Thomas More's oath before Henry VIII in Robert Bolt's play *A Man for All Seasons:*

"If what Master Rich has said is true, then I pray I may never see God in the face!") This oath is resumed and made specific in v. 9, echoing for the reader Jacob's similar oath to Laban when Rachel stole the household gods (31:32). As there, the search here moves by stages toward the location of the cup. One suspects that Joseph has told the steward to search in this order; and again (cf. 43:33b) the brothers must wonder what is going on.

Again they prostrate themselves. To Joseph's inquiry (44:14-15), Judah responds helplessly that they can say nothing in their own behalf, for "God has found out the guilt of your servants." To which guilt is he referring? Their merciless treatment of Joseph (42:21)? Or are they trying to share responsibility for the cup in Benjamin's sack? Joseph replies with the same self-curse (*halilah li*, 44:17) as the brothers used with the steward (v. 7), insisting on keeping only the youngest of them. They must hear Joseph's "go up in *shalom* to your father" as a bitter parody of his earlier inquiry after their father's *shalom* (43:27). As he had with Jacob in 43:8-9, Judah responds with an oath — in Hebrew, "by me" or "by my life" — and then rehearses what has happened since the first meeting. Clearly Judah aims to appeal to Joseph's humane feelings, as at each turn of phrase he portrays Jacob's fatherly heart. He describes the terrible blow to Jacob on hearing of Joseph's loss (44:28); then he quotes Jacob's most poignant words (v. 29; cf. 42:38) and repeats them (44:31); and finally he reports his own oath to Jacob (v. 32; cf. 43:9). Judah can have no idea of the profound effect these words have on this "stranger" who is "like Pharaoh himself" (44:18).

Finally Joseph can control himself no longer (45:1). The emotions he has kept channelled within him overflow their banks, and he weeps so loudly as to be heard even in Pharaoh's house. Is the weeping for joy? Is it a final weeping over all the pain he has endured? Is it a weeping for the pathos of brothers who have moved from preoccupation with mutual competition and brotherly hatreds to a place where their primary feeling and concern is for solidarity with what family they have left? Is it also for Rachel and the wet nurse? It is perhaps all of these and more — a weeping that arises out of, and at the same time restores Joseph to, his profound connectedness to all the dimensions of the lives with which his own life is bound up (44:30), so that he is finally ready to risk disclosing himself to these his brothers. Ordering all others to leave, Joseph weeps openly before his brothers in a dramatic advance beyond his earlier feelings of mere nakedness and shame before them (42:24).

Although in his knowledge of who they are Joseph has moved in stages toward this self-disclosure, his brothers in their ignorance are caught totally unprepared for it, and his behavior fills them with dismay. So, beautifully matching Judah's poignant candor in 44:18-34, Joseph speaks freely to them from his heart. He begins with words (45:5-8) that he will reiterate in ch. 50, as he lifts the crushing burden of their guilt by placing it within the horizon of God's providential care for the whole family (45:8). Was this too a cause for his weeping a moment ago — the realization of the unfathomable providence of God, which could turn his brothers' long hatred and his subsequent affliction in Egypt to such good account, so that he need no longer try to forget it all (41:50-52) but now can accept it as part of the fabric of his life at God's hands? Joseph weeps again, with Benjamin. Then he kisses all his brothers and weeps on them. Finally they are able to respond.

Pharaoh's response on hearing all this may be said to arise out of the fact that he "knows" Joseph (contrast Exod. 1:8). Egypt has so prospered under Joseph that any family of his is welcome there. Arrangements are quickly made to bring everyone down. Joseph gives everyone festal garments (cf. Luke 15:22). Do the brothers who resented his tunic from Jacob now resent Joseph's fivefold favor to Benjamin (cf. Luke 15:25-30)? Or have guilt and then reconciliation finally worked a change in them on such matters? What does Joseph mean by his parting words (Gen. 45:24)? The verb *ragaz* ("be agitated, quiver, quake, be excited, perturbed"; RSV "quarrel") can describe feelings of terror, awe, rage, or disquiet. Perhaps he senses that what is happening is too much for them to take in, leaving them in a turmoil of conflicting feelings. So he offers them a wry word of caution (don't fall to squabbling again) and reassurance (don't be agitated by what you don't fully understand).

On hearing the news, Jacob's heart stops in disbelief (v. 26).

The shock seems even greater than in 37:33-35. (A similar reaction will greet the news of Jesus' resurrection, as the disciples "disbelieved for joy" [Luke 24:41, RSV; rather than NRSV, simply "disbelieving"]. It is similar also to Sarah's reaction in Gen. 18:12 and then in 21:6.) Like his sons in the disclosure scene in 45:1-15, Jacob has to be told twice before he can begin to take it in. His first word is *rab* (v. 28) — the word Esau used in 33:9. The RSV both times translates "enough." But in places like Exod. 9:28; Deut. 3:26; Num. 16:3, 7 the word implies excess. It is as though Jacob, who once thought he had everything (see above on 33:11) now has even more than that. His two expressions at 33:11; 45:28 touch a profound truth. There is no joy as great as the joy in recovering what was lost (Luke 15). To gain what one never had is a blessing; but to have had — to have loved — and then to have lost leaves a void that no other blessing can fill, a void that seems to mark the limits to life's goodness and meaning. Where the lost is recovered, those limits are exceeded (as in laughter), and life once more opens out onto the plenitude of God.

46:1–47:12

On the way to Egypt, Jacob comes to Beer-sheba. By this time in the ancestral saga this place has become drenched with associations. After the birth of Isaac, Abraham and Abimelech made a covenant to establish Abraham's ownership of a well there. Then Abraham planted a tree there in honor of Isaac's birth, built an altar, and called on the name of the Everlasting God (Gen. 21:31-33). Again, after the trial on Mt. Moriah and God's reiteration of the promise of 12:1-3, Abraham returned to Beer-sheba to live (22:19). When Isaac was called by God not to flee to Egypt to escape a famine (26:1-2), he ended up at Beer-sheba, where God appeared to him and conveyed to him the promise given to Abraham (vv. 23-24). So Isaac too built an altar to God there, pitched his tent, and dug a well (26:25, 32-33). When Jacob fled into exile from Esau, it was at Bethel that God met him to reassure him, but it was from Beer-sheba that Jacob had set out (28:10).

Now Jacob arrives at Beer-sheba on another flight, this time from famine. Given that his grandfather went down to Egypt under such circumstances, given that his father was called by God not to do so at such a time, and given that he had once gone into exile from here, how should Jacob look to tradition to guide him? He might well wonder whether he is doing the right thing in following his heart into Egypt. Given that Yahweh has long since become his own God, why does he offer sacrifices specifically to the God of his father Isaac? Is he seeking specifically the God who had guided his father on such an occasion? Or is he seeking the God of the father who had blessed him when he went into exile in Paddan-aram and who brought him back to Canaan? If tradition by itself provides so many different precedents that it does not guide Jacob clearly in what to do, it guides him at least in how to seek God. The guidance (reminiscent of 28:15) comes: "Do not be afraid to go down" (46:3). His clan will multiply there, and his favorite son will close his eyes. So he sets out with all his entourage.

The fatefulness of this juncture in the saga of this people is signalled by the narrator's pause (vv. 8-27) to take careful stock of exactly who went down. Two features of this stock-taking are noteworthy. First, of the twelve sons, the children on the Leah side total forty-nine (7 × 7), while the children on the Rachel side total twenty-one (3 × 7), for a total of seventy. The character of all these numbers, turning on factors of seven and three, suggests a quality of "rightness" about things as the people set off. (Later, the twelve tribes descended from these seventy will pass from the Red Sea to Elim [Exod. 15:27], after a period of hardship arriving at a place of rest containing twelve springs of water and seventy palm trees.) Second, whereas the genealogies in Gen. 5 and 10 make no mention of mothers, let alone of their names, here all the mothers are named, along with Dinah, and some of the other wives are also mentioned.

In Gen. 46:28 I prefer RSV mg, "he sent Judah before him . . . to show the way," as continuing Judah's leadership in 43:8-10; 44:11-34 and implicitly preparing the brothers for 49:8-12. The restoration scene in 46:29-30 continues the deep emotion seen earlier between the brothers, except that where Joseph wept more loudly then, now he weeps longer. Does the difference correspond to the intensity of the pain endured at their hands and the long separation from a loving and beloved father? Then Joseph makes preparation for a formal arrival. He will go and give Pharaoh advance warning. In the meantime he coaches his brothers to act so as not to offend Pharaoh through deceit or silence, and so as to ensure land in Goshen. This second reference to "abomination" (v. 34; see 43:32) underscores the cultural differences between the two peoples. The irony, again, is that the people who will be abominated as gentile shepherds will in time abominate the eating and herding of pigs which are left to Gentiles (Luke 15:15).

The family gets its wish to live in Goshen, and more. Already impressed with Joseph's ability, Pharaoh solicits herdsmen from among his able brothers (Gen. 47:6). Presumably as king he is beholden to no constraints of etiquette, so why is Pharaoh moved to ask how old Jacob is? Jacob's response, framed in opening and closing blessings, comes as a curiously muted and sorry summary of his life. Why does he put matters this way? This may be the courtesy of self-diminution before an august monarch. Perhaps he wishes to avoid any implicit boast of himself and his God before Pharaoh. Joseph settles everyone in Goshen and supplies them with all their needs — another element in the fulfillment of his first dream.

47:13-26

The impact of the famine on Egypt is narrated between two comments on Israel's well-being in 47:11-12 and 27-28, so that the starkness of the famine is intensified by the contrast with the comments that frame it. The impact is traced swiftly, in three stages, and in a way that depends for its proper interpretation on the reader's social location and economic experience, or on one's capacity to read the story with imaginative sympathy.

To begin, the people of Egypt give Joseph all their money for the food they have not been able to grow but which they need to remain alive. An elementary note is in order here on the advantages of a monetary system. In a barter economy, everyone must make provision for storing surplus goods. In a monetary economy, conversion of surplus value into money allows for centralized storage and easier transactions of value. But monetary value depends on the ability to reconvert money into real goods; and at such a time the seller of the real goods holds some power over price and conditions of sale. Short of the sale, the holder of foodstuffs can always subsist on the goods themselves, while the buyer will suffer or even die unless the transaction is completed. The famine in Egypt makes the grain business a seller's market, and the asking price is all the money the people have.

The people risk their money in hope that next year the famine will end and they will be able to live off the land. But it does not end, and now they have no money to buy food. Joseph points to their cattle as barter. The dilemma — as anyone knows who has lived or worked on a farm — is that in a famine the livestock will die without food, while if the livestock are bartered the family loses its breeding base for future livestock. The people have no alternative but to barter. Now, even if the famine does end the following year, they will only be able to work the land, and the rebuilding of their livestock will be slow and costly.

Still the famine does not end. Now the dilemma is that, if the Egyptians do not barter the land, they will die of starvation, and the land itself will become "desolate" and "die" (v. 19). Its fruitfulness depends on human cultivation (cf. 2:15; 3:17-19). But if they do barter it, they will have no basis at all for self-sufficiency, and will have to sell themselves into slavery along with the land. Again the people have no alternative. They are caught in a seller's market.

As one who grew up on the rim of Western Canada's dust bowl during the "Dirty Thirties" (so-called because of the ever-drifting clouds of topsoil blown about by hot winds in the rainless summers of the 1930s), I find it impossible to read this passage with scholarly or any other kind of detachment. Memories of farmers who lost their lands to foreclosing banks press in to shape interpretation. Memories of those who wrote off the Church for its servility at such times to moneyed interests all but undermine my present convictions as to the reality and truth of the religious dimension, in the Bible or out of it. What is perhaps most painful of all to read is that the priests were not forced into the same situation as the rest of the people. They were allowed to keep

179

their land and live on a royal allowance until, presumably, better times would render their land once again productive.

Why could the people not have been offered a similar or equivalent arrangement? Could the state stores of food not have been used for emergency relief? Could not some scale of repayment have been worked out that was both fair to the state and bearable by the people? If not, why were the priests favored? Was it because they were crucial to Egypt's connection with the divine? But what understanding of the divine would move a society to think the divine more concerned with the sacral symbolic structure than with the people as a whole? One need not suppose that Egypt's double strategy, of buying up livestock, land, and people and of subsidizing the priests and leaving their land to them, was conceived and carried out in a spirit of crass greed for profit. One may suppose, rather, that this two-faced strategy was carried out in the strong conviction that it was the right thing to do, that it embodied the best divine wisdom available. No doubt in any political economy one will find profiteers and crooks. These are not the great danger to human welfare. The greater danger is the mind-set — the theology or worldview — within which human crises are met with a wisdom that is taken to be given by the gods but that is in fact a false wisdom. (Is this not the real issue in Gen. 2–3?)

But to read this passage with grave apprehension, need one have grown up in Saskatchewan in the "Dirty Thirties," or be a farmer in the American Midwest in the 1980s and 1990s, or live in any of a vast number of other local economies controlled by larger economic and political structures? Even if one does not in any material way share the social location of the people of Egypt, but is reading the Genesis story simply to appreciate what is going on in it, how can one help but recall what will arise later in the biblical story? When Israel comes into the Promised Land, the region will be divided up into small plots held in stewardship to Yahweh. So sacred is that trust that when a king like Ahab desires to buy Naboth's vineyard or trade for it, Naboth will say, "*Yahweh forbid* that I should give you *the inheritance of my fathers*" (1 Kgs. 21:3). His objections are both theological and sociological — or rather, these are two dimensions of a single reality in which

Naboth has his identity and his meaning. It is highly revealing that when Ahab reports this refusal to his non-Yahwistic wife (raised as she is to Canaanite conceptions of monarchy), he deprives the refusal of its theological and sociological rationale: "He answered, 'I will not give you my vineyard'" (1 Kgs. 21:6). As a parable of the loss of small landholdings to larger interests in the period of the monarchy, this passage shows how the social and economic injustices under the monarchy constituted a *de facto* secularization of Israel, destroying its ties both with heaven and with its own social past, and provoking sustained prophetic critique.

Such prophetic voices encourage one to read Gen. 47 with grave disapproval. But does the narrator in Genesis give us any nudge in this direction, or only make a silent appeal to our human sensibilities as shaped by the human vocation in Gen. 1 and 2? Perhaps the promise of lands to the ancestors from ch. 12 onward, and the various notices of disputes over wells, and of purchases of land by individuals alert us to the appropriateness of individual and familial landholdings. What of the narrator's threefold notice that Joseph married Asenath, daughter of the priest of On (41:45, 50; 46:20)? Does Joseph's resulting social connection bear upon the special arrangement he made for the priests in this time of famine? Earlier, in the matter of Pharaoh's dreams, Joseph's wisdom had stood out in contrast to that of the Egyptian sages and diviners. Now Joseph's wisdom appears to converge with that of the established interests in Egypt, as in more senses than one he acts to fulfill Pharaoh's dreams. Did Joseph take a fateful turn when — however understandably — he named his children Manasseh and Ephraim (41:51-52)? All his hard and afflicted life, Joseph had acted in innocence and loyal industry toward the realization of a vocation he may only dimly have understood. But when that twofold time of misery ended and he rose to Pharaoh's side, married a priest's daughter, and had two sons, his names for them spoke of forgetting his past, forgetting the hardships of his father's house and his more recent afflictions. But one's past is part of who one is, however painful it may have been. It is a fundamental dimension of one's compassionate connectedness to others. Joseph's policies in ch. 47, grounded in his marital connection with the priests and his political place with Pharaoh, seem to have lost their compassionate ground in his own experience of suffering at the hands of familial and political superiors.

Again, Joseph's reference to his silver cup as a divining cup (44:5, 15) may betray more than a ruse by which to frighten his brothers. It may signal a tendency to think of himself in terms that threaten to betray his vocation. The shift in Joseph is striking. To the butler and baker he had affirmed, "Do not interpretations belong to God? Tell them to me, I pray you" (40:8). When Pharaoh later said to him, "I have heard it said of you that when you hear a dream you can interpret it" (41:15), Joseph had demurred, "It is not in me; God will give Pharaoh a favorable answer" (v. 16). But in 44:15 he says, "Do you not know that *such a man as I* can indeed divine?" One is tempted to suggest that, long before there arose a new king over Egypt who knew not Joseph (Exod. 1:8), there arose a new Joseph over Egypt who had all too successfully forgotten his painful past, and in so doing had forgotten also the old Joseph. As we shall see, the forgetting is not permanent. Yet while it lasts, it initiates sweeping social changes which will come back to haunt Joseph's descendants later. Meanwhile we may note that, though in later Israel the priests and the Levites were put on temple allowance, at least they were not allowed to hold land.

47:27–49:33

For several reasons I take all this material as a complex unit. First, the notice concerning Jacob's age in Gen. 47:28 is completed by his death notice in 49:33. (Compare the genealogies in chs. 5 and 10, and the notices in 23:1-2; 25:7-8, 27; 35:28.) Accordingly the material between 47:28 and 49:33 may be taken as an extreme instance of the sort of narrative detail that is inserted in the genealogy several times in ch. 5 (vv. 3b, 22a, 24, 29), and especially the narrative in 6:1–9:27 which splits the notice in 5:32 and 9:28. Second, the acts of Jacob within this complex passage all are by way of putting his affairs in order on the verge of his death.

Third, the language of 47:27 sounds a Priestly refrain running back through the ancestral stories all the way to Gen. 1:28, where God blesses the first couple so that they may be fruitful and multiply and fill the earth. (The Priestly refrain of 47:27 is picked up again in Exod. 1:7, where, with 1:8-10, it sets the stage for Israel's deliverance from Egypt by Yahweh, "the God of your father, the God of Abraham, the God of Isaac, and the God of Jacob" [Exod. 3:6; cf. 2:24; 3:13, 15, 16; 4:5; 6:2-5].) In Gen. 1 the theme of fruitfulness first arises on the second half of Day Three (1:11). There, God calls on earth to "vegetate" in such a way that plants will yield seed and fruit trees will bear fruit in which is their seed, each according to its own kind upon the earth. Since 1:29 reinforces the notion that vegetation is for human consumption, it is worth noting that before fruit is meant for us to eat, fruit is meant to bear seed to perpetuate its own species. When in 1:22 and 28, then, God blesses other forms of life to "be fruitful," this means that on analogy with the vegetation they are blessed with the capacity to perpetuate their own respective life-forms. The theological significance of this is that God, the source of all existence and all life, communicates to each type of creature a derived yet genuine generative power to communicate its life to others of its kind. Climactically, the sabbath day of rest itself is blessed. This suggests that, after each working week, a day of rest is to refresh, regenerate, and strengthen the whole creation to live and thrive fruitfully through another week of work. One may note that, whereas for God the working week ends in sabbath, for humankind created on the sixth day the first full day of life is a sabbath. This means that the sabbath which follows a working week is a return to the rest that preceded it. Thus hope roots in deep memory to give a vision of wholeness toward which we and all creation may live. Meanwhile, the rhythm of work and rest enables the generative and regenerative process down through the "generations of the heavens and the earth" (2:4a).

The blessings of ch. 49 are individualized for each son. (In 48:20 Manasseh and Ephraim are blessed together.) This individualization is underscored by 49:28, where "blessing each with the blessing suitable to him" may be taken to echo the "each according to its kind" in 1:11. Thus when Jacob blesses his two grandsons in ch. 48 and his twelve sons in 49:1-27, I connect this directly to the Priestly themes in 47:27, and through this verse all the way back to the Priestly creation story in Gen. 1, specifically to 1:28, and indeed back to 1:11 and Mother Earth. Viewed in this way, the whole complex passage in 47:27–49:33 invites us to take the book of Genesis as ending on the theme with which it began — the generative fruitfulness of God's creation — expressed through Jacob's blessing as God has given him the capacity to bless with generative power. The poetic intensity and elaborateness of the blessing fit the point at which the families of the Abrahamic community of regeneration (12:1-3) now will fan out into tribes amid the nations of the world for whose sake they exist (cf. Isa. 49:6).

47:29–48:22 Jacob's first act (Gen. 47:29-31) is to have Joseph swear by a ritual whose significance we have explored at the beginning of ch. 24. There, aged Abraham in the land of promise swore the servant to fetch a wife for Isaac from Paddan-aram, but on no account to take the son back there. Here, aged Israel swears Joseph to do steadfast love and faithfulness with him (see above on 24:27), by taking the father's body back to the Promised Land for burial. (On the relation between *hesed* and memory, see above on 40:14.) Thus the community of the living and the dead are to be held in the steadfast and faithful embrace of the one land. When Joseph swears to him, Israel bows on the head of his bed — the final fulfillment of Joseph's dreams in ch. 37.

Then, on his deathbed Jacob recalls for Joseph the blessing of El Shaddai at Luz (48:3-4), echoing the terms of Gen. 1:28. Why does he draw Joseph's two sons so close to him as to make them his own sons, elevating them to rank alongside Reuben and Simeon? It is as though these two sons of Joseph are to receive the inheritance that would normally go to Jacob's two oldest, who however have disqualified themselves (49:3-7). One suspects that Jacob is also concerned about the two grandsons' half-Egyptian heritage. That his favorite son should have had children by one so culturally removed surely must have troubled him. The rationale in v. 7 may imply that, by this action, Joseph's first two children become the adoptive children of Jacob and Rachel.

The blessing scene itself, beginning with Jacob's near blindness, recalls elements of Isaac's blessing of Jacob. But whereas Isaac had given Jacob and Esau a blessing that focused primarily on the fertility of creation and on relations between the two brothers, Jacob's blessing comes in terms of God's lifelong leading which has redeemed him from all evil. If Jacob's lifelong anxiety operated still in his words to Pharaoh, "The days of my sojourning have been few and evil" (cf. 47:9), here he emphasizes a long life in which God has redeemed him from all evil. Comparison of these two different statements suggests that Jacob remains a divided soul to the end of this earthly life. But whereas he was in the grip of his Jacob self for the first part of his life, since Jabbok — where he received his true name, Israel — he has begun to live up to his true self, so that he dies a redeemed and to some degree a transformed divided self. Thus he testifies to God's faithfulness in keeping the oath to him at Bethel (28:15, 20-21). It is no surprise, and it is highly significant, that it is precisely this occasion that lays the basis (in 48:15-16) for the formula "the God of Abraham, and the God of Isaac, and the God of Jacob." Henceforth (beginning with 50:24) this formula will connote not only the blessing of generativity in the face of sterility, but also God's faithfulness to lead and to protect through all manner of evil. It is this that gives the use of the threefold identification in Exod. 2:23–6:8 its significance in the face of the evils of Egypt. The latter deliverance is foreshadowed in the conviction voiced in Gen. 48:21-22.

The focus on Jacob's care to bless the younger over the older child recalls what was involved in Jacob's gaining the blessing over Esau. In the process, this overturning of primogeniture involves another conventional practice that only now in some parts of the world is being challenged for its ideological content. The preference given to right-handedness, and the disadvantage suffered by left-handed people, is so pervasive in many cultures as to be all but unnoticed except by the left-handed. From young children forced to write right-handed, or at any rate to write left-handed on desks not fitted to their needs, to the sinister overtones in the word "sinister" (literally, "left-handed") in contrast to the positive overtones in the word "dextrous" ("right-handed"), a large part of the world has suffered painfully at the hand of the right-handed majority. The irony is that, in this act of blessing, Jacob may be seen to employ and reinforce one social convention in the act of helping to overturn another. Thus the path to redemption may in part be paved with some of the very inequities from which that path seeks to redeem us. In the present instance the problem is this: how signal the overturning of primogeniture without language? If the language itself has a built-in bias through conventional usage, how signal the overturning of convention? Is there any language that does not contain elements of the very evils from which we seek redemption? What language will we use to declare the full rights (so to speak!) of the left-handed? Is it in part, perhaps, the language of saving humor, as when left-handed people wear T-shirts capitalizing on the way the two sides of the brain are neurologically cross-connected to the hands on the other side — T-shirts celebrating the fact that only the left-handed are in their right minds?

49:1-27 Now we come to what is often called the Blessing of Jacob. In Deut. 33 Moses will similarly bless Israel just before his death, as the people are poised to enter the land across the Jordan. These two blessings have many similarities, but the second one also introduces a number of changes. Given what has been suggested earlier in this section concerning the roots and significance of blessing, it is worth pondering that the Mosaic period ends on the brink of entry into Canaan, as the ancestral period ends on entry into Egypt, with a comprehensive powerful blessing.

A third such blessing can be associated with these two — the words Balaam speaks concerning Israel in Num. 22–24. There, on seeing the approach of Israel, Balak king of Moab fears them for their numbers and sends to Balaam to have Israel cursed. The ensuing narrative is of great interest in its own right, but here we may only note that when Balaam tries to curse Israel, God commands him rather to bless. After the third blessing, and Balak's mounting anger, Balaam says, "If Balak should give me his house full of silver and gold, I would not be able to go beyond the word of Yahweh, to do *either good or bad* of my own will; what Yahweh speaks, that will I speak. And now, behold, I am going to my people; come, I will let you know what this people will do to your people *in days to come*" (Num. 24:13-14). The first italicized idiom echoes words of Laban in Gen. 24:50 (cf. 31:24), where Laban was fully persuaded of God's hand in events and accordingly had no room for his own personal judgment. Here the idiom emphasizes that Balaam's words of blessing are not only his own, but are from God. The second italicized idiom is a set phrase that occurs thirteen times in the Bible, eleven times in the prophetic books (e.g., Isa. 2:2; Hos. 3:5, often translated, "In the latter days" [so RSV]), and elsewhere only here and in Gen. 49:1. The use of the second idiom in Genesis and Numbers gives these two passages the character of a prophecy. The two idioms together in Num. 24:13-14 illustrate the general principle asserted in 2 Pet. 1:20-21, that scriptural prophecy does not arise simply through human interpretation, but ultimately from the moving of God's Spirit.

The connections between Jacob's blessing and that of Balaam are intriguing. First, outside of Gen. 12–50 and Exod. 6:3, the divine name *Shaddai* occurs in the Pentateuch only in Num. 24:4, 16. This usage associates Balaam's blessing of Israel with God's various promises to the ancestors by that divine name. Second, the blessing in Num. 24:9 contains two lines identical to two lines in the blessing of Judah in Gen. 49:9b, while the following two lines in Num. 24:9 take up the "blessed/cursed" theme beginning in Gen. 12:3. One may take Num. 24:8-9a as elaborating Gen. 49:9, both texts celebrating Israel's strength against its enemies. Following Num. 24:8, the image of the couching lion and lioness in v. 9a may refer to the settlement in the Promised Land, as an undisturbed "rest" from enemies. Immediately, then, the words of Gen. 12:3 are carried forward and applied to this people settled confidently in this land.

The third connection is the announcement in Num. 24:17 of a star/scepter arising out of Jacob/Israel, echoing the blessing of Judah in Gen. 49:10. Like that earlier blessing, Balaam's announcement points to a royal figure who will prevail against all enemies. The connection between the references to "lion of Judah," the scepter, and victory in the blessing on Judah in Gen. 49:8-12, and the references to the same themes in the blessing on Jacob-Israel in Num. 24:8-9, 17-19, suggests that the words of Gen. 12:3 are in Num. 24:9 attached not only to Jacob-Israel in general, but also specifically to the ruler who is to arise. This connection becomes explicit in Ps. 72:17b, where the promise of Gen. 12:3 is attached directly to the Davidic king. (We may note that the very first blessing by Balaam ends with the words, "Let me die the death of the righteous,/and let my end be like his" [Num 23:10]. If "the righteous" here is Jacob as just spoken of, then Balaam may be seen here as blessing himself by Abraham's descendant Jacob — again echoing Gen 12:3.)

These three blessings by (1) Jacob (Gen. 49), (2) Balaam (Num. 23–24), and (3) Moses (Deut. 33) act as generative words to accompany and empower the children of Jacob/Israel (1) in Egypt, (2) through the wilderness, and (3) into the land. As such, these blessings themselves are among the firstfruits of Jacob's blessing first given in seed form in Gen. 48:15-16.

Reuben. Jacob's word to Reuben falls into three parts of two lines each. The first two lines say who Reuben is by birth: Jacob's firstborn. As such, he is Jacob's "might" (*koah,* as in 4:12 [RSV "strength"], the sign of fertile power), and he is the firstfruits of Jacob's strength (*on,* the word Rachel used or played on in naming her second son [35:18]). This characterization of the firstborn as the first embodiment of the might of the father underlies the social institution of primogeniture. The second two lines say who Reuben is by behavior: I translate, "Excessive (*yeter*) in pride and excessive (*yeter*) in power,/Unbridled as water, you shall not succeed (*hotar*)." "Pride" is literally "lifting up," as in Ps. 93:3, "the floods lift up." The pride and the power are a surging force. "Unbridled" speaks of reckless, wanton, and uncontrolled behavior. (Elsewhere this Hebrew word occurs only in Judg. 9:4; Jer. 23:32; Zeph. 3:4.) "Unbridled as water" picks up a standard ancient image for chaotic force that knows no constraints except those imposed from without, as in Ps. 93:4. Hebrew *yeter* everywhere else in the OT means "remainder, abundance, excess" (as in Isa. 56:12, "great beyond measure"; cf. v. 11: "the dogs have an excessive [RSV "mighty"] appetite; they never have enough"). Hebrew *hotar* (cognate with *yeter*) everywhere else means "leave over, be overabundant, prosper" (as in Deut. 28:11; 30:9).

188

Reuben's firstborn might and strength has expressed itself in uncontrolled surging power which drives to excess, assuming that its own unbridled actions will assure its success. Jacob's blessing bridles Reuben (as Yahweh bridles the waters in Ps. 93:4).

The third pair of lines shows why Jacob thus bridles Reuben. This firstborn son's act with Bilhah (Gen. 35:22), taking advantage of her after her mistress Rachel's death and during Jacob's grief, was a clear bid to take over his father's authority. Such an act, where the son attempts to displace the father, occurs often in the ancient world. (According to one old Mesopotamian text, the Harab myth, in seven successive generations the son takes the mother and displaces the father.) In terms of individual psychosocial development, such an attempt emerges in the Oedipal crisis as the next critical stage after maternal care and weaning. Reuben's act discloses the root problem with primogeniture: unbridled lust for a power that cannot await its own proper time and context of realization. Jacob's words, "you shall not succeed," sum up the general critique of primogeniture that runs through Genesis. As the very first word to the firstborn of the twelve tribes, Jacob's blessing to Reuben releases a restraining power that is to run through their history, to curb and bridle and finally doom a deep-seated flaw in human enactments of power within the community. Reuben is not the key to who the people of regeneration are called to be.

Simeon and Levi. If Reuben expresses the excessiveness of social power through sexuality, Simeon and Levi express it through the violence of the sword, a violence that enacts vengeful anger, wantonness, and wrath, as in their retaliation for the rape of Dinah (34:25-31). Their "council" and "company" is made up of all those who share their mind-set or wisdom as a way of being in the world vis-à-vis one's enemies. Jacob will not be a part of this council (cf. Ps. 1:1). He withholds his *nephesh,* his own life force, from such a mind-set; for it in no way manifests his glory (so the Hebrew and RSV mg). He thereby at the outset of Israel's history rejects the sword as the basis of Israel's relation to other peoples. Simeon and Levi who thus acted together are to be scattered, just as the people who together built Babel out of fear and in order to instill fear in their enemies were themselves scattered (11:9).

189

Thus, the first two blessings to later Israel deal with funda-mental issues of authority and leadership within the community (Reuben) and of modes of relation to other communities (Simeon and Levi). In each case, all too typical conceptions and practices are rejected. As Jacob, this father knows their "wisdom" all too well from the inside; as Israel, he knows that to bless his first three sons the way he does is, for all its stringency, to call them to their true self as sons of his own true *nephesh* and glory. It is his way of touching them on the thigh to give them a limp that is to mark his descendants to this day (32:25, 31-32), and so to help the children of Jacob become the children of Israel.

Judah. With Judah Jacob's blessing turns positive, picking up Leah's own power of blessing in her naming of this son (29:35) and nuancing this blessing as he declares Judah's leadership within the tribes. Does Jacob thereby contradict Joseph's dreams (com-pare 49:8b and 37:8, 9), or do those dreams and this blessing apply to different periods in the people's history? (One might compare the respective periods of Joseph's and Judah's leadership, in Ps. 78.) The lion of Judah begins as a young whelp who has eaten its fill, then lies down to a rest that is not to be disturbed. If this takes the story as far as the settlement of Israel in the Promised Land, at that point Judah shall enter a period of hiber-nation, so to speak. But the scepter and the staff will nevertheless not depart from him until the time appointed for it, when not only his brothers but the peoples will obey him. (Thus a period of waiting comes between this blessing of Judah and its fulfillment, analogous to the period of waiting betweeen Joseph's childhood dreams and their fulfillment.) Tying up his royal steed after his victory, Judah will wash his garments and sit down to the victory banquet. The third line in Gen. 49:10 most naturally refers to Shiloh (RSV mg). But what can this mean? I propose that the blessing refers to Judah's period of "hibernation" ending with the fall of Shiloh, at which time leadership in Israel will pass from Joseph to Judah (Ps. 78:60-68).

The blessings on the first four sons all deal with issues of social power, internal and external. The contrast between the first three sons and Judah could not be more striking. Reuben cannot wait to inherit his authority, but must seize it in unbridled excess of energy. Simeon and Levi in their wrath do not know how to interact peaceably with their neighbors or to seek reconciliation with their enemies. (A later descendant of Judah will say, "all who take the sword will perish by the sword" [Matt. 26:52].) Judah knows how to wait patiently until the time of his appointed accession to power. Such self-restraint is to be the key to power both internally and externally. Here the long journey to and through monarchy in Israel is set on its way. How long will it be until later royal Judah will fully undergo transformation from the spirit of Jacob to the spirit of Israel, that is to say, until royal Judah becomes its true self in contrast to the three older brothers? Until the vision of the Peaceable Kingdom in Isa. 11:1-10, with its echoes of Gen. 1 and 2? Until the vision of the servant in Second Isaiah, and its outcome in the Davidic vision and a new garden land in Isa. 55:1-13?

Zebulun, Issachar, Dan, Gad, Asher, Naphtali. The following six blessings, spanning the remaining children of Leah and those of Zilpah, differentiate the characters of these brothers succinctly. Each receives individual attention. But they do not figure prominently, since the blessing as a whole is concerned with the larger issues of leadership within the whole people and in the wider world. From a contemporary point of view, the omission of Dinah is troubling. One is encouraged by her mention in Gen. 46:15; but her absence from a blessing concerned with leadership may be taken as a silent sign of the need for further transformations in the community of Jacob/Israel — transformations, perhaps, under the reign of Jesus as the seed of Abraham (Gal. 3:28-29; cf. 6:16).

Joseph. Jacob now comes to his favorite son. The opening image (Gen. 49:22) poignantly recaptures Jacob's first sight of Rachel at the well. The second image (v. 23) vividly evokes the animosity of Joseph's ten brothers after her death. Literally, "They showed bitterness toward him, they ganged up on him,/they hated him (*satam*), the masters of arrows (*ba'ale hitstsim*)." The use of the verb *satam* as in 50:15 secures the allusion to the brothers (cf. 37:4, 5, where "hated" translates *sana'*), while "masters of arrows" stands in ironic contrast to their taunting arrow of scorn, "here comes the master of dreams" (*ba'al hahalomot*) in 37:19. Through all this long internal strife — and through the affliction Joseph suffered in Egypt — "his bow remained unmoved" (49:24). The bow here (as with the brothers' arrows) is Joseph's own strength. RSV "unmoved" translates *eytan*, which literally means "perennial, ever-flowing," especially of water (in contrast to a wadi, or "deceitful brook," in Jer. 15:18). His strength is not so much unmoved (though it is that) as it is unfailing. The image is of a source of life that from birth if not before is ever-flowing (like living waters). This contrasts with earlier imagery associated with Jacob's birth and rebirth, and reinforces the possibility that Joseph is not twice-born like his father but once-born. If this be the case, another mystery emerges. Joseph's mother Rachel was for a long time childless, just like Jacob's mother Rebekah. The temptation of some contemporary students of human development is to explain all aspects of a person's development and character in terms of parental and other social and material factors in the world. Joseph's contrast to his father and his mother is a salutary caution against confining the activity of God to the influence of parents and other finite factors in the world.

Joseph's strength derives from the God of Jacob, characterized initially in a variety of images: First, God is imaged as *abir ya'aqob*, the Mighty One of Jacob (Gen. 49:24). Hebrew *abir* (RSV "Mighty One") is often now associated with *abbir*, "bull," as in Isa. 10:13. The image then is one of fertility and might, both qualities being appropriate to Gen. 12–50 generally, and especially to Joseph in the face of all his early enemies. But the word may also be associated with *eber* and *ebra*, "pinions," in which case the phrase *abir ya'aqob* refers to God as also depicted in the wings of the eagle in Exod. 19:3-6; Deut. 32:11; Isa. 40:31 ("on wings [*eber*]," i.e., on Yahweh's back, not RSV "with wings"). These wings also then appear on the cherubim above the ark, as in Ps. 132 where twice (vv. 2, 5) Yahweh is named *abir ya'aqob* (cf. also Isa. 1:24; 49:26; 60:16). The image then may be one of the parent bird's care and protection of its young, an image again appropriate to Gen. 12–50 generally and to Joseph in particular.

The second image, of God as Shepherd, likewise connotes nurture, care, and protection. The third image, of God as the Rock of Israel, may again (as often in the OT) connote steadfast-

ness and reliability. In the present context it may also carry connotations of fatherly and motherly fertility and nurture, for in
Deut. 32 God as Rock is faithful father (vv. 4-6) who made and
redeemed Israel (v. 15), and who in feminine terms begot and
birthed Israel (v. 18). But in Deut. 32 the Hebrew word is *tsur*,
a word often elsewhere applied to God, while in Gen. 49:24 the
word is *eben*, "stone, rock," a word not otherwise applied to
Israel's God. Why this peculiar use of *eben*? It may be that the
poet wished simply to play on the partial similarity in sounds and
in letters between the two parallel phrases, "Mighty One of Jacob"
= "Rock of Israel," that is, *abir ya'aqob* = *eben yisra'el* (the root
letters are *'bn* = *'br*). But *eben* does occur also in the context of
fertility concerns, where it is associated with feminine divine
powers that give birth (Jer. 2:27; cf. 3:9). So here, in coherent
sequence after God as strong-pinioned parent bird and as
Shepherd, Rock or Stone may image God who births and faithfully
sustains Israel. This image perhaps should also be associated with
occurrences of the word "stone" (*eben*) encountered in Gen.
28:11, 18, 22; 35:14, passages in which Jacob himself memorialized God's faithful promises to him.

Genesis 49:25 finally comes around to name this God. The
"God of your father" is none other than El Shaddai (RSV "God
Almighty"), appearing as such to Abraham in 17:1 to promise a
child, coming on Isaac's lips in 28:3 to bless Jacob with fruitfulness, appearing to Jacob after his return to Bethel to reiterate the
ancestral promise (35:11), coming on Jacob's lips in a prayer for
divine mercy (*rahamim*, "compassions of the womb") in the face
of prospective bereavement (43:14), and most recently recalling
for Joseph the promise of 35:11 just before blessing Joseph's two
sons (48:3-4). By this time the core connotations of this name
should have become clear, focusing closely on birth, nurture, and
compassion as the matrix of family and clan relations. Now these
connotations are poetically elaborated. It is as El Shaddai that
God grants the life-giving blessings, not only of family and clan,
but of the whole creation. (The lines "blessings of heaven
above,/blessings of the deep that couches beneath" echo Isaac's
words to Jacob in 27:27-28 and Esau in v. 39.)

These cosmic blessings are at the same time the blessings of breasts (*shadayim*) and womb (*rehem*). Such blessings are mighty to prevail (*gabar*) over the blessings of the eternal mountains and the everlasting hills. What is the significance of the connection as well as the contrast between mountains and Shaddai's blessing? The divine name El Shaddai is perhaps the most puzzling of ancestral names for God, and its meaning continues to exercise scholars. Here I would build on the work of Frank M. Cross, who traces the divine name *Shaddai* back to a Semitic word *thadu/shadu* originally meaning "breast" (cf. the Hebrew dual form *shadayim* in 49:25; *Canaanite Myth and Hebrew Epic*, 55-56 and n. 44). This Semitic word then came to mean also "mountain." (Cross compares the French-named American mountain range "The Grand Tetons," literally, the large breasts.) Now, a mythological connection between divine breasts and earthly mountains appears in the Babylonian creation story Enuma Elish, where the breasts of the primordial goddess Tiamat, mother of all the gods and the cosmos, are identified with mountains having gushing springs.

On the basis of these and other associations, I take the divine name El Shaddai to identify God not just in relation to human fertility and nurture in general, but specifically in relation to the feminine role in these fundamental processes. In v. 25, then, the similarity in sound between *shadayim*, "breasts," and the name Shaddai is a poetic play that conveys a profound meaning. In vv. 22-26 Joseph is blessed in the name of divine parental care, imaged in both feminine and masculine terms. Such a blessing is "mighty beyond the blessings of the eternal mountains,/the bounties of the everlasting hills." This may mean that the blessings on Joseph will endure as long as the fruitfulness of the earth itself, and beyond. Such a blessing will be mighty enough to enable Joseph to prevail (v. 24) over against all the forces that have opposed him and will oppose him, hostile forces that would call in question the belief that the divine is appropriately imaged in nurturing and protecting parental terms. Such a blessing will also enable him to prevail over against all that has been imperfect or inadequate in his own parenting. (In our own day, amid mounting disclosures of instances of child abuse extending back into infancy and who knows how much earlier, what might it mean to minister to such victims, and to pray for them and bless them, in the name of El Shaddai?)

Narratively speaking, the name El Shaddai was introduced as early as 17:1. There and in subsequent occurrences, as we have seen, it occurred always in the context of the gift of children and of (parental) protection. In 49:25 the meaning of the name is all but stated as giver of cosmic fertility and as "giver of blessings of breasts and womb." We can see that the "blessing of womb" celebrates the God who opens the wombs even of Sarah, Rebekah, Rachel, and Tamar. But the "blessing of breasts" seems to be much less prominently featured in the ancestral narrative. Therefore we might well have expected a divine name in 49:25 playing on the word *rehem*, "womb," rather than on *shadayim*, "breasts." (That God could bear a name associated with *rehem* is suggested by the fact that in Canaanite religion the high god El had a divine female consort named Rahmay.) But closer study shows that the theme of nourishing breast is also present in the narrative, explicitly or implicitly. First, there is the fact that Rebekah's wet nurse Deborah is mentioned twice, in 24:59; 35:8. (In the second instance she is memorialized in a remarkable way.) Second, there is Jacob's specific concern in 28:20 for food and clothing — a concern that has its first form in the infant's need for its mother's breast. Third, there is the repeated theme of famine in the land (12:10; 26:1; 41:53-54). In such famine, the earth proves unable to provide food for the life that has issued from it (cf. Gen. 1 and 2; also 3:17-19; 4:12). The thematic connection between earth's fertility and breast-feeding is established in 49:25. Fourth, in the most extreme of the three famines, it is Joseph whose first dream speaks of a plentiful supply of food. (In this context, he takes after his grandfather Isaac the farmer [26:12-13].) These observations should show that it is under the divine parental care of the ancestral God El Shaddai, giver of the blessings of breasts as well as womb, that the ancestral story unfolds. It is a story of recurring barrenness, insufficient breast milk, and famine, under God's care brought to fertility, nurture, and economic plenty.

Two further observations may be made concerning the names of God. First, though the divine name El Shaddai occurs several times throughout Genesis, beginning in 17:1, its meaning is most fully developed only at the end of the ancestral period, in 49:25. This is similar to the treatment of the divine name Yahweh, which occurs frequently throughout the present form of the text of Genesis, yet is given its meaning only later, at the burning bush (Exod. 3:13-15). This is really not surprising, in light of our own experience. We learn one another's names long before we come to know fully what those names stand for and thereby what they mean.

The second observation turns on the fact that it is not El Shaddai but Yahweh who opens Leah's womb (Gen. 29:31). Similarly, though it is God (*Elohim*) who opens Rachel's womb (30:22), nevertheless in naming Joseph she says, "May Yahweh add to me another son" (v. 24). This variation in usage might suggest that we should abandon the attempt to read the text canonically, as a unified text, and recognize that the variation in divine names is to be accounted for merely as evidence for a plurality of earlier sources, J, E, D, P, and so on. The question, however, is whether earlier sources, referring to God in different ways, have been drawn together into a story that gives those differences a new function, in which they subtly shift the focus or emphasis in references to God. According to the narrator in Exod. 3:14, Yahweh gives the meaning of the name Yahweh as "I will be who I will be." Among other things, this makes room for Yahweh to be present to a particular people or person under any name appropriate to this or that particular circumstance. In that case, Yahweh can be revealed or made known to the ancestors as Yahweh, simply as God (*Elohim, Eloah,* or *El*), or under circumstantially appropriate titles such as God Most High (*El 'Elyon,* Gen. 14:19, 22), the Everlasting God (*El 'Olam,* 21:33), or El, God of Israel (*El Elohe Israel,* 33:20) — but most frequently, and most climactically in 49:22-26, as El Shaddai.

It is as El Shaddai, then, that the biblical God Yahweh is imaged in parental terms, in contrast to the blessings manifest in the earth itself (v. 26a), and indeed over against all other potential rivals in such blessing and power. (Babylonian royal inscriptions often celebrate that city's walls as eternal and as mountains; cf. also Isa. 40:4; 41:2, 15.) In the present context, the lines in Gen. 49:26 structurally balance the opening reference to Joseph's brothers as his enemies and rival claimants of parental blessing and power. The final two lines make the application explicit. Thus, the two largest and most positive blessings, to Judah and to Joseph, lift up and perpetuate through these two brothers conceptions of power as patience, and generative nurture and protection, in the face of those who live out of a different mind-set. This is the legacy into which Jacob/Israel's descendants are called to enter.

Benjamin. Like the second group of six in vv. 13-21, the final blessing comes as an anticlimax, falling on the head of Jacob's very youngest son. In view of the words to Reuben, does its content reflect the fact that this youngest one, born in his father's old age, became spoiled and unbridled, and that even in this blessing the father — still after all in part Jacob — no longer has the desire or the energy to curb him? The irony is that Israel's first king will be Saul, of the tribe of Benjamin. Saul's early successes against Israel's enemies will embody the energies imaged in this blessing of Benjamin. But he will be betrayed by those very energies, when he impatiently offers sacrifice before going into battle instead of waiting for Samuel (1 Sam. 13:8-15), and when he saves the best of the spoils of battle for the people instead of observing the stringent rules of sacral war with their restraint of the lust for spoils (1 Sam. 15). Another irony — perhaps redeeming Benjamin's memory — lies in wait for another Saul of the tribe of Benjamin. This Saul in his zeal for God will go about "breathing threats and murder against the disciples of the Lord" (Acts 9:1), until (like Jacob) he encounters God. There he will be transformed in the light of an "unworldly" (that is to say, an unconventional) vision of wisdom and power (cf. 1 Cor. 1:21–2:7). Such very much later outworkings are perhaps some indication of the regenerative potency of Jacob's blessing amid its historical conditionedness, a potency meant to give blessing to all the generations of heaven and earth (Gen. 12:3).

49:28-33   Having blessed the sons, "blessing each with the blessing suitable to him," Jacob repeats to them the request to which he had made Joseph swear (47:29-31). This time Jacob carefully names all the deceased ancestors, husband and wife, as well as his wife Leah, buried in the cave of Machpelah. His silence in respect to Rachel is deafening. Her burial place was duly noted earlier, with fresh recollection of his sorrow (48:7). Given the importance of the burial of all the other ancestors together in one place, what are we to make of his silence concerning Rachel, and of her absence from this tomb? With what meaning may we fill this silence and this absence? Is Rachel the matriarchal monument to all who die in exile, ungathered? Or should we allow Rachel herself, and her God, to fill the gap with their own voices, as in Jer. 31:15-22, where another return of the children of Jacob — specifically Ephraim — is promised? Meanwhile, what are we to make of Jacob's last action, as he "gathered up (*wayye'esoph*; RSV "drew up") his feet into the bed, and breathed his last, and was gathered (*wayye'aseph*) to his people" (Gen. 49:33)?

We may begin by supposing that such an action would not be surprising in a culture where the dead were buried in a fetal position. "Drew up his feet into the bed" might even be a way of saying "died," like "breathed his last" or "went to his last resting place." The question then is why the narrator uses such a figure of speech precisely and only of this individual. The following elements in his life may be suggestive: (1) Jacob recently has referred in two different ways to his whole life as a journey (47:9; 48:15-16). (2) His name is Jacob, cognate with the Hebrew word for "heel." (3) At the point where his name was changed to Israel, he was touched on the thigh and left to limp for the rest of his life (32:31). (4) In his prenatal fetal position, Jacob was felt to struggle mightily with his twin brother (25:22). However we take the verb there (see above), it is clear that that struggle involved a thrashing of the limbs, among which the legs would undoubtedly figure most vigorously. If the verb in 25:22 is in fact a form of Heb. *ruts*, "to run," or plays on the sound of that verb, then we have an even more vivid thematic connection between the very beginning and the very end of Jacob's life.

The implication of such a connection may be that, after a life of struggle and of continuing sojourn and travel, Jacob — who has suffered all his life from a deep-seated abandonment anxiety — is now content to curl up and die quietly in a land far distant from home. Having gained the assurance that he will be buried with his ancestors, he ceases his struggles and his travels in Egypt, "gathers up" his feet, expires, and is "gathered up" to his ancestors. His very act of yielding up his breath comes as an act of resignation to God in trust (cf. Luke 23:46). Given that his anxiety may have begun already in the womb and, as I have speculated, may have had to do with his mother's problems in conceiving (and nursing?); and given the way he named the oak under which he buried Deborah, Rebekah's nurse (Gen. 35:8); and given the fundamental conceptions reflected in such idioms as found in Job 1:21 ("naked I came from my mother's womb, and naked shall I return"), the careful naming of those to whom he will be gathered (or return) may be one clue to Jacob's ability finally to gather up his restless feet in the peace of death. Dying in a land of exile, he is not exiled from his wider family, but in fact is united with them.

50:1-26

The last chapter of the book opens and closes on the same theme: the embalming of an ancestor in Egypt with a view to his eventual burial in the land of promise. After the period of the embalming, and according to Egyptian practice, all Egypt is portrayed as weeping seventy days for this Semitic ancestor of later Israel. I suggest that Gen. 12:3 provides the theological frame within which to reflect on this remarkable observance. Two aspects of this frame are relevant. On the one hand, Joseph has been a blessing to Egypt, in saving Egypt from the famine that is ravaging the earth. In this respect he has fulfilled God's charge to Abraham to "be a blessing" (12:2). One may assume, then, that the Egyptians' mourning, and their subsequent state escort of Jacob's family for the interment at Machpelah, comes as an expression of their gratitude to Joseph for the blessing they have received through him. On the other hand, in so honoring Joseph's father, the grandson of Abraham, they are blessing him and not belittling him or holding him of no account (12:3). Thereby, according to the original promise (of which Egypt presumably was unaware), Egypt stands to receive further blessing from God.

One cannot help but think of 50:7-9 in reading Isa. 49:22-23a. Second Isaiah contains numerous echoes of ancestral experiences, as grounds for the exiles' hope of return from Babylon. To take a pertinent example, in Isa. 40:11 (1) the word "lambs" translates *tela'im,* literally "striped/spotted" (as in Gen. 30); (2) the phrase "those that are with young" translates *'alot,* evoking the image in Gen. 33:13 where the same word is translated "giving suck"; and (3) all these are Yahweh's "reward" (*sakar,* Isa. 40:10), echoing the reference to Jacob's "wages" in Gen. 30:28-33. These echoes between Isa. 40:11 and the Jacob story give a picture of Yahweh as not only being with Jacob in exile (Gen. 28:15), but as in some sense the one who in and through Jacob *was* in exile working for Laban and then finally returning to the land of promise with the reward. If Jacob's return from Paddan-aram is echoed in Isa. 40:10-11, his return from Egypt is echoed in Isa. 49:22-23a. Thus we see another example of how the book of Genesis generates fundamental themes that shape the life of the community of regeneration.

What does it mean, now, for another people, the Canaanites, to memorialize Jacob's death and burial by giving to the threshing floor of Atad the name Abel-mizraim, "mourning of Egypt" (Gen. 50:11)? Why do they not give it a name that means "mourning for Jacob"? Perhaps the Canaanites wish to honor the Egyptian display of grief (regardless of whom it is over) because Egypt is a great international power that at times controls part or all of Canaan. It is a diplomatic thing to do. That the ancestral burial place should be named by the Canaanites in honor of Egypt will surely continue to have ironic overtones for Israelites of later times — in the time before Solomon, or in the time of Solomon, or after Pharaoh Neco slew King Josiah at Megiddo (2 Kgs. 23:29). Through this long, complicated, and often bloody history of international relations between Egypt, Israel, and the Canaanites, the name Abel-mizraim — Egypt's mourning of a dead Israelite — will continue in its own quiet way to bear its strange witness. Is it a witness only to a brief cross-cultural harmony that since has been lost, or is it also a witness of hope for a harmony that may yet again be possible? In such a case the lamentation of Egypt at Abel-mizraim joins the lamentation of Rachel at Ramah, until such a day of cross-cultural reconciliation as is envisioned in Isa. 19:24-25.

Meanwhile, the ten brothers face an immediate problem. With Jacob dead, their guilty consciences rise up again to press on their minds the possibility of retribution from Joseph: "It may be that Joseph will hate us and pay us back for all the evil which we did to him" (Gen. 50:15). So they send a petition that they hope will stand between them and such "paying back." As in the case of Jacob's prayer to God in 32:9-12 (see above), the form of their petition is worth studying closely:

a. "Your father gave us this command before he died, '[Thus you shall] say to Joseph,

b. Forgive, *na'*, the transgression of your brothers and their sin, because they did evil to you.'

a'. So now,

b'. Forgive, *na'* the transgression of the servants of the God of your father.' "

The first thing to notice is that the brothers' petition to Joseph takes the form of a message that Jacob has sent to Joseph through them. The expression, "Thus you shall say to X," is a standard introduction to a message from a first party to a second party through a messenger. (Jacob had used it, e.g., in sending a message to Esau under similar circumstances; cf. 32:3-5.) This means, then, that the prayer for forgiveness in b is not a petition by the brothers on their own behalf, but an intercession by the father with one of his sons on behalf of his other sons.

So far as the brothers are concerned, they feel more confident that Joseph might heed a request from his father and theirs than that he would heed one from those who had sinned against him. Yet in b Jacob does not say, "forgive the transgression of my sons," but "forgive the transgression of your brothers." Joseph should forgive those who sinned against him, not simply out of regard for his father's wishes, but because these men are his brothers. (Cf. the similar shift between "son" and "brother" in Luke 15:24, 30, 31, 32.) Moreover, Jacob's threefold emphasis is remarkable: (1) the transgression; (2) their sin; (3) they did evil. Joseph's forgiveness does not mean that what they did could or should be made light of. He is to forgive them in full view of what they have done.

The second thing to notice is that the brothers then take up their father's intercession (b) and make it their own as a petition (b'). When they do so, they shift the emphasis in two ways. On the one hand, they abbreviate the charge against them to its first term, "transgression." (One can easily understand this!) On the other hand, however, they shift the reference to them as "your brothers" to "the servants of the God of your father." Here they are not sons, nor brothers, but servants. And the focus now shifts from "your father" (Gen. 50:16) to "the God of your father" (v. 17). If Jacob appeals to Joseph to forgive his brothers, the brothers appeal to Joseph to forgive the servants of the God of his father (cf. the similar reference to "the God of your father" in the first line of 49:25).

Third, we should notice the particle of persuasion, *na'*, that occurs both in the intercession and in the petition. As indicated earlier (see above on 12:11; 16:2), this particle indicates that the speaker is appealing to something mentioned or implicit in the situation, as a basis on which the request should be granted. In the present instance, the appeal seems to be threefold: (1) to Joseph's relation to his father (he should obey his father's request); (2) to Joseph's relation to his brothers (he should have compassion on his own kin; see above on 43:14); and (3) to the brothers' relation to the God of Joseph's father. What is especially noteworthy is that the brothers do not appeal to their relation to Jacob, as his sons. This may be because the evil they had done to Joseph arose over the question of which son stood in the closest relation to their father as eventual heir. In such a context, and according to the character and customs of family and clan religion in those days, the brothers' concluding phrase, "the servants of the God of your father," is a formal recognition that it is now Joseph, and not any of the other brothers, on whom Jacob's mantle has rightfully fallen. This is confirmed when the brothers go on to say, "Behold, we are your servants" (cf. Luke 15:18-19).

The final observation on this prayer has two closely related aspects. First, it illustrates how the religious logic of forgiveness nests in the bosom of family relations ("your father" is the opening and closing phrase in the brothers' message). But since "the God of your father" is imaged in Genesis in parental terms, the religious logic of forgiveness ultimately nests in the divine parental bosom. Second, the brothers' appeal in the name of the father Jacob follows the example of Jacob's own petition in 32:9-12, where he prays to God in the name of God's promises to the ancestors Abraham and Isaac. The brothers' prayer for forgiveness thus lays down the logic of appeal that Moses follows in Exod. 32:11-13 (esp., climactically, v. 13; cf. Deut. 9:13-29, esp. v. 27). The same logic underlies Paul's affirmation in Rom. 11:28 leading to the conclusion that God will have mercy on all (v. 30). Indeed, Rom. 9:3-5 may be translated to mean that Paul had intercessorily offered himself in place of his Jewish kin and for their sake, and then recalled that the ultimate welfare of his kin is assured in the ancestral promises and the coming of Christ in the flesh. If the groaning travail of the whole creation (Rom. 8:22) is held in the groaning intercession of the Spirit (v. 27) and of Christ (v. 34), this groaning nests in the bosom of the God whom Paul in v. 15 and often elsewhere calls Father. In terms of the stages in the biblical narrative, it is thus God's divine parental relation to the ancestors, resting in God's election and the ancestral response, that is the matrix within which all problems are to be prayed about and finally resolved.

How does Joseph respond to the brothers when they say they are his servants? Or rather, which Joseph will answer? The Joseph who has become "such a man" (Gen. 44:15) in Egypt that he can command a royal retinue at his father's funeral? The Joseph who still smarts under his brothers' hatred toward him in his youth (42:7)? Or the Joseph who began to emerge compassionately in the earlier reconciliation scenes?

At 37:4 Joseph's report of his brothers' hostile words against him was like Jeremiah's report in Jer. 20:10 and the psalmist's complaint in Ps. 31:13. In the psalm, the speaker concentrates primarily on the enemies' attacks and on God as deliverer, but he prays also that the wicked may be put to shame and go dumbfounded to Sheol (Ps. 31:17). Jeremiah is not much easier on his foes. He affirms that they will be greatly ashamed and that their eternal dishonor will never be forgotten; and he asks God to let him see God's vengeance upon them, for he has committed his cause to God (Jer. 20:11-12). But at least neither Jeremiah nor the psalmist takes vengeance into his own hands (as does Lamech in Gen. 4:23-24, and as do Simeon and Levi in 34:25-29). Rather, they leave it to God to avenge as God sees fit. This shift is significant. To take vengeance into one's own hands (and perhaps even to take forgiveness into one's own hands as though it were a possibility entirely within human capacity) is to act in God's place as God's agent of judgment. In the OT vengeance — an extreme form of judging and setting right — is said to belong only to God (Deut. 32:34-35), so that to carry out vengeance in God's place is to displace and reject God in favor of one's human action. Paul picks up this issue in Rom. 12:19 in a way that bears directly back on Joseph, as he writes, literally (cf. RSV mg), "Beloved, never avenge yourselves, but *give place* to the wrath of God; for it is written, 'Vengeance is mine, I will repay, says the LORD.'" Since vengeance belongs only to God, the Christian is to give place to that wrath, that is, not to act wrathfully in its place, but to leave vengeance to God. However one may *feel* (and the Psalms indicate that there is plenty of room to feel wrath where it is provoked), one's own *actions* are to be confined to doing good to the enemy, thereby overcoming evil with good. This now leads directly back to Joseph's words, "Fear not, for am I in the place of God?" (Gen. 50:19).

In 44:15 Joseph had said to his brothers, "such a man as I can indeed divine," seeming to claim for himself a power that earlier he had attributed only to God: "Do not interpretations belong to God?" and "It is not in me; God will give Pharaoh a favorable answer" (40:8; 41:16). Now he returns to that earlier attitude. (With an eye to Luke 15:17 we might say that, in his own way, Joseph "comes to himself.") Thus when we compare Joseph's statement here with Paul's in Rom. 12:19, we might at first suppose that when one has been wronged one ought to do nothing of any sort and leave the whole matter to God. But Joseph's words in fact help to shed light on how Paul's words are to be taken.

Consider what it means to forgive. When one has been wronged, one feels moved to retaliate in kind or in equivalence

— or, like Lamech, sevenfold. The spirit of retaliation presupposes that one need allow no margin for error or for evil in God's world. As Job's friend Bildad will put it, the world makes no place for the evildoer, who instead is driven out of his place so that no one will even know that place any more (Job 8:22; J. Gerald Janzen, *Job*. Interpretation [Atlanta: John Knox, 1985]). To forgive is to leave others room for a margin of error or evil — in hope of eventual restitution, reconciliation, and the fuller life thereby made possible.

In this sense, God's forgiveness is part of what establishes the horizon of God's providence, a horizon which both creates and bears with human freedom, suffering its abuse on the way to redeeming its evils. As for the human capacity for forgiveness, anyone who has hated deeply under another's terrible wrongdoing knows exactly what Joseph means. Like Laban in Gen. 24:50; 31:24, Joseph dare not make an autonomous decision for good or evil toward his brothers. If the matter were up to him, Joseph would opt for retaliation. He has to make way for God, give place to God, and leave it to God to act in accordance with God's providential wisdom. In so making way, Joseph gives up his own claims to vengeance — and even his own supposed powers of forgiveness. But the wonderful paradox is that, in leaving a space for God to deal with his brothers, Joseph in fact images God, for he embodies in himself the same horizon of patient bearing as God does! The happy irony is that precisely in refusing the presumption of acting in God's place, Joseph in fact does act in God's place. (He does not realize this, but if Jacob's experience of Esau's forgiveness in 33:10 is any guide, his brothers will see in his face the face of God.) What enables Joseph (constrains him? frees him?) to do so is the realization that the brothers' actions toward him, though evil, occurred within the horizon of God's ultimate intention to save life, a horizon that has patiently and hiddenly borne this evil in order to bear the fruit of this reconciliation.

(It may be noted that Joseph's words, "Am I in the place of God?" echo the words of his father to his mother in 30:2, words which had marked the beginning of Jacob's recognition that he could not in fact control all relations and shape all events by his

own power of action. The specific problems are different: barrenness in the one case, hatred and estrangement in the other. Yet
their solution is similar: making room for God's power of action
and waiting patiently on that power. This similarity of solution
amid difference in problem is perhaps analogous to Jesus' comment on forgiveness and healing in Mark 2:9. But insofar as
estrangement and barrenness are both a form of death — the
death of relationship, and the death of the power to pass on life
— perhaps even the different problems are really different forms
of the one fundamental problem, of death working against life.
This is implied in the Gospel of John, where on the one hand
Jesus' interaction with the woman at the well [see above on Gen.
38] gives rise to a well of water in her springing up to eternal
life, and on the other hand the gift of the Spirit of Jesus risen
from the dead enables his disciples to forgive [John 20:19-23].
In this sense, one may see the promise of resurrection implicitly
embedded already in a passage such as Gen. 50:15-21. It is the
various stories of the opening of barren wombs, the reconciliation
of estranged brothers, the exodus from Egypt in accordance with
the promises to the ancestors [Exod. 2:23–3:15], and again the
forgiveness of Israel's idolatry for the sake of the ancestors [Exod.
32:11-14], which should perpare one for the event and the message of resurrection in Jesus. That is to say, it is a matter of
knowing the Scriptures and the one life-giving power of God that
is manifest in their pages in these different yet connected ways
[cf. Mark 12:24, 26-27].)

Joseph's forgiveness does not change the character of the
brothers' wrongdoing, but it shows a change in Joseph, a change
reflected in his recognition of God's providence. He now sees
that, within that providence, what the brothers meant against him
evilly, God took up and used for good, "to bring it about that
many people should be kept alive, as they are today." The tragedy
of retributive dynamics is that, though they may be intended to
serve a tenacious demand for justice, the "justice" that is thereby
served becomes a lie, for it kills instead of making alive. If the
end of justice is the overcoming of the power of death by the
restoration of life, then forgiveness is the true form of justice in
cases like these. Needless to say, where forgiveness is the true

form of justice, repentance such as the brothers show is also part of the picture.

Having confessed God's saving providence, and so conveying God's miracle of forgiveness, Joseph reiterates his "fear not," and goes on to reassure them of his practical and material support of them and their families. His words to them are literally, "thus he comforted them (*niham*), and spoke upon their heart" (Gen. 50:21). The latter idiom is the one we encountered when Shechem spoke to Dinah after he had raped her (Gen. 34:3; see above), but it is used here in the sense it has in Hos. 2:14, and especially in Isa. 40:1-2, which uses *niham* and the idiom in the same sequence as Joseph. When Joseph comes to his own deathbed, he prophesies that God will bring all his people out of Egypt in accordance with the oath to Abraham, Isaac, and Jacob. He also binds them, as did his father, to take his bones with them when that time comes.

The stage is set for the book of Exodus, with its divine deliverance (Exod. 1–15) and then forgiveness (chs. 32–34) of Israel in faithfulness to the covenant made with the ancestors (Exod 2:23–3:15; 32:13; 33:19; 34:6-7). Two ancestral words will powerfully accompany the children of Abraham and Sarah out of the book of Genesis and into the long pilgrimage to their eventual land of promise: Those words are Jacob's blessing in Gen. 49 and the words of Joseph in 50:19-21. In speaking as he does, Joseph speaks out of the power of Jacob's blessing bestowed on him. He answers the fierce arrows of his brothers' hatred (49:23) by turning Shaddai's blessing of fertility — the blessing of breasts and womb (*shadayim* and *rehem*) — into the blessing of forgiveness which arises out of his compassion (*rahamim* as in 43:14). These words proclaim the divine power and wisdom that will ever go with God's people, blessing them and keeping them, causing God's face to shine on them and having mercy on them, lifting up God's face to them until they enter finally into God's peace.

AFTERWORD

Genesis is the story of origins. As such it obviously comes first in the Bible. But it has more than a temporal relation to the stories that follow. A good deal of the ensuing plot line, and many of the fundamental issues and character types that arise later, are already foreshadowed in Genesis. The various foreshadowings do not rigidly predetermine the rest of the story. By the way they cast their shadow forward, they image a divine providence that establishes a horizon for all that follows, and they witness to that providence as working before, within, and after all the real but finite actors and factors in the world. This horizon makes room — sometimes we feel, with Job, altogether too much room — for freedom, decision, novelty, surprise, cross-purposes, multiple perspectives, and multiple interpretations (as when the name of a place like Beer-sheba or Bethel, or of a person like Ishmael or Isaac, is given several explanations). What this horizon does promise, already, is that the untidy roominess of the world — what William James called this "blooming, buzzing confusion" — is embraced within a steadfast love and faithfulness which will bring all things — through good and evil, suffering and laughter, drama and banality — to a good end.

Genesis as it stands, then, appears to frame what follows by foreshadowing it, and in so doing to offer an inexhaustible resource of encouragement and renewed energy for the reader to see the story inside or outside the Bible through to the end. But can such a reading of the book survive historical-critical study? Regardless of when we date the component sources of Genesis — and the Priestly source in its final form is quite late even if we do not follow some in dating the Yahwist to the Exile — a good deal of what we read in Genesis may be taken as retrojection of experiences and understandings arising much later in Israel's history. Are not its so-called foreshadowings, then, actually shadows cast backward by later Israel? If they are, how seriously can we take the narrative as a witness to the nature of things, rather than a fiction after the fact?

Yet is providence often if ever experienced as such at the time, let alone in advance? Is it not mostly if not always recognized in retrospect? On the human level, children are only dimly or fitfully aware of their parents' providence at the time when they are most dependent on that horizon of nurture, guidance, and protection. Only later, as they find themselves being provident with their own children, do they begin to appreciate with any depth and fullness of detail what it was within which compass they in such blithe obliviousness grew up.

If Israel only in retrospect tells its story of origins as providential, that should occasion no surprise, and certainly no theological unease. What should give dissatisfaction is the tendency to dismantle a narrative so judiciously built up over such a long period of communal experience and reflection within that providential horizon we have traditionally called inspiration — to dismantle it, and then to try to interpret the component parts in relation to their supposed historical contexts of origin. Thus, for example, one widely used introductory textbook begins with the Exodus of Israel from Egypt, considers the ancestors and the Garden story in connection with the United Monarchy of David and Solomon, and takes up the Priestly stories of Creation, Flood, circumcision, and the tabernacle at Sinai only in connection with the Exile. As illuminating as this is for understanding aspects of the history of the religion of Israel, it fails miserably to address the great culminating stage in that history: the coming of all the various traditions into the final form of the Bible as we have it. It is in this final form, I am persuaded, that the biblical text may most fruitfully be read.

To benefit fully from the ancestral narratives of Genesis is to be schooled by them in the art of reading our own experience as occurring within God's providential horizon. Such a schooling should move us, not so much to read off the details of the future either from our own past or from the Bible, but to make our fallible decisions with trust in or at least belated recognition of a providence that goes before us like Joseph into Egypt. We may even learn haltingly to read and brokenly to trace (with mounting excitement as over clues in a treasure hunt) a family resemblance between these old stories and the shapes of our own individual and communal lives.

This, at any rate, seems to have been Paul's conviction. After speaking in Rom. 8 of God's foreknowledge and predestination (or pre-horizoning), in chs. 9–11 he takes up that case in point which causes him the greatest perplexity and tests his trust and his understanding to the utmost: the relation between Jews and Gentiles in God's redemptive providence as disclosed in Jesus Christ. It is surely no accident that (1) Paul encompasses all this within an interpretive frame provided by the Hebrew ancestors (Rom. 9:6-14); (2) in 9:15 he quotes a divine word from Exod. 33:19, which itself was elicited by Moses' appeal to the covenant with the ancestors (Exod. 32:13); (3) at the other end of the argument he returns to the theme of God's faithfulness to Israel for the sake of the ancestors (Rom. 11:28); and (4) he concludes with an affirmation of God's mercy upon all (v. 30) which echoes and applies 9:15. Paul's last word in this whole section sums up the divine providence in what may be the most theologically freighted sequence of prepositions in the Bible: "From him and through him and to him are all things" (Rom. 11:36). If the "through" be allowed a figuratively spatial connotation, then all things are here envisioned as having their origin, horizon, and destiny in God. Within the intermediate phase opened up by God as the divine horizon of the world, the affairs of our lives have their jostling and often conflicting ways. That their destiny is finally in the hands of the One to whom they all owe their origin is a vision traced for us already in the ancestral narratives, and especially in the climactic story of Joseph and his brothers.

SELECTED BIBLIOGRAPHY

Commentaries

Brueggemann, Walter. *Genesis*. Interpretation (Atlanta: John Knox, 1982).

Cassuto, Umberto. *A Commentary on the Book of Genesis*. Vol. 2 (Jerusalem: Magnes and London: Oxford University Press, 1964).

Coats, George W. *Genesis, with an Introduction to Narrative Literature*. Forms of the Old Testament Literature 1 (Grand Rapids: Wm. B. Eerdmans, 1983).

Davidson, Robert. *Genesis 12–50*. Cambridge Bible Commentary (Cambridge and New York: Cambridge University Press, 1979).

Gowan, Donald J. *From Eden to Babel: A Commentary on the Book of Genesis 1–11*. International Theological Commentary (Grand Rapids: Wm. B. Eerdmans and Edinburgh: Handsel, 1988).

Hamilton, Victor P. *The Book of Genesis: Chapters 1–17*. New International Commentary on the Old Testament (Grand Rapids: Wm. B. Eerdmans, 1990).

Jacob, Benno. *The First Book of the Bible: Genesis* (New York: Ktav, 1974).

Kidner, Derek *Genesis*. Tyndale Old Testament Commentary (Downers Grove: Inter-Varsity and London: Tyndale, 1967).

von Rad, Gerhard. *Genesis,* rev. ed. Old Testament Library (Philadelphia: Westminster and London: SCM, 1972).

Sarna, Nahum M. *Genesis*. JPS Torah Commentary (Philadelphia: Jewish Publication Society, 1989).

————. *Understanding Genesis* (New York: Schocken, 1970).

Speiser, Ephraim A. *Genesis,* 3rd ed. Anchor Bible 1 (Garden City: Doubleday, 1979).

Vawter, Bruce. *On Genesis: A New Reading* (Garden City: Doubleday, 1977).

Wenham, Gordon J. *Genesis 1–15.* Word Biblical Commentary (Waco: Word, 1987).

Westermann, Claus. *Genesis 12–36* (Minneapolis: Augsburg, 1985).

————. *Genesis 37–50* (Minneapolis: Augsburg, 1986).

————. *Genesis: A Practical Commentary.* Text and Interpretation (Grand Rapids: Wm. B. Eerdmans, 1987).

Monographs

Alter, Robert. *The Art of Biblical Narrative* (New York: Basic Books and London: Allen & Unwin, 1981).

————. *The World of Biblical Literature* (New York: Basic Books, 1992).

Arendt, Hannah. *The Human Condition* (Chicago: University of Chicago Press, 1958).

Clines, David J. A. *The Theme of the Pentateuch.* JSOT Supplement 10 (Sheffield: JSOT Press, 1978).

Cross, Frank Moore. *Canaanite Myth and Hebrew Epic* (Cambridge: Harvard University Press, 1973).

Fishbane, Michael. *Biblical Interpretation in Ancient Israel* (Oxford and New York: Oxford University Press, 1985).

Fokkelmann, J. P. *Narrative Art in Genesis* (Assen: Van Gorcum, 1975).

Hays, Richard B. *Echoes of Scripture in the Letters of Paul* (New Haven: Yale University Press, 1989).

Hendel, Ronald S. *The Epic of the Patriarch: The Jacob Cycle and the Narrative Traditions of Canaan and Israel.* Harvard Semitic Monographs 42 (Atlanta: Scholars Press, 1987).

Humphreys, W. Lee. *Joseph and His Family: A Literary Study* (Columbia: University of South Carolina Press, 1988).

Jacobsen, Thorkild. *The Treasures of Darkness: A History of*

Mesopotamian Religion (New Haven: Yale University Press, 1976).

Jeansonne, Sharon Pace. *The Women of Genesis: From Sarah to Potiphar's Wife* (Minneapolis: Augsburg Fortress, 1990).

Lambdin, Thomas O. *Introduction to Biblical Hebrew* (New York: Scribner's, 1971).

Longacre, Robert E. *Joseph: A Story of Divine Providence: A Text Theoretical and Textlinguistic Analysis of Genesis 37 and 39–48* (Winona Lake: Eisenbrauns, 1989).

McKane, William. *Studies in the Patriarchal Narratives* (Edinburgh: Handsel, 1979).

Mann, Thomas W. *The Book of the Torah: The Narrative Integrity of the Pentateuch* (Atlanta: John Knox, 1988).

Moberly, Robert W. L. *The Old Testament of the Old Testament: Patriarchal Narratives and Mosaic Yahwism* (Minneapolis: Fortress, 1992).

Redford, Donald B. *A Study of the Biblical Story of Joseph (Genesis 37-50)*. Supplements to *Vetus Testamentum* 20 (1970).

Rendsburg, Gary A. *The Redaction of Genesis* (Winona Lake: Eisenbrauns, 1986).

Van Seters, John *Abraham in History and Tradition* (New Haven: Yale University Press, 1975).

Westermann, Claus. *The Promises to the Fathers* (Philadelphia: Fortress, 1980).

Whybray, R. N. *The Making of the Pentateuch: A Methodological Study*. JSOT Supplement 53 (Sheffield: JSOT Press, 1987).

Williams, James G. *Women Recounted: Narrative Tninking and the God of Israel*. Bible and Literature 6 (Sheffield: Almond, 1982).

Articles

Anderson, Bernhard W. "Abraham, the Friend of God," *Interpretation* 42 (1988): 353-366.

Biddle, Mark E. "The 'Endangered Ancestress' and Blessing for the Nations," *Journal of Biblical Literature* 109 (1990): 599-611.

Cohn, Robert L. "Narrative Structure and Canonical Perspective in Genesis," *Journal for the Study of the Old Testament* 25 (1983): 3-16.

Donaldson, Mara E. "Kinship Theory in the Patriarchal Narratives: The Case of the Barren Wife," *Journal of the American Academy of Religion* 49 (1981): 77-87.

Evans, Carl D. "The Patriarch Jacob — An 'Innocent Man,'" *Bible Review* 2/1 (1986): 32-37.

Exum, J. Cheryl. "The Mothers of Israel: The Patriarchal Narratives from a Feminist Perspective," *Bible Review* 2/1 (1986): 60-67.

Fox, Everett. "Can Genesis Be Read as a Book?" *Semeia* 46 (1989): 31-40.

Goldingay, John. "The patriarchs in Scripture and history," in *Essays on the Patriarchal Narratives*, ed. Alan R. Millard and Donald J. Wiseman (Leicester: Inter-Varsity, 1980, and Winona Lake: Eisenbrauns, 1983), 11-42.

Haran, Menahem. "The Religion of the Patriarchs: An Attempt at a Synthesis," *Annual of the Swedish Theological Institute* 4 (1965): 30-55.

Holmgren, Fredrick C. "Faithful Abraham and the *ᵃmānâ* Covenant: Nehemiah 9:6–10:1," *Zeitschrift für die alttestamentliche Wissenschaft* 104 (1992): 249-254.

———. "Holding Your Own Against God! Genesis 32:22-32 (In the Context of Genesis 31–33)," *Interpretation* 44 (1990): 5-17.

Klein, Ralph W. "Call, Covenant, and Community: The Story of Abraham and Sarah," *Currents in Theology and Mission* 15 (1988): 120-27.

Kselman, John S. "The Book of Genesis: A Decade of Scholarly Research," *Interpretation* 45 (1991): 380-392.

Mann, Thomas W. "'All the the Families of the Earth': The Theological Unity of Genesis," *Interpretation* 45 (1991): 341-353.

Martin, John Hilary. "Can Religions Change? A Hierarchy of Values in Genesis," *Pacifica* 3 (1990): 1-24.

Miller, Patrick D. "Syntax and Theology in Genesis XII 3a," *Vetus Testamentum* 34 (1984): 472-76.

Miscall, Peter D. "The Jacob and Joseph Stories as Analogies," *Journal for the Study of the Old Testament* 6 (1978): 28-40.

Moberly, Robert W. L. "The Earliest Commentary on the Akedah [Gen. 22]," *Vetus Testamentum* 38 (1988): 302-323.

Neufeld, Ernest. "In Defense of Esau," *Jewish Bible Quarterly* 20 (1991-1992): 43-49.

Olbricht, Thomas H. "The Theology of Genesis," *Restoration Quarterly* 23 (1980): 201-217.

Robinson, Robert B. "Literary Functions of the Genealogies of Genesis," *Catholic Biblical Quarterly* 48 (1986): 595-608.

Sutherland, Dixon. "The Organization of the Abraham Promise Narratives," *Zeitschrift für die alttestamentliche Wissenschaft* 95 (1983): 337-343.

Wcela, Emil A. "The Abraham Stories, History and Faith," *Biblical Theology Bulletin* 10 (1980): 176-181.

Weizman, Z. "National Consciousness in the Patriarchal Promises," *Journal for the Study of the Old Testament* 31 (1985): 55-73.

Wenham, Gordon J. "The religion of the patriarchs," in *Essays on the Patriarchal Narratives,* ed. Alan R. Millard and Donald J. Wiseman, 157-188.

West, Angela. "Genesis and Patriarchy," *The New Blackfriars* 62 (1981): 17-32, 420-432.